How Was Your Week?

Bringing People Together
In Recovery the LifeRing Way
– A Handbook

Second Edition

Martin Nicolaus

LifeRing Press
Oakland

For additional copies of this publication, contact:

LifeRing Press
1440 Broadway Suite 400
Oakland CA 94612
Tel: 800-811-4142
publisher@lifering.org

Quantity discounts available.

To arrange for LifeRing speakers to address your audience, contact the LifeRing Service Center at 800-811-4142 or service@lifering.org.

Alpha versions 9/8/2002 – 3/24/2003
Version 1.00 7/3/2003
Version 1.9 5/18/2015
Version 1.99 6/16/2015
Version 2.0 7/15/15

ISBN 10 1515286568
ISBN 13 9781515286561

Contents

Chapter 1: Introduction 1

1.1: The Purpose of this Book 1

1.2: Chapter Two: The Convenor's Vision 2

1.3: Chapter Three: How Was Your Week 4

1.4: Chapter Four: Openings and Closings 5

1.5: Chapter Five: Newcomers 5

1.6: Chapter Six: Nuts and Bolts 6

1.7: Chapter Seven: The Meeting's Money 6

1.8: Chapter Eight: LifeRing Online 7

1.9: Chapter Nine: Meetings in Special
Settings 7

1.10: Chapter Ten: The Meeting of Meetings 7

1.11: Chapter Eleven: Sobriety 8

1.12: Chapter Twelve: Secularity 8

1.13: Chapter Thirteen: Self-Help 9

1.14: Chapter Fourteen: Building a Personal Recovery Program 9

1.15: Chapter Fifteen: Getting Started 10

1.16: Chapter Sixteen: About This Book 11

Chapter 2: The Convenor's Vision 13

2.1: About This Chapter 13

2.2: The Convenor Brings People Together 13

2.3: Why the Group Process Works 16

2.3.1: Two Forces At Work Inside 16

2.3.2: When "A" Connects With "A" 18

2.3.3: When "S" Connects With "S" 20

2.4: The Convenor Sees the Good in Bad People 23

2.5: The Convenor Facilitates Connections 25

2.6: The Convenor Empowers Others 28

2.7: The Successful Convenor Can Step Away 31

2.8: Seven Reasons to Become a Convenor 33

    2.8.1: It Helps My Recovery 34

    2.8.2: To Give Something Back 35

    2.8.3: Because of the Golden Rule 35

    2.8.4: For More Meaning in Life 35

    2.8.5: Because Someone Has to Do It 36

    2.8.6: Because It Feels Good 36

    2.8.7: Because Convening is Love 36

2.9: In Appreciation of Convenors 37

Chapter 3: How Was Your Week? 39

3.1: About This Chapter 39

3.2: A Newsreel of Highlights and Heartaches 39

3.3: Planning Ahead 41

3.4: Gory Details Please 43

3.5: Making "I" Statements 46

3.6: Your Week In Recovery 48

3.7: Similar But Different Formats 49

    3.7.1: The Life Story Format 50

    3.7.2: My Feelings Now 50

3.8: What "How Was Your Week?" Really Asks 51

3.9: Down with Drunkalogues 52

3.10: Crosstalk 54

    3.10.1: Crosstalk Is Voluntary 56

    3.10.2: Crosstalk Is Supportive 57

3.10.3: Some Common Issues in Crosstalk 60

3.10.4: Timing Crosstalk 64

3.10.5: Crosstalk: Conclusion 66

3.11: Where to Start the Process 67

3.12: Handling Dead Airtime 68

3.12.1: Topic on the Fly 69

3.12.2: Stock Topic 69

3.12.3: "Quaker Meeting" Mode 70

3.13: How Much Should the Convenor Talk? 71

3.14: When the Convenor Must Speak 73

3.15: Threats of Harm 77

3.16: A Camaraderie Like No Other 78

3.17: The Format in Perspective 80

3.18: Lifetime Recovery Agendas 82

3.19: Partners and Loved Ones 83

3.20: Variations on the Theme 84

Chapter 4: Opening and Closing 87

4.1: About This Chapter 87

4.2: Primacy, Latency, and Ritual 87

4.3: The Opening Before the Opening Statement 88

4.4: Starting On Time 89

4.5: The Opening Statement 89

4.6: Personal Talking Rituals 93

4.6.1: Label or Not? 94

4.7: Closing the Meeting 96

4.8: Everyone Here Is Above Average 98

4.9: After the Meeting 101

Chapter 5: Newcomers 103

5.1: About this Chapter 103

5.2: Newcomers 103

5.3: Offering Direction 105

5.4: Sponsorship? 106

5.5: E-Pals 109

Chapter 6: Nuts and Bolts 111

6.1: About This Chapter 111

6.2: The Message of the Chairs: Circle Format 111

6.3: Table or Not? 112

6.4: When We Outgrow the Room 113

6.5: The Box and Where to Keep It 115

6.6: Door Signs and Directional Signs 117

6.7: Attendance Slips 118

6.8: The Clipboard 122

6.9: Books and Handouts 124

6.10: Literature Racks and Bulletin Boards 126

6.11: The Basket 127

Chapter 7: The Meeting's Money 131

7.1: About This Chapter 131

7.2: The Three B's 131

7.3: Book Sales 133

7.4: Shoe box or Checkbook? 134

7.5: The Meeting's Surplus 136

Chapter 8: Online Meetings 139

8.1: About This Chapter 139

8.2: Online Recovery Support Works 139

8.3: The Varieties of LifeRing Online 141

8.4: Issues with Narrow Bandwidth 143

8.5: Online Format Issues 144

8.6: Proof of Attendance Online 146

8.7: Conclusion 146

Chapter 9: Meetings in Special Settings 149

9.1: About This Chapter 149

9.2: Introduction 149

9.3: The Variety of Special Settings 151

    9.3.1: Settings that Filter the People 151

    9.3.2: The Institution's Policy and Staff 152

9.4: LifeRing in the Psychiatric Crisis Setting 154

    9.4.1: Struggling to Find Level Ground 154

    9.4.2: A Focus Group Like No Other 156

    9.4.3: Topics for Minds in Turmoil 157

    9.4.4: Crosstalk in a Psychiatric Setting 158

    9.4.5: The LifeRing Uplift 159

9.5: Meetings in High Turnover Settings 161

    9.5.1: Working up a LifeRing Intro 162

    9.5.2: "Talked Out" Settings 165

    9.5.3: The "LifeRing College" 166

9.6: Professionals in the Room 167

    9.6.1: Professional Backups 167

    9.6.2: Professionals as Convenors 169

9.7: Professionals and the *Recovery by Choice* Workbook 171

9.8: Sticking Together On The Inside 172

9.9: A Constitutional Right to Secular Support 175

9.10: Corresponding with Prisoners 176

    9.10.1: Guidelines for Prisoner Correspondence 178

    9.10.2: Prison Visits 179

    9.10.3: Quotations 180

9.11: Special Rewards 181

9.12: Delegates From Meetings in Special Settings 183

Chapter 10: The Meeting of Meetings 185

10.1: About This Chapter 185

10.2: LifeRing Is a Network of Meetings 185

10.3: The Annual LifeRing Meeting and Congress 186

10.4: Key Points in the Bylaws 187

10.5: Conclusion 189

Chapter 11: Sobriety 191

11.1: About this Chapter 191

11.2: Sobriety Is Our Priority 191

11.3: Sobriety Means Abstinence 192

11.4: Poly-Abstinence: One-Shop Stopping 198

11.5: Quitting the Easy Ones 199

11.6: Take Your Medications 201

11.7: Methadone 203

11.8: Support to Quit Nicotine 204

11.9: Medical Marijuana 207

11.10: Other Addictions 208

11.11: Conclusion 209

Chapter 12: Secularity 211

12.1: About This Chapter 211

12.2: Where Is Secularity? 211

12.3: Secularity is Trending 213

12.4: The Engine of Recovery is Secular 215

12.5: Secularity Includes All Beliefs and None 216

12.6: Keep Whatever You Believe 217

12.7: LifeRing Is Not an Atheist/Agnostic AA Meeting 219

12.8: Secularity Lets People Come Together 223

12.9: Secularity Lets People Relax and Be Real 224

12.10: Secularity is Research-Friendly 225

12.11: Knowing Our Limits 227

12.12: Recovery as Liberation of the Spirit 229

Chapter 13: Self-Help 231

13.1: About This Chapter 231

13.2: Two Dimensions of Self-Help 231

13.3: Self-Help As An Organizational Principle 232

13.3.1: Our Spiritual Ancestors, the Washingtonian Total Abstinence Society 233

13.4: Self-Help as a Therapeutic Strategy 236

13.4.1: Honor Thy Original Sober Self 239

13.4.2: You Have More Sober Time Than You Think 240

13.4.3: Building on Strength 241

13.5: Some Clinical Examples 242

13.5.1: Dr. Stewart 242

13.5.2: Evelyn 243

13.5.3: Marillac 243

13.6: Denial of the Sober Self 244

13.7: Protagonists of Our Own Recovery 245

13.8: The Clinical Verdict: Alcoholics Recover Because They Heal Themselves 247

13.9: Open Architecture on an Abstinence Foundation 248

13.10: The Approach Needs to Fit the Person 250

13.11: Lessons from Learning Theory 252

13.12: Choice Is the Mother of Motivation 254

13.13: Dealing with Cognitive Distortions 256

13.14: You Make the Path by Walking 257

Chapter 14: Building a Personal Recovery Program 259

14.1: Two Methods 259

14.2: Origin of the Workbook 261

14.3: Exercises for the Choice Muscles 262

14.4: A Tool for Making Sober Choices 263

14.5: The Nine Domains 264

14.6: Quality Control: Relapse Prevention 266

14.7: Writing Your Personal Recovery Plan 266

14.8: Start Point and Sequence 267

14.9: The Workbook in Perspective 267

14.10: Workbook Groups 269

14.11: Less is More 271

Chapter 15: Getting Started 273

15.1: About This Chapter 273

15.2: What It Takes To Be a Founding Convenor 273

15.3: Bootstrapping 276

15.4: Finding and Reaching Our People 277

    15.4.1: Who Are Our "Customers"? 278

15.4.2: Broadcasting and Narrowcasting 279

15.4.3: Twelve-step Meetings: Off Limits 282

15.5: Sobriety Is the Key to the Door 284

15.6: Treatment Programs: A Convenor's Primer 291

15.7: Gaps in the Wall   292

15.7.1: Professionalization 292

15.7.2: Internal Developments in the Twelve-step World 294

15.7.3: Public Criticism 295

15.7.4: Court Decisions 297

15.7.5: Patient Resistance 298

15.7.6: Growth of Alternative Treatment Approaches 300

15.8: Clients as Educators 302

15.9: A Two-Way Street 302

15.10: Abstinence, Abstinence, Abstinence 305

15.11: The Strategic Goal is Choice 307

15.12: Accent on the Positive 308

15.13: Team Presentations 310

15.14: Using LifeRing Press Literature 311

15.15: Approaching Others 311

15.16: Other Ways to Reach Out 312

15.17: Dealing with Obstruction 318

15.18: If We Build It, They Will Come 323

15.19: Leveraging Outreach 325

15.20: The Meeting Room 326

15.21: The LifeRing Charter 329

15.22: Leases, Insurance, Rent 331

15.23: Growing the Meeting 332

15.24: Turning it Over 334

15.24.1: Convenor Candidates 334

15.24.2: On-the-Job Training 336

15.24.3: When to Pass It On 337

Chapter 16: About This Book 341

16.1: Pre-history 341

16.2: A Period of Ferment and Frustration 342

16.3: New Energy, New Publications 344

16.4: Sobriety Becomes the Priority 345

16.5: The Need for an Update 346

16.6: What's Different 346

16.7: The Experience Base of This Book 348

16.8: My Convenor Mentors 350

16.9: Treatment 353

16.10: Acknowledgements 354

Chapter 1: Introduction

1.1: The Purpose of this Book

The demand for an abstinent recovery path other than the twelve steps of Alcoholics Anonymous has brought a growing number of recovering people to LifeRing. LifeRing Secular Recovery is a network of mutual aid recovery groups based on the "Three-S" philosophy: Sobriety (meaning abstinence), Secularity, and Self-Help. For reasons explained below, the people who organize, lead, and support LifeRing groups are called convenors. At this time, the demand for LifeRing groups outstrips the supply of convenors ready and able to lead them.

The main purpose of this book is to assist and encourage more people to become LifeRing convenors. Accordingly, the main focus of the present book is on the convenor's role: the practical and theoretical tools that the person leading LifeRing recovery meetings will want to acquire.

The person looking for a general introduction to LifeRing, with no present intent to become a convenor, may be better served by reading *Empowering Your Sober Self: The LifeRing Approach to Addiction Recovery* (2nd ed., LifeRing Press 2014).

The person looking for a structured recovery pathway along LifeRing lines may find a good fit in *Recovery by Choice: Living and Enjoying Life Free of Alcohol and Other Drugs, a Workbook* (4th ed., LifeRing Press 2011).

The content of the present book is divided into three main parts. The first part, comprising Chapters Two through Ten, discusses the ins and outs of existing LifeRing meetings. The second part consists of Chapters Eleven through Fourteen. These explicate the three basic principles on which LifeRing is founded: Sobriety, Secularity, and Self-Help, and provide an outline of what it means to build a personal recovery program (PRP). The third part consists of Chapter Fifteen, a long discussion of how to get a LifeRing meeting started in a new area. There is an appendix, Chapter Sixteen, which gives a short history of LifeRing together with acknowledgements. A section of references and an index complete the volume.

Here, by way of introduction, is a short summary of the chapters.

1.2: Chapter Two: The Convenor's Vision

The history of addiction recovery shows a great variety of groups, but little insight into the process that makes groups helpful. The LifeRing convenor's vision begins with the recognition that addiction splits the personality into two parts. One part, which we label "A," is the inner voice of the addiction. Its message is "drink and use, no matter what." The other part is the inner voice of survival, sanity, and sobriety. We label this the "S" or sober self. This is the voice that is sick and tired of drinking/using and wants to get free of it. Addicted persons live with this inner war.

Social reinforcement decides which party wins the inner conflict. Typically, when addicted persons come together in a drinking/drugging setting, the "A" in the one connects with the "A" in the other, and this connection empowers the "A" in both of them, and undermines the sober self in each of them. If the "A" succeeds in gaining 100 per cent control of the person, eliminating the sober voice, then the person will die.

In a sobriety support group, by contrast, the connections link the "S" within each participant. This connectedness reinforces the sober selves, and with each connection they become more prominent within the person, pushing the "A" into a smaller sphere of influence. As this process continues, the person reaches a tipping point when the "S" rises to the top and pushes the "A" into the inferior position.

The group process transforms the person from an addict with a little sober voice inside into a clean and sober person with a little addict voice inside. So long as the person remains abstinent, they can live a full and normal life and develop all the potentials that lie within them. The general aim of this process, and the LifeRing motto, is empowerment of the sober self.

When the average person sees someone who is addicted, they see only the alcoholic/addict – the "A." The LifeRing convenor sees more. We see also the "S" – the person's innate goodness, health, and sanity. We see it as our role to facilitate the release and the rise of that inner goodness. We understand that the active ingredient in bringing about this transformation is the positive connections between and among meeting participants. As convenors we are not healers or gurus or counselors or physicians or other kinds of authorities. We are peers in recovery, whose special contribution consists of bringing people together.

LifeRing convenors are the core of the LifeRing network. People become convenors for a variety of reasons. High among them is the boost that convening provides for the convenor's own recovery work. Convening makes demands on the convenor's time and energy, but the rewards are beyond measure.

1.3: Chapter Three: How Was Your Week

Chapter Three answers the question, "What do people do at a typical LifeRing meeting?" This chapter assumes that the meeting is all set up, that an opening statement has been read, and that the convenor has asked, "How was your week?"

The invitation to talk about "how was your week" asks the meeting participants to give a newsreel of the highlights and heartaches of their recent days in recovery. This kind of report is commonly called a check-in. People are also asked to look ahead to the coming week to spot any challenges or celebrations relevant to their recovery. It's most helpful when people talk in concrete details rather than generalities and cliches. Also useful is for people to make "I" statements in place of "you should" statements. This format is focused on the here and now, and does not ask for people's life stories. Drunkalogues and drugalogues are strongly discouraged.

A key element in this format is "crosstalk." Crosstalk means dialogue, feedback, conversation. After each person has reported on their past and coming weeks, we open the floor to conversation. Other people can ask the person questions, make comments, share similar stories. Feedback from peers creates two-way connections that are much more empowering than one-way communications. There are some rules about crosstalk: it is voluntary, it is positive and supporting, and it is considerate of the group's time. The chapter reviews some of the issues that sometimes crop up in crosstalk and suggests ways that the convenor can handle them.

Bottom line, this meeting format aims to create a living room atmosphere where people feel safe and free to engage in sober, supportive conversations with their peers.

We abbreviate this format as "HWYW," and this is what most LifeRing meetings use. The chapter also points to a number of variations on this format, including topic formats and hybrid formats, which are discussed in more detail in other chapters.

1.4: Chapter Four: Openings and Closings

This chapter looks in more detail at the start and end of the meeting format. It points out that it's important for the convenor to come a bit early to set up the room. It's important to start on time. The chapter discusses the opening statement and variations on it.

There's also discussion here whether individual meeting participants should begin their shares by labeling themselves "alcoholics" and "addicts" or not.

Most LifeRing meetings end with a round of applause. Some convenors adjourn from the meeting to a coffee house or a pizza place.

Some LifeRing participants benefit from having a more of a social life in the company of others, in addition to the meetings, and convenors may want to arrange social get-togethers to the extent possible.

1.5: Chapter Five: Newcomers

Welcoming newcomers is a pleasant task for the convenor. We have no special ritual for it. The convenor can try to learn the newcomer's needs and interests and connect them with others in the meeting who have a similar profile. Depending on the newcomer's wishes, the convenor can offer them recovery direction by referring them to the *Recovery by Choice* workbook, which provides a structured pathway toward empowerment of the sober self.

The chapters also explains why we do not do "sponsorship" (like twelve-step groups) in LifeRing. We have other ways of providing support between meetings and of providing evidence, where necessary, of a person's sustained commitment to recovery work. The chapter also explains the E-Pals program that provides online orientation and support for people approaching LifeRing for the first time.

1.6: Chapter Six: Nuts and Bolts

This chapter discusses the physical setting and the tangible tools of the convenor's role. LifeRing meetings generally set up chairs in a circle so that people can make eye contact with one another. A room without a table is preferable if there's a choice. When meetings get too big, it may be useful to split into two rooms. Supplies like the opening statement, the clipboard, signup sheets, brochures, books, and the basket are usually kept in a box. It's important to post directional signs and door signs before the meeting starts so that newcomers can find it. Some participants bring attendance slips that the convenor needs to sign. Books and handouts need to be made available. The chapter also discusses different ways of passing the basket for donations.

1.7: Chapter Seven: The Meeting's Money

Most meetings pass the basket for donations. The chapter talks about different ways of handling the money. When the meeting has a surplus of donations over its expenses (for example, for room rent) it can contribute to the expenses of the LifeRing Service Center, which maintains the *lifering.org* web site, publishes meeting schedules and brochures, runs LifeRing Press, and much else. LifeRing is a 501(c)(3) nonprofit and all convenors, regional reps, officers and directors are volunteers, serving without pay.

1.8: Chapter Eight: LifeRing Online

Some people have accumulated impressive amounts of clean and sober time in LifeRing exclusively through online participation. This chapter discusses LifeRing's online presence, starting with the *lifering.org* website and the numerous online venues that radiate from it: chat rooms (including voice and video), email lists, a Delphi forum, a Ning network, a Facebook page, and others. LifeRing online meetings have the same status in LifeRing's internal democratic process as face-to-face meetings.

1.9: Chapter Nine: Meetings in Special Settings

This chapter reports on LifeRing convenors' experiences in special settings such as inpatient treatment centers, locked psychiatric wards, and prisons. These challenging settings call on convenors to raise their game and make adjustments in attitude, meeting format, and other points. Relationships with professionals become particularly important here. LifeRing has proven itself not only viable but highly valued in these settings, and convening there is among the most rewarding experiences a convenor can have. Even convenors who do not convene in special settings can learn from these experiences.

1.10: Chapter Ten: The Meeting of Meetings

This chapter zooms out to show the LifeRing meeting as part of a larger organizational network centering on the annual meeting. This consists in part of educational programs and social events and culminates in the Delegates' Assembly, also known as the LifeRing Congress. The chapter explains that every LifeRing participant has one vote, and that each meeting is entitled to one delegate. The delegates elect the Board of Directors and vote on Bylaws amendments or other policy issues discussed at the Congress. The chapter provides an introduction to key points of the Bylaws that provide LifeRing with its independent and democratic structure.

1.11: Chapter Eleven: Sobriety

This chapter begins the section of the book dealing with the "Three S" philosophical foundations. Sobriety is the primary and most fundamental principle in LifeRing. Sobriety in LifeRing always means abstinence. We practice abstinence across the board, meaning not only from alcohol but also from all other medically non-indicated drugs. Our meetings are open to anyone who wants to practice abstinence, regardless of their "drug of choice." People who relapse are always welcome back so long as they evidence a desire to become clean and sober. People who desire to moderate or control their drinking/using, or to substitute one drug for another, are politely referred out to other groups. We encourage but do not require LifeRing participants to quit the use of tobacco. We support people taking prescribed psychoactive medications, e.g. for depression or other concurrent diagnoses, provided they have been honest with their physician and their physician is competent in addiction medicine. We do not interfere in the doctor/patient relationship. The chapter has an extensive discussion of issues contained in the "sobriety" concept.

1.12: Chapter Twelve: Secularity

Secularity is the second "S" in the philosophical trilogy. In a few words, secularity means that LifeRing meetings are open to people of all faiths and none. Meetings are free of prayer, and the engine of recovery (see Chapter Two) requires no higher power or other divine intervention. Neither religious witnessing nor atheist/agnostic advocacy are appropriate in our meetings. This format is in tune with the rapidly growing trend away from religious affiliation in the United States. The chapter discusses a number of other issues related to the secularity principle.

1.13: Chapter Thirteen: Self-Help

Self-help or self-direction is the third of the "Three S" principles. This chapter deepens the explanation of how the LifeRing meeting process works, presented in Chapter Two. It addresses the popular misconception that people who are addicted to alcohol or other drugs are incapable of helping themselves. Quite the contrary. A wide range of clinical evidence demonstrates that alcoholics/addicts not only can help themselves, but that their own self-help is the only thing that really works. Treatment professionals who understand this point direct their efforts at drawing out, facilitating and encouraging the patient's motivation to get well. The LifeRing self-help principle rests on the soundest clinical experience.

LifeRing does not buy into the fallacy that there is a magic bullet, a cure that always works if you work it, or a protocol that fits everyone. Research makes clear that treatment needs to be individualized. In LifeRing, each participant builds a personal recovery program (PRP). All personal recovery programs are based on abstinence, but on that foundation a broad diversity of approaches arises, each tailored to the individual whose program it is.

1.14: Chapter Fourteen: Building a Personal Recovery Program

Many LifeRing participants build their personal recovery programs by the random access method, picking up key ideas that work for them as they happen to encounter them in the course of meetings or elsewhere. They place these random gems into a mosaic that constitutes their recovery plan.

LifeRing also offers a structured way of doing the same thing, in the form of the *Recovery by Choice* workbook. This chapter is an introduction to the workbook method and to the nine domains or work areas that are at its core. The workbook does not contain a program; it is a tool for building personal recovery programs in a cohesive, organized way. The domains are somewhat like machines in a gym, designed to exercise different muscle groups. It does not matter in what order you work them. There is a relapse prevention chapter near the end, which serves as quality control on your program building project. At the end, you put all the partial plans from each domain together into a written recovery plan for your life.

The random access method and the structural pathway are complementary strategies for empowering your sober self. Whatever the recovering person's preference, the LifeRing convenor has the resources to serve them.

1.15: Chapter Fifteen: Getting Started

This chapter discusses what it takes to get the first LifeRing meeting started in a new area, and to grow the number of meetings once established. The convenor needs to have at least six months clean and sober before starting the meeting, and needs to be aware that starting a first meeting in virgin territory can be challenging. The most effective way to start is by targeting chemical dependency treatment centers, because they all have numbers of people with alcohol/drug issues who need support groups. Although most of the rehab centers are twelve-step, the doors are not as closed to LifeRing today as they were twenty years ago. The chapter contains guidelines on how to approach treatment professionals and how to make presentations in treatment settings. There are ideas about how and where to get meeting rooms. The chapter also summarizes a long list of methods that LifeRing convenors have used to get the word out. It takes energy and perseverance to get a startup movement like LifeRing up and rolling, but it can be done and is being done, and this chapter shows how. Finally, when the meeting is established and the convenor sits in a room filled with people, there is one more task: identifying and orienting a successor convenor, turning the meeting over, and starting the next one.

1.16: Chapter Sixteen: About This Book

The history of this book is intertwined with the birth of Life-Ring. This chapter sketches the prehistory and the emergence of LifeRing, describes the experience base on which the book is built, and acknowledges the people who helped in one way or another to produce the first edition and the current edition of this volume.

References are in the "(Smith 2000:99)" format. To find the cited source, go to the References section at the end of the book, look in the alphabetical author index for Smith, find the title published in 2000, go to page 99.

This book is unofficial. I have tried as far as possible to express the consensus view of the LifeRing network and to explicate the fundamental philosophy, embodied in a few words in the Life-Ring charter, as accurately as I know how. On some issues I have expressed my personal views without attempting to give voice to a consensus, and I have flagged the passages where that is the case.

Only the LifeRing Congress can expound the official position of LifeRing Secular Recovery. Except for the portions of the text that reflect the LifeRing Bylaws – to date our only official publication – the views expressed here are, therefore, entirely unofficial, and readers are encouraged, as always, to think for themselves.

Chapter 2: The Convenor's Vision

2.1: About This Chapter

People who lead and support LifeRing meetings are called "convenors." This chapter is a basic orientation to the LifeRing convenor's role. Much of the rest of the book is based on the points introduced here. If you read nothing else, read this chapter.

2.2: The Convenor Brings People Together

The word "convenor" comes from the Latin, and has two parts. The prefix "con-" means "with" or "together," as in "chili con carne" – chili together with meat. The stem "venor" comes from the verb "venir," which means, "to come." To "convene" therefore means "to come together," and a convenor is one who convenes others, who causes them to assemble; in other words, one who brings people together. Dictionaries show the word with either an "-er" or an "-or" ending, but the "-or" spelling is more consistent with common words such as "conveyor" and "surveyor" that are built in a similar way.

The convenor, in a nutshell, is one who brings people together. It is an apt name for someone who facilitates recovery from addiction to alcohol and other drugs.

The indigenous peoples of North America discovered already in the 1700s that an effective method to break the power of the European's firewater was for the victims to come together in circles of mutual aid. "Our first experience of individuals turning their own negative experiences with alcohol into a social movement of mutual support occurs within Native American tribes." (White 1998:6)

Since that beginning, American history shows a long and almost uninterrupted sequence of different organized efforts at recovery from addiction to alcohol and drugs, most of them built around the same core concept.

From the original Native American circles, through the Washingtonians of the 1840s, the fraternal orders of the late 19th century, the Keeley Leagues of the early 20th, Alcoholics Anonymous in the mid-20th century, and many others, underneath all kinds of different paintwork and ornamentation, the core concept is the same: bring people together.

Samson Occom (the Mohegan abstinence leader), John Hawkins and John Gough (Washingtonian orators), Nathaniel Curtis (Sons of Temperance), Leslie Keeley (Keeley Leagues), Bill W. and Dr. Bob (Alcoholics Anonymous), Jean Kirkpatrick (Women for Sobriety), Charles Dederich (Synanon), and many others – no matter their culture, creed, or treatment technology, they were all convenors. (White 1998)

Exactly why it works to bring people together is a topic of much confusion. Many of the convenors in the history books seem to have concluded that the actual healing power lay in themselves, or in some sure-fire clinical protocol or magical potion, or in a supernatural being. Thus, in a sense, having once understood that the key thing is to bring people together, they immediately forgot it again, and went running off in a different direction.

Around the turn of the 20th century, the dominant treatment protocol was the Keeley Institutes' Double Chloride of Gold formula. Tens of thousands credited the Keeley potion with their recoveries. With hindsight, the historian White concludes that the formula was "a gimmick that engaged addicts' propensity for magical thinking." The real formula that made the Keeley system successful was the social chemistry among those standing in line to receive the injections, and the support they gave one another in "engineering their own personal reformation" after the treatment. (White 1998:63, 336)

Future historians will likely refer to today's dominant recovery protocols in similar terms.

The challenge for LifeRing is to go forward without gimmicks and without pandering to the craving for magical solutions – to approach sobriety soberly. That requires recognizing the power to recover within those who are recovering.

There is much that remains mysterious about recoveries. How the impulse to get clean and sober begins to awaken and become active inside a given addicted individual – surely one of the most important events in a person's recovery career – is little studied. But once that impulse has awakened and has established so much of a beachhead in the person's mind that they show up on the door of a treatment center or a recovery support group, the processes are less obscure.

The great engine of recovery is the everyday process of social reinforcement. The same energy of social support that can lead two drunks on bar stools to their deaths, can give two recovering people in meeting chairs the strength to live sober lives. The alcoholic/addict has these two powers contending within: to die stoned/drunk or to live clean and sober. Which one prevails depends mainly on which one finds social reinforcement.

2.3: Why the Group Process Works

The recovery group process works by connecting the "good" within each of the assembled individuals so that these parts re-inforce one another and grow stronger. There is a two-minute animated version of this explanation on the *lifering.org* website. Here is a longer text version.

2.3.1: Two Forces At Work Inside

Reduced to its simplest elements, a map of the forces at work inside a person approaching recovery looks like Drawing 1. This is not brain anatomy, it is a schematic diagram. The "A" represents the addiction. It does not matter a great deal what name one gives to it. You can call it the disease, the beast, the devil, the god in the bottle, the little bastard, the lizard brain, or any number of other names. By any label, this is the voice that urges you to drink/use, invents reasons why you should and must, and shifts blame for the harmful consequences. It isn't simply an urge but a highly complex tangle of habits, feelings, skills, and ideas; it is the management center that takes care of the considerable amounts of hard work required to maintain an addiction.

Also active in the mind of the person approaching recovery is another part, which I've labeled "S." This is the sane voice, the part that wants to become clean and sober. The voice of this part argues with the first voice, and says things like "I'm sick and tired of this drug stuff," and "I want to have a life." It picks apart and refutes the rationalizations that the addict self fabricates. I've labeled this part "S" to stand for "the sober self." Some people call it the inner survivor, or other names. The labels

aren't important. What is very important is to be aware that both of these forces – not just one alone – are present and active in the mind of the person approaching recovery.

I've spoken with hundreds of people approaching or in recovery, and almost without exception they report that some version of these two forces is at work inside their minds.

Some people see the "A" and the "S" as choices floating before their eyes. Some people see the "A" and the "S" embodied in metaphorical fighting dogs, Sumo wrestlers, armies, etc.

Many people experience the "A" and the "S" as opposing sides of an ongoing argument in the committee in their heads. Many have discovered something similar to dual personalities within themselves: the sober Me and the drunken/drugged Me, Dr. Jekyll and Mr. Hyde. Some people actually hear voices.

In these and other variations, the same basic theme forms a common core experience of recovering people.

This is a fact long noted by writers who have listened carefully to people in recovery. Here are four among many writers who could be cited.

The historian William White, summing up a consistent thread running through more than 200 years of recovery, writes:

> Addicts simultaneously want – more than anything – both to maintain an uninterrupted relationship with their drug of choice and to break free of the drug. Behaviorally, this paradox is evidenced both in the incredible lengths to which the addict will go to sustain a relationship with the drug and in his or her repeated efforts to exert control over the drug and sever his or her relationship with it. (White 1998:335).

The physician/journalist/photographer Lonny Shavelson, whose portrait of five addicts in San Francisco (*Hooked*) is one of the most empathetic and realistic descriptions of addict life ever penned, writes:

[T]he fierce power of an addict's obsession with drugs is matched, when the timing is right, by an equally vigorous drive to be free of them. (Shavelson 2001:36)

The senior academician Prof. Edward Senay of the University of Chicago, speaking from decades of clinical experience, writes:

The majority of substance abusers [...] are intensely ambivalent, which means that there is another psychological pole, separate from and opposite to denial, that is in delicate, frequently changing balance with denial and that is a pole of healthy striving. (Senay 1997:364)

Similarly, Prof. George Vaillant of Harvard, summing up a study that followed a sample of alcoholic men for more than 55 years, writes:

Alcohol abuse must always create dissonance in the mind of the abuser; alcohol is both ambrosia and poison. (Vaillant 1995: 298)

These writers attest that the urge to become free of the drugs of addiction is part of the addicted person's core life experience, alongside and in conflict with the urge to drink/use. Although the individual in whose mind this dissonance plays out experiences it typically as intense discomfort, even agony, there lies the root of change for the better.

I've purposefully drawn the "A" in Drawing 1 as larger and on top of the "S," to represent the fact that most of the time, in people who are still actively using alcohol or other drugs, the "A" governs them and is in control of their thoughts and actions. In reality, this is an ever-shifting mental balance that can tip back and forth in fractions of a second. What the drawing shows is the average state, the default condition, of the person still drinking/ using, before they have entered and become stable in recovery.

2.3.2: When "A" Connects With "A"

Out in the world, most of the time, when two or more people connect who look like Drawing 1 inside, the addict part in the one reaches out and touches the addict part in the other. They establish addict-to-addict communication, as shown by the arrows in Drawing 2 (below), where the two people are sitting on stools at a bar. If we start with the person on the left, the outgoing arrow might be something like, "Let me buy you a drink," and the incoming arrow, which completes the circuit, would be something like, "Sure thing, and I'll get the next one."

It's important that the arrows go both ways – that the communications form a circle. Psychologists call this a reinforcement or feedback loop. Compare this with jumper cables. Jumper cables have two wires. If you just connect one wire, nothing happens. Power flows only when both conduits are hooked up.

For simplicity, the drawing only shows two arrows. In real life, the addict-addict dialogue would consist of many incoming and outgoing messages, all with the same basic content, forming an active closed circuit connecting one "A" with the other.

What happens to the strength and scope of the "A" inside each participant in this loop as this kind of energy flows back and forth? Everyone knows what happens within each addict when addicts connect as addicts: the "A" grows bigger and more powerful within them. Drawing 3 shows the progression of the addiction within both persons at a more advanced stage of the connection. The "A" has grown bigger and more dominant, and has squeezed the "S" into a smaller area of influence.

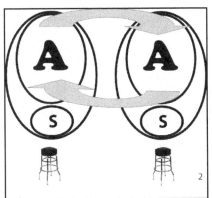

If this circuit continues unbroken, eventually the "S" will lose all traction within the person's thoughts and actions. There will no longer be a voice within the person that says "Whoa!" At that point it is only a matter of time and money before they die. If they have enough money to get all the drug they want and enough undisturbed time to do it, only luck will save them. Maybe someone will find

them, pick them up and call 9-1-1 before it's too late. Otherwise, it's over. When a person is 100 percent "A," they are dead (Drawing 4 right). Addiction has claimed another victim.

2.3.3: When "S" Connects With "S"

Although the lethal feedback loop between "A" and "A" is very common, it is not inevitable. If people come or are brought together in an environment that blocks or attenuates the "A"-to-"A" connections and facilitates connections between the sober selves, "S"-to-"S", then a different outcome is probable. Drawing 5 (below left) shows the initial connection. Here the individuals are in a sober setting such as a LifeRing meeting.

Here, the initial outgoing message (left to right) might be something like, "I feel it's time to do something about my drinking." And the return message might be, "That's why I'm here too." The

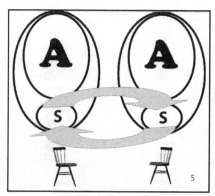

drawing shows only a single set of arrows, but in a real connection there are many messages with a similar content going back and forth continuously in an active feedback loop between "S" and "S."

As in the other case, the product of an ongoing sober-sober connection is reinforcement of the sober areas. Drawing 6 (previous page, bottom right) shows an advanced stage in this process. Each message in the circuit is like a little jolt of energy that sends more power to the connected area.

Gradually, over time, as the loop keeps working, the "S" in each participant grows stronger and larger, and forces the "A" to retreat into a smaller sphere of influence.

At some point in this positive progression, the balance of forces inside the recovering person reverses or tips over. The "S" rises to the top and replaces the "A" in the dominant position in a more or less stable, resilient manner.

Turnovers of this kind in both directions are common during the person's career and even during any given day, hour, or minute. The key achievement of the "S"-to-"S" social reinforcement process is the stability, resiliency, and security of the new, "S"-dominant position.

Before, the person was an addict with a suppressed urge to be sober. Now, they are a sober person with an addiction locked up inside (Drawing 7, below).

If they take care to keep their sober self active and supported, the "A" will lie dormant for life. So long as they do not put alcohol or drugs into their body, they can lead a perfectly normal life. They can realize all the potentials that are within them and seize all the opportunities that life presents.

But if they drink or use again, they revert sooner or later to Drawing 1.

The shorthand description for the progression from the "before" to the "after" condition is empowerment of the sober self. That is, by engaging in a focused, purposeful connection with others similarly situated, the individual frees up the sober potentialities that were latent within, so that this sober force now surfaces in a stable, resilient manner, rises to the top, and defines the person's identity.

In slogan form, the aim of the group process is, "Empower Your Sober Self." You will find this slogan embedded in much of the LifeRing literature, and it forms the title of a book that describes the process in greater depth. Some further discussion of this point is in the chapter on Self-Help in the current volume.

The process here described is not the only possible method for getting to a recovery outcome. Just as there are many ways to obtain fire – for example, lightning, rubbing sticks together, mixing chemicals – there are many processes that can yield recoveries.

I've focused on this particular process because it is the one that is central to what convenors do in LifeRing recovery meetings. Over the years, I've found the metaphor of the "A" and the "S" helpful in understanding what is happening within and between individuals in meetings, and in guiding my work as a convenor.

Now let's take a look at what Life-Ring convenors see and do.

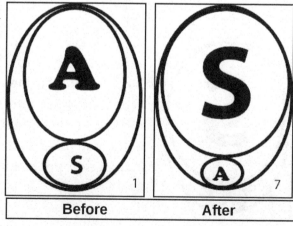

Before   **After**

2.4: The Convenor Sees the Good in Bad People

The LifeRing convenor looking at a person who is approaching recovery sees more than meets the average eye. Most of the world sees only the addict, the alcoholic, the person who is bad, sick, weak, dumb, vicious, self-destructive, insane, etc., and who supplies an endless catalogue of depravity – theft, fraud, murder, molestation, incest, hallucination, mutilation, arson, attempted suicide, etc. – for the morbid fascination of the outsider. The convenor's knowing eye takes in that whole dismal panorama at a glance. The convenor neither condemns nor excuses the person for their bad history. It is what it is. It does not capture the convenor's attention for long.

What the convenor looks for and speaks to in the person approaching recovery is not their addiction (their "A") but their good side, their sober self ("S").

The LifeRing convenor knows that the heavy user of drugs and/or alcohol who comes to a recovery setting only appears to be one person, but is really two. The addict/alcoholic inside the person, who has dictated the person's conduct for most of the recent past, lives in a state of war with a clean and sober doppelganger.

- Within the person there is not only the bad but also the good.

- There is not only the disease but also the immune system.

- There is not only the lunatic bent on self-destruction, but also the sensible person who wants to survive.

Helping someone toward recovery means finding, recognizing, activating, reinforcing and facilitating the empowerment of that healthy striving inside the person.

Therefore the convenor treats each person approaching recovery with respect and kindness, no matter how deeply they have fallen and how much they have harmed themselves and others.

The convenor stands before the person approaching recovery as an equal, and conveys the absolute expectation that the person can succeed in leaving the past behind them and building a new life founded on sobriety.

Sometimes the LifeRing convenor has to maintain this vision in the face of considerable resistance. Society in general views the addict from above, with a mixture of pity and disdain. The healing professions have a long history of contempt for addicts and alcoholics; and this is often mutual. (White 1998:332)

Even in the field of chemical dependency treatment, which arose in part to provide the addicted patient with a shelter from the disdain of other professionals, it is not unusual to find staffers who see only the addict in the addict.

Addiction lecturers frequently present the disease concept of addiction in a one-sided, antiquated manner, as if the innate immune system that engages with and fights disease had not yet been discovered, or did not apply to this condition.

The faith-based recovery model, where healing depends on the outside intervention of a "higher power," starts from the assumption that when it comes to the power for recovery, the alcoholic's tank is empty.

Each of these visions is blind to, ignores, dismisses, or steps on the addict's own inner sober resources, the "S." These models look inside the addict and find nothing to admire and nothing to work with. In essence, they have given up on addiction and on the addict.

The person in active addiction all too often echoes these paralyzing views and displays little persuasive evidence that contrary, healthy forces are working within.

At times, the LifeRing convenor's vision that there is good inside of people who are so very obviously bad – that there is health inside of people so obviously sick – seems merely a hypothesis, a metaphysic, a faith, or an illusion.

The convenor's vision finds regular empirical validation in the successful conduct of a recovery meeting. If addicts were only bad, there could be no good meetings. If addicts were only sick, the meetings would only spread the infection. If addicts had no recovery power, they would have nothing of their own to contribute to groups except the chronicles of their depravity.

If addicts were only addicts, then there would be no difference between recovery meetings and bar room or drug house gatherings.

Yet anyone who has ever attended a LifeRing meeting will have witnessed a remarkably positive, healthy, sober, lively, and frequently laughter-filled encounter.

Where did all those horrible people go, who caused so much grief to others and themselves? Where did all these likable, vulnerable, interesting and bright individuals come from who populate the meeting? The answer, of course, is that both personas have been in the same bodies all the time, and still are.

It just took someone to see the good in them and bring them together in a way that validated, connected and reinforced that goodness.

2.5: The Convenor Facilitates Connections

The LifeRing model of recovery differs from many others in that we locate the healing power within people and in their togetherness, and not in something external to them. The force that heals arises from within people and gains power when they connect so that it flows between them. The convenor's art and science lies in aligning the connections in a purposeful way.

In chemistry, a catalyst is an element that makes it possible for two or more other substances to react with each other and to become transformed. The catalyst is not a fuel or an ingredient in the reaction; it merely lines up the molecules of the other substances in a way that allows the reaction between them to take place.

The LifeRing convenor is a kind of catalyst. The convenor's actions make it possible for others to connect with each other and to become transformed. The energy and the material for the transformation came from within them; all that the convenor did was to line them up properly so that they could connect and start the reaction between them.

Some people command a high price for this wisdom that the LifeRing convenor gives away for free. Witness Marshall Goldsmith, ranked among the top ten executive coaches by the *Wall Street Journal* and profiled in the *New Yorker* and *Harvard Business Review*. Says Goldsmith:

> A key thing is, I really don't hold myself up as 'coach as expert.' I'm much more 'coach as facilitator.' Most of what my clients learn about themselves they don't learn from me. They learn from their friends and colleagues and family. Anybody around you can help you change your behavior, and they can help you more than an executive coach can. (Goldsmith 2000:22,24)

Although convenors may help to bring about extraordinary transformations, they are ordinary persons in recovery and do not possess or require extraordinary powers. The traditional superhero costumes do not fit the convenor. For example:

• The LifeRing convenor is not a power figure like a surgeon who slashes people open, fixes the mess in their innards, and stitches them up again all better.

• The convenor is not a psychiatrist who develops deep theories about what is wrong with the patient and prescribes appropriate therapies and medications to cure them.

- The convenor is not a chemical dependency treatment counselor or therapist, who assigns a clinical protocol and supervises the patient's progress through it.

- The convenor is not a shaman or priest who channels the power of a supreme being to heal people or save them from evil.

- The convenor is not the mother or father of others' recoveries.

- The convenor is not a performer who puts on a transforming spectacle.

- The convenor is not a professor, wise man, sage, or guru.

- The LifeRing convenor is not the disciple of any prophet nor the scholar of any particular doctrine.

- The convenor is not a recovery expert and is not the owner of any special truth.

This last point bears emphasizing. The LifeRing convenor does not have, and does not pretend to have, a Truth, a Way, a Magic Bullet, or some other sure-fire cure for addiction, other than the homely wisdom that you will stay clean and sober if you don't put drugs or alcohol into your body.

The LifeRing convenor refrains from telling other people what they must do in order to get or stay sober.

I have been clean and sober more than twenty years now and I have a good idea how to keep me that way. I do not know how to get you clean and sober and keep you there.

There are many different ways to do it. What worked for one person often fails another. There are no panaceas for addiction. White, after surveying nearly 300 years of recovery history in the United States, concludes emphatically:

> There is no universally successful cure for addiction – no treatment specific.... [A]ddiction professionals who claim universal superiority for their treatment disqualify them-

selves as scientists and healers by the very grandiosity of that claim. (White 1998:342)

I do have complete confidence that you can find a way that works for you. You probably already know the way, or sense it, from the experience of living in your body.

As a convenor I offer you my best efforts to create and to sustain a supportive social framework in which you can pursue your work of self-transformation. There is more detail about this topic in the chapter on Self-Help.

The LifeRing convenor's role, then, is to facilitate a process that runs between and within others. At given moments, in a pinch, the convenor might have to do a bit of healing, a bit of enlightening, and a bit of bossing around, but all those things are incidental and exact a price.

The core of the convenor's role and the source of the convenor's renewal is to connect people with each other in a way that empowers their own inner urge to be free of alcohol and other addictive drugs.

2.6: The Convenor Empowers Others

In an established LifeRing meeting where everyone is familiar with the format, the convenor may be almost invisible and the role may seem trivial. Apart from speaking a few ritual words that signal the opening and closing, and handling a few chores with the clipboard and the basket, the convenor seems to be nothing more than an ordinary participant. If you come in a few minutes late and leave a little early, and the meeting is humming along smoothly, you may not have a clue which member is the convenor. You are probably then in the presence of a convenor who has mastered the role.

It's only when there is a snag in the meeting's process that you may discover who the convenor is. For example, someone goes on much too long. The next person who wants to speak is squirming in their seat. Other members are tapping their feet impatiently. The convenor is the one who interrupts and asks the talker to please look at the clock.

The convenor did not interrupt because the convenor wanted to speak, but because others wanted to. (The convenor will also personally refrain from going on too long, on the same ground.) In general, what distinguishes the convenor's role from that of the ordinary member is its other-directedness.

Almost every meeting participant in time connects with others and allows others to connect with them. That is the core process within a well-run meeting; it embraces everyone including the member who also wears the convenor hat. The convenor's distinct responsibility as convenor is to facilitate and protect the sobriety connections of others with each other.

When the convenor has laid the foundations properly, then people in the meeting will engage in sober-sober communication with one another all around during the course of the session. In a good LifeRing meeting there is broad participation and active crosstalk involving practically everyone at some time during the session.

The person who believes the convenor's primary function is to gather people into a circle focused on the convenor is not yet thinking like a LifeRing convenor at all. The meeting is not about the convenor. The meeting is about facilitating sober connections between the participants all around, so that the participants themselves become connected and empowered.

If you were to draw a chart showing who has talked or responded directly with whom at some time during the meeting, you could get a picture like Drawing A, next page, bottom left. Drawing A shows a meeting in which every participant connected with at least three other participant at some time during the session. (Assume these are all "S"-to-"S" connections.) This sketch rep-

resents an ideal rarely achieved in real life, but it indicates the
general aim of the convenor's work. A meeting in which everyone
established a bond of supportive communication with everyone
else is the strongest possible meeting.

By contrast, if a meeting only has connections running between
the convenor and the other participants, without more, it is a weak
meeting; see Drawing B, below right. The convenor in Drawing
B is acting like a lecturer, a guru, a healer, doctor, or shaman, not
yet like a convenor. Such a person may feel a sense of control,
enjoy being the focus of attention, and receive many strokes, but
they have not yet begun the actual work of convening, which
consists of facilitating others to connect with each other.

Eye contact shows the pattern. If every meeting participant
looks at the convenor when sharing the story of their week, the
convenor is being seen as an authority with healing powers. If this
happens to me, I make it a point not to return eye contact, but to
look around at the group instead. It may be necessary to ask the
person speaking to address the group.

Similarly, if some member other than the convenor were to
monopolize the airtime, the purpose of the meeting would be
diverted.

A good meeting is one where at the end all the members feel
stronger and more connected in their sobriety than at the begin-

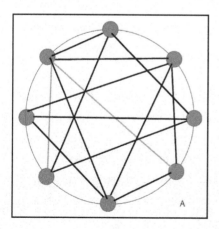
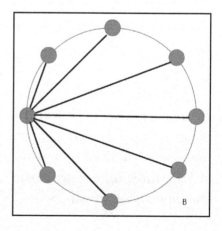

ning. The process-centered LifeRing meeting format, with its emphasis on participation, on everyday real-life issues, and its broad scope for crosstalk, is well adapted for this purpose. There is more detail about this in the next chapter.

Outside the meeting, the same concept of other-directedness defines the convenor's role. To bring another person to the meeting you attend is a form of outreach, and that is a form of convenor work. Convenor work also includes bringing a person you don't know to a meeting you yourself don't attend.

Members who give LifeRing presentations, who write for publication, who maintain an online platform, who do computer entry, answer phones, fulfill literature orders, keep the accounts, or any of the scores of other services that are required to get and to keep others connected with each other – these are also doing convenor work. To do convenor work means to facilitate and to empower other people to get together in recovery, including people whom the convenor doesn't know and may never meet.

A person may have read many books and have a deep understanding of drug and alcohol issues, but if this person does not play a role in bringing people together in recovery, this is not a convenor. A convenor disconnected is a contradiction in terms. A convenor alone is powerless. All the convenor's power to effect change comes from bringing people together.

2.7: The Successful Convenor Can Step Away

The ultimate test of whether a convenor has succeeded in bringing people together in recovery is whether the convenor can walk away.

In an established LifeRing meeting, the convenor has laid the foundations so well, and the participants have become so connected with one another, that they almost run the meeting themselves without the convenor's intervention.

That is the ideal, and the convenor who achieves it deserves the highest esteem. In order to earn that gratification, the convenor needs to be able to pass on the clipboard and the rest of the convenor role to a successor.

There is nothing more personally gratifying for a convenor than to come back to a meeting two years or five years or more after having been its convenor, and find it still up and running and helping people stay clean and sober. In that sense, the convenor's role is similar to a parent's: nothing is more heartwarming than to see the offspring thriving on their own.

When I convene a LifeRing meeting, I make it my Rule One to work myself out of the job and to prepare to hand over the role to a successor. I make it a conscious policy from the first session to identify the likely people who in due time will become convenors, and to prepare them to take over the role. (In some special settings this policy needs to be adapted; see Chapter Nine.) As a LifeRing convenor I do not teach people how to get sober, but I do teach sober people how to become LifeRing convenors. There are more details about how and when and to whom to pass the baton in the Chapter Fifteen of this book.

Being able to hand over the clipboard, step away, and watch the meeting thrive is not only a matter of intense personal gratification for the convenor. The motto "Pass It On" is essential to the survival of the meeting and to the health and growth of the LifeRing network.

I have seen convenors in our predecessor organization who remained the leaders of the same community-based meeting for years and years. They came to treat the meeting as their personal property and to see themselves as indispensable. They made no efforts to attract or train successors or to rotate the convenor role. When those convenors eventually burned out or moved away, "their" meetings collapsed. The participants had become dependent on that convenor and could not proceed on their own. This is hardly a model for an addiction recovery organization, is it?

A community meeting where the only person capable of convening is the current convenor, and where no one has emerged as a likely successor, is either a new meeting just getting off the ground, or an old, dried-up meeting that is waiting to die. Such a meeting is fragile, brittle, liable to be shattered by the smallest reverse, and doomed to disappear when its current convenor cannot continue.

The mature, resilient meeting is one that has a core group of past and future convenors in it. Such a meeting has a depth of experience and ability that will carry it through any challenge and any change of personnel.

Moreover, such a meeting will spawn new meetings as it outgrows its rooms and as its experienced members seek the challenge and satisfaction of bringing more people together in recovery elsewhere.

At this time, the demand for LifeRing meetings outstrips the current supply of convenors ready to lead them. Convenors with the experience of starting new meetings are especially valuable.

When they have successfully started one and turned it over, they will be needed somewhere else to start another. The principle of "Pass It On" ensures that there will in time be LifeRing meetings everywhere that people in recovery want to have them.

2.8: Seven Reasons to Become a Convenor

People who become convenors do it for a variety of good reasons. The following seven are the ones I hear most often. One: it helps their recovery. Two: it expresses gratitude. Three: it's a moral obligation. Four: it gives a higher meaning to their life. Five: somebody has to do it. Six: it feels good. Seven: for love.

2.8.1: It Helps My Recovery

Being a convenor can be helpful to one's personal sobriety in several obvious ways. For example, the convenor is expected to appear at the meeting on a regular basis, and any kind of regular sobriety practice is usually an effective recovery tool. (For examples, see *Recovery By Choice*, Ch. 3, Sec. 11, My 'Daily Do.')

The convenor has a higher profile as a person in recovery than the average participant, and is therefore likely to have a larger and more active support network. Acting as convenor involves a deeper emotional commitment to recovery than the average person. Relapsing while in the convenor role would be a serious setback not only for the convenor (it would end their current usefulness as convenor) but also for others in the meeting who may have come to look to the convenor as a role model.

For these and similar reasons, many persons who already have their personal recovery programs well launched choose to take up the convenor role for its ongoing supportive benefits. There is more discussion of this issue in the final chapter.

LifeRing Convenor Mary S.:

Tonight's meeting was just one of those wonderful gatherings in which I felt tremendous love and connectedness with each person present.

A member with eleven months' sobriety convened the meeting. It's such a joy to see the transformation that has taken place in him, as he moved from viewing sobriety as a straitjacket to really unfurling his sober wings....

I felt the love of those who truly understood my struggles. I felt gifted by a generosity I never experienced prior to my recovery.

It hasn't always been a rose garden, but my decision to become a convenor, rooted in the purely selfish need for a viable f2f alternative to AA, has been one of the greatest joys I've known.

2.8.2: To Give Something Back

A second reason to become a convenor is gratitude. When I decided I had to do something about my drinking, I found a support group already functioning and available to me. A handful of convenors had arranged for the room, put out literature, and got the meeting up and running. I derived an enormous lifetime personal benefit from their effort. Most newcomers are in a similar situation. After one accumulates some sobriety time one begins to feel grateful to the group. The dollar or two that the average member puts into the basket falls far short of compensation either for the benefit one has received or for the effort that others expend to keep the group running. Donating one's time as convenor is one way to show gratitude and give something back.

2.8.3: Because of the Golden Rule

A third reason to become a convenor is similar to gratitude, but on a different level. It is based on the golden rule of ethics: what goes around, comes around. When I sowed addiction, I reaped addiction and fed on despair. Becoming a convenor is an ethical affirmation of one's individual responsibility for the messages circulating in the social network. The convenor sows a message of sobriety and prepares a harvest of hope and positive transformation.

2.8.4: For More Meaning in Life

A fourth reason to become a convenor is to reach a higher sense of meaningfulness in one's life. Meaning in life arises from connectedness with others. Drugs and alcohol led many people into social isolation, or into a set of phantom relationships with drinking/drugging partners or codependents. Participating in a self-help recovery group over time means re-connecting with people (or connecting for the first time) and establishing authentic relationships. This is a great improvement, and it is enough for many people. However, some people seek a meaning in life beyond self-repair and self-transformation. Becoming a convenor is a way of dedicating oneself to a mission of service to others, and this can yield a deeper sense of purpose and direction in one's life.

2.8.5: Because Someone Has to Do It

A fifth reason why people become LifeRing convenors is because they feel that something has to be done. Despite more than 60 years of nearly everyone being funneled into recovery on the 12-step pattern, the drug and alcohol problem shows no signs of abatement. There is a great deal of room for improvement in the way we as a society approach the issue. Someone has to step in and help build another road. The LifeRing convenor is the agent of an unspoken social consensus that it is time to give people a meaningful choice of recovery paths.

2.8.6: Because It Feels Good

A sixth reason why people become LifeRing convenors is for the emotional rewards. The convenor's efforts frequently result in profound changes for the better in others' lives. To be a witness to so much transformation is already a privilege. To be a catalyst in such a process can stir one's feelings with indescribable force, bringing up tears of gladness. When I leave a meeting at which things have gone well, I feel a sense of warmth in my gut, unlike any other satisfaction I have experienced. Being a convenor not only does good, it feels good.

2.8.7: Because Convening is Love

A seventh and final reason why people become convenors is love. When people have been clean and sober for some time, they sometimes feel an upwelling of love pent up inside during the long winter of their addiction. Now it surges out of them and seeks an object. No flesh-and-blood person has sufficient magnitude to absorb this force. It requires a transcendent object. The role of convenor affords such overflowing love a worthy channel. Love the good in bad people. Nurture the health in people who are ill. Take people whose instinct is to hide and isolate, and bring them together. Connect them, protect them as they recover their self-respect and exercise their sober legs. Bringing people together in recovery is a transcendent embrace. To convene is to love.

2.9: In Appreciation of Convenors

The whole LifeRing network exists so that people in recovery can come to the meetings, talk about their current recovery issues, get their sobriety charged up, help strengthen others' sobriety, put a couple of dollars in the basket, applaud, feel good, and leave. This meeting process keeps people clean and sober, week after week. Thanks to their sobriety, people develop new lives, new relationships, new interests, new everything. They become transformed in diverse and wonderful ways that no one, not even they themselves, could have anticipated.

People can have perfectly satisfactory recoveries without becoming missionaries. We are a pragmatic organization, not an evangelical one. But there will always be some among our members who get inspired by what they see happening and leap up to get involved. Whatever their mix of motivations, when they see the need for a meeting, they step in and start one. When they see a lack of literature they get it or make it. When they see anything that needs to be done, they get down and do it. They are both talkers and doers, but above all doers. They not only dream, they convert their visions into nuts and bolts and make them work. They are producers, makers, shakers, people who move mountains. They are LifeRing convenors.

Convenors are the core of our organization, and the bridge to its future. Those comfortable meetings with their friendly process, the week-to-week recharge of people's sobriety energies, all the benefits that spin off from sobriety – none of that would have started, and none of it would keep going very long, without someone to found the meeting, set up the room, establish the meeting format, keep the conversation rolling, provide the literature, connect the meetings together, and perform scores of other services in and outside the meeting context. People emerging from the cave of alcohol and drugs need people who can bring them together. Recovery requires convenors and members who do convenor work. The convenors of yesterday and today need to pass on their accumulated experience and knowledge to the convenors of tomorrow, so that our network of hope, choice, and transformation may have continuity and growth.

Chapter 3: How Was Your Week?

3.1: About This Chapter

This chapter answers the question: "What do people do at a typical LifeRing meeting?" It discusses the main body of the process-focused LifeRing meeting format. This consists mainly of first-person reports about current events in each participant's recovery, combined with supportive conversational feedback, also known as crosstalk.

This chapter assumes that the room has people in it, that someone has already read the opening statement, and that the only thing required now to get the participation flowing is for the convenor to pronounce the opening line, "How was your week?"

3.2: A Newsreel of Highlights and Heartaches

"How was my week?" Most convenors have seen a first-timer at a LifeRing meeting look startled when it comes to their turn and blurt out, "What am I supposed to do? Oh, talk about my week? OK, I can do that." They go on and do it, immediately.

Everyone has had a week. Talking about the current events in their life is something almost anyone can and will do. This invitation has a low entry barrier. Using this format, people can be successful and comfortable at participating in a recovery meeting from Day One. A common term for this kind of participation is checking in or doing a check-in.

The most productive "How Was Your Week?" check-ins resemble a newsreel of highlights and heartaches. Like a weekly "news in review" program, the speaker pulls out one, two, or a handful of emotionally meaningful anecdotes from recent days that stick in their mind, and relates those in rich detail.

The material that people bring to the meeting is as broad and varied as real life. No two meetings will have the identical content. But certain concerns come up time and again. In no particular order, the anecdotes that LifeRing participants frequently contribute in their weekly "highlights" newsreel come from these general areas:

- Close encounters with alcohol/drugs. For example, being in a scene where alcohol/drugs are present, having it offered to you, having a craving for it, running into a former dealer, having a drinking/using dream, finding a forgotten stash in the house, etc.

- Relationships. For example, a Significant Other who is clueless about one's recovery, or is supportive at a critical moment; a family member who said something hurtful or helpful; true friends and so-called friends; getting respect and understanding in a relationship; breaking up or starting something new; dealing with a death in the family; responsibilities toward children, and much else.

- Feelings. For example, feelings of depression one felt this week; grief, anger, boredom, love, abandonment, loneliness, happiness, pride – any other emotion, up, down or sideways, that had an impact on one's recovery one way or another.

- Work issues. The whole gamut: unemployment, interviewing, promotions, boss problems, issues with fellow workers, retirement, etc. – whatever impacts a person's recovery.

• Money problems. For example, paying for treatment or for sober housing; getting on disability; having "too much" money (temptation to use); dealing with debts, child support, bills, bankruptcy, windfalls, other sources of financial stress.

• Health issues. Medications the person is taking, dual diagnosis issues, doctor stories, evaluating different treatment programs, dealing with surgeries, injuries, sicknesses, pregnancy, etc.

• Spare time issues. Vacations, holidays, barbecues, parties, sports, hobbies, concerts, trips, TV programs, films, etc.

And much more. A fairly comprehensive collection of the topics that people bring up in these meetings can be found in the Table of Contents of the *Recovery by Choice* workbook. Whatever has touched the person's recovery that week is a fair topic to contribute to the check-in. The typical meeting thus will feature a variety of topics, depending on who is present and what is happening in their recoveries at this particular time.

The underlying assumption of this meeting format is that recovery is an ongoing project, a work in progress, a continuing voyage. The check-in is similar to a progress report such as would be given by a project manager, author, navigator, or other responsible person.

A person may pass, but this is rare; most people participate from their first meeting. Simple arithmetic will indicate the average amount of time available to each one. The expectation is that everyone in the meeting will get some air time to present their current ongoing recovery progress report.

3.3: Planning Ahead

Although it's put in the past tense, the question "How Was Your Week?" is shorthand for a larger invitation to talk that also includes the week ahead. The opening statement usually spells out this point.

One of the most useful things the participants can do for one another is to help make plans for challenges coming up. For example, a member has to attend a relative's wedding next week, and asks for ideas for how to survive it clean and sober. Others contribute their experiences and thoughts.

The person selects the ideas that seem most useful and makes a plan. Then, next meeting, the person can report how it went. Birthdays, anniversaries, and family gatherings all may present challenges to a person's recovery and are good topics to discuss in advance.

Making plans for the week ahead is particularly important before notoriously difficult passages such as holidays. Every year a proportion of recovering people in the U.S. relapses on Valentine's Day, St. Patrick's Day, July 4, Labor Day, Halloween, Thanksgiving, Christmas, and New Year's. This clockwork massacre could be largely avoided by anticipating and planning ahead.

The LifeRing convenor will want to nudge and encourage the meeting participants in the weeks before every holiday to talk in detail about how they are going to survive it sober. Where will I be? Who will I be with? How will I handle the foreseeable challenges that usually come up? A person prepared is a person more empowered.

If people are habitually forgetting to talk about their next week, the convenor could change the format by opening the meeting with the question "What's coming up next week in my recovery?" or "How will I survive Halloween clean and sober?" Or the convenor could nudge a person after they have talked about their previous week by asking, "And what does your next week look like, Sandy?"

Or, if no one has talked forward, the convenor could start a second go-round on the topic, "What is coming up for my recovery next week?" One way or another, the convenor will encourage people gradually to raise their eyes from the ground, at least occasionally, and look up the road toward the next meeting.

3.4: Gory Details Please

The "How Was Your Week" format works best if people enrich their contributions with significant detail. Details are the handles that allow people to grab on to someone else's truth and take it in.

"Yesterday I got so depressed I almost left the house to get a supply. Instead I lay down and took a nap. When I woke up I felt better." Listeners may take from this specific detail not only the particular idea that the speaker laid on the table ("take a nap") but also the broader concept that our feelings at any given moment are not commands that we must unquestioningly obey. (See *Recovery by Choice*, Ch. 6, Sec. 15.) We can take actions that defeat our urges to use or drink. These truths are important tools for the recovering person.

A young man in a meeting I convened recently shared that his biggest sobriety challenge this past week was watching football on television. He found his arm reaching out, reflex-like, for the can of beer. How did he get through it? He bought a six-pack of root beer. He watched the game with another sober friend in recovery. When the triggers got uncomfortable (such as during the beer commercials) they turned off the set. Three valuable tools in three sentences!

In the lively crosstalk that followed, people contributed more. Watch college ball instead of pro ball (no beer ads). Tape the game and watch the replay after you know the final score. Sit farther away from the set and turn down the volume so that the stimulus doesn't overpower you. Screw football, go for a walk instead. And more.

Sometimes people have no tools in their toolbox. For example, they don't know any good ways of saying, "No, thanks" when alcohol is offered, and so they stammer, stumble, and give in.

Working in a LifeRing group, they could probably learn an array of twelve tested answers in about six minutes. The *Recovery by Choice* workbook has a good collection of them (Ch. 5, Sec. 14).

Or they don't know how to protect their sober glass in a drinking situation. A simple old trick like, "Keep a rubber band around your glass and always keep it topped up" might turn the tide for them. Or they don't plan ahead; they don't have their own transportation home when it's time to beat an escape.

Whether it's taking a nap, taking a class, taking a shower, going for a walk, having a talk, volunteering at the library, cleaning the house, reading a book, or any number of other things – the meeting is a constant stream of vivid, practical ideas that worked to keep someone sober, someone you can see and talk to.

Over time, the accumulation of tools contributed in this concrete, nonthreatening, easily accessible fashion affords each participant the opportunity to select and assemble a personal tool set appropriate to their particular needs.

As the meeting's convenor, I sometimes have the opportunity to pull some general truths out of the diversity of concrete details that participants have laid on the table. For example, I may venture something like, "Urges are to be expected, but we don't have to let them overpower us." "There's lots of ways to beat a craving." "We don't have to act on every feeling." "We have choices about our voices." As long as I don't overdo it and become repetitive or pedantic, a few well-chosen generalities can help to bring the diversity of details into a sharper, more coherent focus.

At other times, I have to look beyond a wall of bland generalities to get at a vivid core of detail. In new meetings, people sometimes answer the invitation to talk about their week with a drab cliche: "My week? Fine. Just taking it day by day. Thanks." Then they look to the next person.

Of course, the person has a right to pass, and if that was their intent, then the convenor needs to respect it. But if the person simply doesn't know what is expected, the convenor may want to invite a more detailed contribution.

For example, "OK, Ronnie, I'm glad you stayed clean and sober. Can you share with the group how you did it? Did you run into any situations this week that in the past you would have drank or used over? What did you change this time so that you were able to stay clean and sober?"

Or, "What specifically are you doing different each day now from what you did when you drank or used every day? Can you share the secrets of your success?"

Telling a story rich in significant detail comes naturally for some people, but others need help to overcome talking in cliches. The convenor who has people unclear on the concept may want to model the detailed narrative, or begin the check-in with a participant who is particularly skilled at speaking in colors.

Details also matter when looking forward. A general plan such as "I'm going to stay sober at my sister's wedding" is weak. The convenor or another participant may want to ask questions such as, "OK, Alex, what exactly will you do when all the wedding guests are raising their champagne glasses to the bride and the groom?" – "Where will you get an amber nonalcoholic beverage to put in your glass?" – "How will you get that beverage into your glass in time for the toast?" – "How will you prevent the server from filling your glass with champagne while you're not looking?"

The more experienced group participants can help Alex put together the nuts and bolts that will make the plan work. (For a worksheet that encourages detailed event planning, see *Recovery By Choice*, Ch. 4, Sec. 3, "Learning to do one activity clean and sober.")

Details, gory details, also make people laugh, and laugh hard – a very frequent side-effect of the LifeRing meeting format. A counselor walking by in the hall stuck his head in the door of one of our meetings recently and looked around sternly: "You guys are having too much fun in here!" We cracked up again.

Addiction to drugs/alcohol is a grim business indeed, but getting clean and sober needn't be. Laughter sometimes comes welling up irrepressibly when people get sober. Sober laughter breaks down barriers and helps people bond in sobriety. Laughter is great recovery medicine.

3.5: Making "I" Statements

A good habit that tends to bring out significant, colorful details is making "I" statements. "I" statements begin with "I experienced ..." or "I felt ..." or "I did ..." and the like.

"I" statements have many virtues in self-help meetings. They are based in personal knowledge or belief, and this tends to keep the talk grounded in reality – at least someone's reality. More important, "I" statements are modest; they respect other people's boundaries and their freedom of choice.

By contrast, statements that begin with "you" (as in "you have to do such and such") or with the royal "we" (as in "we alcoholics always ...") are bossy and disempowering; they invade other people's space and tend to repel and shut people out.

The recovery writer Charlotte Kasl recalls feeling violated and alienated by the constant use of generalizations and stereotypes in twelve-step literature – "We" all did this and "we" all did that, usually selfish reprehensible things. This practice, she feels, "echoes the authoritarian righteous father speaking down to the children." (Kasl 1992:227)

Ironically, the people most liable to bless their peers with instant diagnoses ("Your problem is ..."), universal truths ("We alcoholics always ...") and infallible solutions ("You have to...") are usually those with about fifteen minutes of personal sobriety. The delusion that they possess magical healing powers seems to be a stage in some people's early learning process.

Most people learn with experience that I-statements tend to have more basis in reality and tend to be more effective in motivating change.

Compare these two statements:

• "We alcoholics have to continue to develop in our sobriety in order to prevent relapse."

• "I signed up for a Saturday morning class to give myself another reason not to drink Friday night."

The first statement has the cast-iron clang of Absolute Truth, and few would dare argue with it. But in pronouncing it, the speaker postures as an Authority entitled to lay down The Law, and this heavy-footed pose tends to send about half the audience into mental flight and the other half into rebellion. It conjures up no specific consequences for action that would allow anyone to get a handle on it.

The second statement expresses a similar idea as the first, but the emotional response to the speaker is likely to be warm, affectionate, approving: "Good girl, you're taking care of business, that is a clever idea!" The statement makes no claim to lay down a rule for others, and so it inspires little fear or resistance.

Listeners are likely to pick up the concrete detail (sign up for a class) and generalize from it to fit their own particular circumstances (for example: play soccer, go for a walk with my grandpa, volunteer at the animal shelter). The person who laid the concrete detail on the table as an offering is more likely to motivate positive change in some listener's lives than the one who brandished The Truth as a sword over everyone's head.

Participants may well bring in news articles or research summaries they have read, or share interesting recovery books, and engage in vigorous discussion of general recovery issues, but the talk always arises from and returns to the personal dimension. "I read this really interesting book, *Hooked*, by Shavelson. He argues the treatment industry needs to be reformed. Specifically (...). The book really helped me make sense of my own experience because (...)."

Or, "Did you read that Caroline Knapp died? I was really moved by her book *Drinking, A Love Story*. She was only 42. Lung cancer. Hmm." These meetings are not graduate seminars in a course on chemical dependency. The discussion always comes back to what is useful to the participants' own recovery.

Even when a person has specifically asked for advice, the use of I-statements is always appropriate. I-statements promote the good mental habit of taking responsibility for one's own recovery program.

3.6: Your Week *In Recovery*

The question "How Was Your Week" contains an implied limitation: the week *in recovery*. Sometimes the connection between a topic and recovery is not obvious on the face of it. I remember one meeting where a diesel mechanic and a fisherman spent quite a while talking about marine engines. I let it go on because they obviously found the topic fascinating, the meeting was small that night, and I was intimidated by their expertise; but I was fighting an urge to step in and ask "And what does that have to do with your recovery?"

I realized later that I probably did the right thing to be quiet in that instance. Neither of them had ever talked shop before without a joint in one hand and a beer in the other, and didn't think it was possible. The meeting was very liberating for their sobriety.

Now they were freed to talk shop sober anytime; they knew they could do it.

Addiction is not a localized ailment like hemorrhoids. It is systemic; it can invade and attack every facet of a person's life. Therefore, the range of issues that may be relevant to an individual's recovery is very broad, and no two persons are likely to present exactly identical profiles.

For a sample of the broad range of issues that can be relevant to recovery, see the *Recovery By Choice* workbook. Therefore the convenor will want to give a participant the benefit of the doubt that a given topic is related to that person's recovery. In a sense, everything is linked with recovery somehow; one just has to look for the connection.

But there are limits. If a participant talks about nothing but marine engines week after week, then the convenor or another member may want to say a word to this person on the side and ask them what is really going on in their recovery.

Sometimes such a person is facing very difficult recovery issues and is afraid to open up to the group. In other cases the convenor may want to tackle the issue head-on: "Terry, what does this have to do with your recovery?" If nothing were done, the meeting could in time drift off its recovery anchor and become a marine mechanics' social club.

3.7: Similar But Different Formats

The question "How Was Your Week?" focuses the meeting on current events in the participants' lives between meetings. As a rule of thumb, the time span of interest is the period since the last meeting and until the next one. Most commonly, that's a week in each direction, but the format can easily be compressed or expanded to a day or a month or a season.

With some regularity, I run into people who are accustomed to meeting formats that sound similar but have different time horizons. At one extreme, a person may think the format is "What Is Your Life Story?" At the other extreme, someone may believe that the format is to talk about "What I Am Feeling Right Now."

3.7.1: The Life Story Format

LifeRing meeting participants will usually get to know one another's life stories over time. The autobiography comes out in installments. For example, when people have a current relationship heartache, they may flash back to previous events in that relationship or in previous relationships.

Occasionally someone has an experience that seems to project their whole life onto a screen, and they share it at the meeting. Sometimes they just feel like telling their life story, and they do.

That's wonderful. But "telling your life story" is not the everyday LifeRing meeting format. One's whole life story changes little from week to week, and repeating it week after week like a broken record would soon put people to sleep.

More important, the "autobiography" format conveys the message that one's life story is already basically finished and "in the can." The LifeRing format, by contrast, tries to convey the message that one's life story is very much unfinished, and that the really vital parts of it are here now, fresh clay in our hands, for us to design and shape as we choose.

3.7.2: My Feelings Now

At the other end of the time scale is the topic "How (or What) Am I Feeling Right Now?" This is an exercise some counselors use in group therapy sessions to help people get in touch with their feelings.

Often this topic leads people to analyze how they feel right now about the other people in the group, about the counselor, and about the meeting process. This is a useful therapeutic exercise for its purposes, and if the LifeRing meeting participants want to try it out some week, why not? But as a regular practice, this focus is misdirected.

The meeting is not, as a general routine, directed inward on its own process, and the meeting is not psychotherapy. We help each other to stay clean and sober regardless of how we are feeling. The main business of the meeting is for people to touch base, to present an account of their lives outside the meeting, and give one another support in recovery.

The convenor who sees that newcomers are misconceiving the LifeRing meeting format may want to nudge a participant toward the topic. For example: "OK, Ricky, but what was the highlight of your life story in the last week, and what new chapter will you write in your autobiography next week?" Or: "Thanks, Marty, how does your feeling good right now tie into what has been happening in your recovery since the last meeting?"

3.8: What "How Was Your Week?" Really Asks

There is nothing magical about the seven-day period. It could be a day or a year. I've been in wonderful meetings where a person talked only about what happened to them that morning, and in others where people hadn't been to this meeting for six months.

What we're really asking here is "How have you been since last we got together?" It is as if the members of an extended family had scattered and gone their various ways and had various adventures, and have now assembled again, and everyone wants to hear everyone's stories.

The point is to express pleasure at being together again, and to communicate interest and concern for the other's life in the interval since the last meeting, and in the period until the next one. The question "How Was Your Week" basically says that we care about each other, we want to learn from each other, we are family. The message between the lines is one of love and empathy.

3.9: Down with Drunkalogues

The general observation that the weekly check-in benefits from "gory detail" is subject to an important exception. If a person at a meeting has spent their last week drinking/drugging, then the fewer details, the better.

A vivid, detailed account of this activity is the last thing that people at a recovery support group meeting need or want to hear. Detailed descriptions of the drink/drug (for example, the quantity and type and brand of liquor, the amount and color or purity of the drug), blow-by-blow accounts of how they connected and how much they used and where and with whom, the quality and

---

LifeRing Convenor Njon W.:

One of the things that I love most about LifeRing is that when I was going to my very first few weeks of meetings, folks with lots of long-term sobriety spoke to me about things that were going on in their lives that were difficult and how they were dealing with them.

They could also relate to what I was going through because not only had they been through it, but they realized that even in sobriety, life continues to throw us difficult situations and that being clearheaded and facing these difficulties is easier in the long run. They showed me the courage to face these issues and I reminded them of the turning point when they decided to choose sobriety.

Our sober selves supported and strengthened one another as opposed to the "take the cotton out of your ears and put it in your mouth" reception I had come to know from other programs.

length of the high, and the like, tend to trigger the listeners' dormant cravings.

In twelve-step meetings these recitals are called drunkalogues or drugalogues. That kind of recital reinforces the inner "A;" it does not belong in a sobriety meeting.

Even descriptions of the tolerance level people reached ("I was drinking two fifths of vodka every day, when I got to the hospital I blew a .32") can trigger people. Paradoxically, such recitals can make people feel that they don't really have a problem and don't belong in the meeting since they never drank in that quantity.

It may be difficult in some cases for the convenor to draw the line where the detail becomes inappropriate, but it's important to be aware of the issue. The convenor may want to watch faces and body language carefully, and be aware of their own gut reactions, as a guideline for when to call a halt to the parade of "wet" detail.

Many people have reported that meetings where speakers told extended "war stories" awakened powerful urges to drink and use within them. They came out of such meetings with their sobriety undermined, and sometimes dove back into the drinking/drugging life immediately afterward. Such meetings were engines of relapse for them.

The purpose of LifeRing meetings is to strengthen the sober impulse within us, not to stir up and energize the addiction. We are here to connect on the sober-sober circuit, "S" to "S." Unnecessary details about drinking/drugging are messages from the "A" and stimulate reactions from the "A" inside ourselves.

There is no problem with people describing at length the negative consequences ("I rolled my car, I landed in the Emergency Room, I got busted for DUI, my significant other walked," etc.), but when it comes to the actual drinking/drugging, the fewer words the better: "I drank" or "I used." That's enough.

Since the usual LifeRing meeting format does not feature an extended recital of life stories, there is usually no occasion for people to talk at great length about the drinking/using periods of their lives.

If a participant in a LifeRing meeting commences a detailed description of their past drinking/drugging adventures, the convenor may want to head them off at the pass immediately: "We're not here to brag about what big drunks we used to be, Sandy. We're here to support each other in living clean and sober right now. What are you doing, specifically, to stay clean and sober until the next meeting?"

3.10: Crosstalk

In general terms, crosstalk means dialogue, two-way communication. A says something, B says something in direct response to A. Crosstalk is what people do in normal conversation.

All LifeRing meetings allow crosstalk. When meetings use the format described in this chapter, crosstalk is usually OK throughout the whole meeting. The opening statement generally so indicates.

Why conversation got this strange name and why it is generally banned from twelve-step recovery meetings are questions beyond the scope of this book. Whatever the reasons, crosstalk is a settled feature of LifeRing meetings, and its presence is one of the first contrasts that people accustomed to twelve-step formats usually notice when they first visit LifeRing.

Our meetings strive for a living-room atmosphere: a group of sober friends, relaxed, spontaneous, secure, letting their hair down and talking about the current concerns in their lives. Crosstalk is a vital part of that atmosphere.

Crosstalk provides feedback, and feedback is a powerful recovery tool. Studies show that getting feedback is much more influential in bringing about change than passive one-way communications. A research-based study of a broad range of treatment methods concludes:

> One general finding in the motivation literature is the persuasiveness of personal, individual feedback. Lectures and films about the detrimental effects of alcohol on people in general seem to have little or no beneficial impact on drinking behavior, either in treatment or in prevention settings. (Hester & Miller 2003:138)

Crosstalk is important in the LifeRing recovery model because it closes the loop of sober-sober connections. People who can dialogue with one another are more likely to reach a meeting of the sober minds than people who talk past one another in a series of monologues.

Many recovering people have reported that a format without crosstalk feels isolating to them. Without crosstalk, people appear to be together but they are really talking as if they were alone. Many are slumped in their seats daydreaming instead of paying attention, because they will have no opportunity to respond. Even if they are listening, they are passive, as if at a movie or lecture. Meetings without crosstalk make for a lonely crowd.

Meetings with crosstalk tend to be lively. Most of the participants are likely to be sitting up and paying attention most of the time, because they can ask questions if something is unclear, and they can respond immediately if they have something to contribute.

One of our meetings took place at night in the front room of a building with big bay windows facing the street. There were no blinds or curtains. Recently a person in recovery who lives across the street telephoned to say that it looked like a good meeting: people were sitting up, looking attentively at one another, and there was a lot of laughing. Just watching the body language made her want to join in. The secret of that inviting quality is crosstalk.

3.10.1: Crosstalk Is Voluntary

Because crosstalk can be so powerful, participants and convenors will want to be clear about the concept and handle it with care. Crosstalk in LifeRing is voluntary and it is supportive.

Crosstalk in LifeRing is always within the power of the person talking. If a person doesn't want any comment on their personal "News of the Week in Review," they can say, "I just wanted to put that out there; I don't want any feedback on it right now." The other participants need to respect that, and the convenor will protect the member's wish if required.

This point may be particularly urgent if there are members who are overflowing with unsolicited advice. Unsolicited advice is disempowering and tends to repel people.

If unsolicited advice is a persistent problem in the meeting, the convenor may want to say a few words about it at the outset, for example, "Crosstalk generally is welcome but please only offer advice after you're sure that the person has asked for it. Sometimes people only want to vent."

Normally crosstalk is "on" by default, and a person needs to turn it "off" if they don't want it. But in some meetings in special settings (see Chapter Nine) where people are likely to feel very vulnerable, the convenor may opt to turn it off by default and specifically empower each person to turn it on: "Sam, did you want any feedback on that?"

LifeRing Convenor Michael J.:

We just had our first LifeRing meeting here in Madison on Saturday. Ten folks total. It went well but I think everyone is so used to AA and the "captive audience" syndrome, that once they realized that the floor was open, well, the flood gates broke! It was nice, but very much not about sobriety. I think everyone was just so thrilled to be able to talk and ask questions and laugh....I need to find tips to keep the topic at least related to sober living. Any little mind tricks would be much appreciated!

Crosstalk is always optional with the listeners. Nothing in the LifeRing format requires anyone to provide feedback. The convenor may ask generally, "Does anyone have any feedback on what Chris just said?"

The convenor can make a more specific request: "Chris, I bet you're not the only person to have had a drinking dream. Can we have a show of hands? How many people have had a dream where they drank or used?" But the convenor doesn't usually buttonhole a specific participant to pull feedback out of them: "Pat, what do you think about what Chris just said?"

If somebody wants to maintain silence, that is their prerogative. Participation is voluntary.

3.10.2: Crosstalk Is Supportive

Crosstalk in LifeRing is a method for obtaining a higher quality of sober mental and emotional connection between the par-

---

LifeRing Convenor Thomas H.:

I was lucky to have five people present for my first meeting, and it went quite smoothly.

Many of the folks actually looked up LifeRing before they came so they obviously showed their interest.

One lady said she has been sober for eighteen years and a die-hard twelve-step follower, but is getting bored with it and wants to move onto another avenue of recovery groups.

She said she is not used to the crosstalk, but said that aspect is what she really enjoys, and welcomes it, along with her looking down the road to maybe helping spread the joy as a convenor.

This statement was also reiterated by other members. One gentleman said "Wow, this is odd" and he liked it and he too was another avid AA member.

Overall the interaction and crosstalk is what these people enjoyed and I am looking forward to next week to see how many show.

ticipants than is possible with serial monologues. For that reason, crosstalk needs to be supportive of the person's sober striving.

Some treatment programs use crosstalk as a weapon of attack. They see their mission as attacking the "A" rather than reinforcing the "S" inside the recovering person.

This approach is called "confrontation therapy" or "attack therapy." Although it may work in some cases – anything works for some people – research into its effectiveness generally has been strongly negative. Confrontation therapy has "one of the most dismal track records in outcomes research […] with not a single positive study." (Hester & Miller 2003:96)

If anything, confrontation is effective in promoting relapse. In one study, the more the therapist used confrontation, the more likely the patient was to be drinking a year later. (Hester & Miller, 1996:101)

We do not use confrontation or attack therapy approaches in LifeRing. Crosstalk in LifeRing is always affirmative of the other person's sober self.

Neutral questions asking for relevant information are among the most common items in crosstalk. For example: "Did you detox in a clinic or on your own?" – "Who was your case manager?" – "Did the Naltrexone work for you?" – "How long had you quit drinking before you stopped smoking?" – "What are you going to do if your former dealer phones you again?" – "Are you on antidepressants?" – "Does your mother know that you're in recovery now?"– "Do you have a sober place to go for Thanksgiving dinner?"– "How old are your children?" And so on.

Sometimes the questions can have an edge. For example: "Is it your plan to go back to drinking as soon as your probation time is up?" – "Were you as hesitant to spend money on your drinking/drugging as you are to spend money on your recovery?" – "In what way have you changed your program since you last relapsed?" Those are challenging questions. But the questions never cross the line into confrontation or attack.

Crosstalk in LifeRing is also a method of giving direct and immediate feedback to the person who has just spoken.

Feedback works best when it is positive. "That was awesome what you did, coming back in right away!" – "You must have felt so terrible when they said that to you!" – "That's a great idea, thank you, I'll borrow that!" – "I wouldn't beat myself up too much over that. The main thing is you stayed sober." – "I had a similar situation, and I can really relate." – "I really admire the way you handled that."– "Your participation in this meeting has meant a lot to me" – "You look so much better than you did last week!" And so on.

Supportive feedback does not all have to be warm and fuzzy. Warm and fuzzy is good, but too much is nauseating.

Feedback can positively reinforce a choice that the person receiving the feedback did not happen to make. It will still be effective, provided it refrains from attacking the person or telling them what they should do.

Making I-statements, always useful in participation generally, is doubly effective when giving this kind of feedback. "Personally I stay away from non-alcoholic beer because it wakes up my cravings for the real thing." – "I could safely go to a rock concert now but I don't think I would have risked it when I only had a few days clean and sober." – "I always feel stronger at social events if I hang with somebody else who is not drinking." – "I have a friend who took an anger-management class and it helped him a great deal." And so on.

Comments from peers coming immediately after the person has spoken, and addressed directly to the speaker, can have a powerful effect on their feelings and their future behavior.

Crosstalk is also a way for the person speaking to solicit advice if they want it. "I don't know whether to go to the football game with my drunken boss, does anyone have any advice?" – "My Dad says I should partner up with Frankie in a truck driving business but Frankie is on meth and is always offering me some. What should I do?" – "Since I quit drinking two weeks ago I feel like I'm on a roller coaster. Should I ask my doctor for some kind of meds? What do you all think?"

Getting and giving advice, when asked for, can be an effective way of creating sober connections between people and energizing every participant's sober brain activity.

Crosstalk is also a natural channel for wisecracking and kibitzing. Artful wisecracking can greatly lighten up a meeting. But it's useful to remember that some people in the meeting may be raw, anxious, vulnerable, irritable, or in any number of other troubled emotional states. Tact and consideration for the other person's feelings are always appreciated. Sarcasm is rarely appropriate.

The person who has a warm sense of humor and can make people laugh at themselves in a good-natured way is always a valued crosstalk contributor.

3.10.3: Some Common Issues in Crosstalk

Crosstalk is ordinary friendly conversation, and most of the time people handle it without any difficulty and without any need for the convenor to speak up. But people vary in their conversational skills, and some may be a bit rusty after years of isolation or drug-talk. Others have only experienced crosstalk in very different settings with very different ground rules, such as the "attack therapy" used in Synanon-style "therapeutic communities." (For a vivid illustration, see Shavelson 2001:149-154.) Some people have never experienced crosstalk at all.

Consequently the convenor may need to get things unstuck from time to time. Here are some points to watch out for:

- *Interrogation.* Asking questions is a normal part of cross-talk. But sometimes a participant overdoes it. Question follows question like a courtroom cross-examination. The convenor will want to watch the person being questioned for signs of discomfort (read the feet!) and step in quickly before the experience becomes hurtful. For example: "OK, Ronnie, if you have more questions for Alex maybe you two can talk after the meeting. Let's move on."

- *Private conversation.* Occasionally two people in a meeting discover that they have friends in common, or went to the same school, or are planning to attend the same social event, etc. They may use the crosstalk format as a way of having a private conversation on group time. The convenor needs to invite them to do it later.

- *Lost focus.* Occasionally the meeting may lose focus and several people start talking at once in a chaotic manner, either across the room or to their neighbor. The convenor will want to restore focus, for example by recognizing one person to speak, and asking the others to be patient and wait their turn.

- *Spinning the Wheels.* If a person has an emergency or other urgent issue in their life, it makes perfect sense to focus much of the meeting's time in crosstalk on that person's situation. But sometimes a person becomes the focus of the meeting and takes

---

LifeRing Convenor Laura M.:

One skill that is extremely important for a convenor to work on is that of time management.

Knowing how to get people back on track if they have wandered off on some other path besides recovery and how to rein in the excessive talkers.

Having a sense of humor can be helpful, as well as giving kind reminders. I have to call a member of my group to recommend she need not comment on everything a person says.

Sometimes addressing the group helps people get the point about managing their own time so I don't have to do it for them.

up a lot of its time for no productive reason, and the meeting gets stuck, spinning its wheels. For example, sometimes a newcomer (often female) will be deluged with "helpful suggestions" from other participants (usually male).

• *Hogging the stage.* Sometimes a person misuses the opportunity of crosstalk to hog center stage at a meeting because they crave to be the focus of attention. In such cases, the convenor needs to step in and move the meeting along. How and when to step in is a judgment call for the convenor to make. Often the other participants will signal their discomfort unconsciously by jiggling or twisting their feet. One positive way for the convenor to get the meeting moving again is to ask the participants to give the person in the spotlight a round of applause by way of support, and then ask the next person to share their news of the week.

• *Jumping out of turn.* Sometimes one person's weekly review stimulates another person to share something in crosstalk that turns into that person's own weekly "highlights and heartaches." That's fine, but the convenor then needs to remember who's next.

• *Attack mode.* Occasionally a first-timer at crosstalk will go into confrontation therapy mode: "I think the way you're looking at yourself here is bullshit. You're just putting up this big defensive wall. This is a fatal disease and you're in denial, goddam-

LifeRing Participant Dona B.:

My Kaiser program recovery group includes some drama queens. They do have life debilitating problems, and they dominate the group discussions. But after each meeting, I usually feel drained, exhausted, hopeless.... My issues seem miniscule in comparison to the care of disabled children, abusive spouses, nasty divorces, stalkers, prospective jail time, and no money.

One of my f2f LifeRing meetings is better in that the convenor keeps the meeting moving so no one person can dominate, but this type of situation must be a real challenge for any convenor.

mit!" Whoa! The convenor will want to step in immediately and remind the attacker that this is a support meeting, not an attack meeting. When people feel safe, they may let down their defensive walls; but if they are attacked, they never will. Occasionally people say things in meetings that with hindsight don't seem very perceptive. That happens in life. Among the most helpful things that other people can do when this happens is to keep silent and move on. Attacking the person is not the answer.

• *Unsolicited Advice.* The convenor may want step in quickly to shut off any flow of unsolicited advice before it becomes a deluge. "Pat, don't forget that you need to ask Gloria whether she wants advice or is just putting her stuff out there."

• *Dead Silence.* Occasionally in a new LifeRing where most of the people have experienced nothing but twelve-step meetings, they sit there as if in a coma until it comes their turn to speak. The convenor may have to invite crosstalk repeatedly before people wake up. "OK. Any comments, questions, or other feedback for Sandy?" The convenor may have to model crosstalk, but has to make sure that people understand that crosstalk is for everyone, not just for the convenor. This is not easy. Sometimes the convenor may have to create general silence until someone opens up with crosstalk. In time and with modeling and patience people will come to life.

• *A Crosstalk Monopolist.* Occasionally one person has a crosstalk comment for everyone on just about every issue. After the

---

LifeRing Convenor Martin C.:

It is a lot easier than you might imagine. I have been convening the types of meetings that you might imagine would be on the hard side, where a pretty large chunk of our member have had mental illnesses and/or spent years living on the street, but I have almost never had any difficulties at a meeting that required me to really step in. Just about the only times when peer pressure has not been enough and I have had to step in is when people talk for too long, and that is easy to be polite about.

pattern is clear and saturation has been reached, the convenor can ignore the person and not give them the nod, or ask them directly to hold off and give other people a chance to get their two cents in. "Thanks, Pat, but I asked if anyone *else* had a comment for Alex." The convenor may also want to ask people to raise their hands for crosstalk, and call on them by name or with a glance and a nod. The convenor can then ignore the hand of the compulsive talker. If the person is an incurable monopolist, a quiet word on the side after the meeting may be called for.

3.10.4: Timing Crosstalk

As the number of people in a meeting grows, the convenor will want to become more attentive to the clock. LifeRing convenors regularly lead meetings with crosstalk with 18-24 people in the room. However, in order to fit that many people into one hour, we have to keep an eye on the clock. When about half the time is gone, we need to be about halfway around the room.

Finishing up on time involves a bit of guesswork, a bit of nudging, and the goodwill and cooperation of the participants. All it usually takes to move things along is to catch a moment's break in the flow, look at the clock, look at the next person and ask "And how was your week?"

In the box on the next page is an outline of how a typical meeting of that size runs. You can see that in this meeting I guessed a bit wrong about the finish. The last few people's time was a bit tight, and the very last person had an issue that probably would have raised up a good bit of crosstalk.

Still, everyone could see that an effort was being made to provide time for everyone, and everyone was cooperative. Everybody got to talk. Quite a few people had a chance to get feedback on their issues. Lots of people had a chance to give feedback. People left the meeting pretty much alert and upbeat. This had the feel of a successful meeting.

Outline of a Meeting With Crosstalk, 23 people

Minute	*Discussion Summary*
0	Opening Statement
1	Al: Was away visiting family two weeks, did OK. Details.
3	Bob: Dealing with depression this week. Crosstalk by Meg, by Ed, by Rick, by Meg again, by Tami, by Ed again, and others. *When it gets repetitive I move it forward by calling on Cal.*
12	Cal: Out of work, concerned. Sober.
13	Dee: OK week, dealing with parents visiting. Crosstalk by Ung.
15	Ed: Main issue this week whether to start Antabuse. Crosstalk about Antabuse by Al, Tami, Meg, Fawn, Al again, Dee, Ung, Tami again, and several others. *Looking at the clock, I nudge us forward.*
22	Fawn: Got into argument with ex. Stayed sober.
23	Gal: OK week, going to Mexico next week on business, former big drinking hangouts, but has guard up. Crosstalk by Cal, Lon.
25	Huynh: Doing OK, no details.
25 ½	Irene: Doing fine, nothing special coming up.
26	Joe: Graduating from program, going back to job, worried whether people will know. Crosstalk from Al, Sandy, Vik, Nora.
31	Kit: Routine week, stayed sober.
32	Lon: Had court appearance for DUI.
33	Meg: Main problem this week: boredom.
34	Nick: Had cravings most of the week, stayed sober though. Crosstalk by Vik, Ed, Joe.
40	Pop: OK this week, nothing special next week.
41	Quill: Report on visit by parents. Crosstalk by Al, Dee.
43	Rick: First day clean and sober. Brief attaboy-type crosstalk by Al, Ed, Joe, Nick, others.
46	Sandy: Watched a football game clean and sober first time in years. Crosstalk by Fawn, Gal, Lon, Al, several others. *I nudge us forward, pointing to clock.*
57	Tami: Very brief report, doing fine.
57 ½	Ung: ditto
58	Vik: ditto
58 ½	Wendy: Problems in relationship, will tell details next time.
59	Closing round of applause

As people become more familiar with the format and with each other, the convenor will have less and less of a management burden.

I've participated in meetings using this format with as many as 32 people in the room, but allowing 90 minutes. Convenors with meetings in this size range will want to give serious thought to splitting into two rooms; see the chapter that follows.

Time management is obviously easier in smaller meetings. At some point it becomes unnecessary for the convenor to move the process forward from one person to the next; people will do it on their own by nudging the next person. Most people also have a pretty fair sense of time and will tailor their talking to fit the time available.

3.10.5: Crosstalk: Conclusion

Crosstalk presents the convenor with its own problems and challenges. But because crosstalk is what people normally do with their friends, most meetings quickly catch on to the concept and handle it well with minimal nudging from the convenor.

Crosstalk makes for stronger and clearer connections between the members, stimulates people to listen actively, stay alert, and

---

LifeRing Convenor Dan C.:

I've been convening the Tuesday night "How was your week?" CDRP (Kaiser) Oakland meeting since May.

It's an amazing meeting, with usually about 20-30 people in recovery from many substances, not just alcohol. Most are new to recovery, with "old timers" having as many as three to four months substance-free. Most of the meeting attendees have been in meetings and sessions all day at the outpatient treatment center where the meeting is held. Many express appreciation for Lifering's lack of rigidity and openness to all, regardless of the substance they abused. The stories are raw and unfiltered, and make me appreciate my own sobriety every day.

participate more, and makes the LifeRing meeting experience richer and more rewarding for everyone.

Sometimes when people ask why we have crosstalk, I compare it to connecting jumper cables between two cars. If you just connect one wire of the jumper cable, nothing much happens. Crosstalk connects the other wire. It completes the circuit and lets the energy flow.

When people are asked what attracts them to the LifeRing meeting format, crosstalk is usually high on the list.

3.11: Where to Start the Process

It's the convenor's call where in the room to start the round of "How Was Your Week?" reports. Since the convenor is also a person in recovery, the convenor will ordinarily be taking a turn. The convenor can go first, or turn to the first person on their left and right, or start with someone across the room, either at random or with a purpose. Here are some points to consider:

• When the convenor knows that someone in the room has an urgent issue, it is often good practice to start with that person, regardless where they are sitting. For example, it's good to open the floor immediately to a person who has relapsed during the week and is ready to talk about it, or who is in a crisis, for example an illness or death in the family. Starting with that person assures that their concern will get airtime. Anytime there is bad news it is good to get it out and deal with it first thing, or as early as practical.

• If there are a lot of first-timers, some convenors organize the check-in in two rounds. In the first round, people only say their names and perhaps a few things about themselves and their week (25 words or less), and they indicate whether they have an urgent concern that they want to raise in the meeting. Then in the second round, the convenor starts with the person or persons who have the urgent concern(s), and goes around from there with a more detailed check-in. Other convenors handle this function by asking at the outset, "Does anyone have any urgent issues?"

• Generally it's preferable not to start the check-in with a first-timer because they may feel on the spot without a clear idea what's expected. The convenor might, however, ask the newcomer how they heard about the meeting; sometimes that gets them talking about their week without further modeling.

Usually after the first person is called on, the check-in proceeds around the room one by one in predictable fashion. If the convenor starts with someone across the room, the convenor may leave it to that person to decide whether the progression goes to the left or the right.

The convenor may want to encourage members to pass the turn among themselves, for example, by nudging the next person, without first looking to the convenor to give a nod or say a word.

I have also seen meetings where people checked in seemingly at random; whoever felt like going next, did.

3.12: Handling Dead Airtime

Simple arithmetic will tell any member if the meeting is on track with the clock. At about midway in the meeting time, about half the people present need to have finished. In most sessions, the check-in with crosstalk just about fills up the available time with little nudging from the convenor.

However, there are sessions where everyone has finished sharing about their past week and their next week, and everyone has run out of crosstalk, and there's still a substantial chunk of time available. This situation can arise no matter how many people are present.

At that point, the pressure is on the convenor to restart the ball rolling. The convenor now has three basic options. They are to suggest a topic on the fly, to suggest a stock topic, or to go into "Quaker meeting" mode.

3.12.1: Topic on the Fly

Experienced convenors prepare ahead for possible dead time at the end of the meeting by keeping a mental scorecard as people are talking about their weeks.

When the check-in is done, the convenor knows that five people this week are concerned about problems with their relationships, three are worried about job issues, two have had drinking/using dreams, and the rest have scattered miscellaneous concerns.

All other things being equal, when the check-in is done this convenor will suggest a topic having to do with relationships. "Let's talk about ways and means that we can get our family members, lovers, and friends to understand better what we're going through and what we are asking them to do for us at this time."

Not surprisingly, such a proposal will probably start at least five members talking immediately. The convenor who consistently applies this method may acquire a reputation for innate genius at meeting leadership, but it's really just a matter of keeping score of people's concerns and reflecting them back.

3.12.2: Stock Topic

The convenor may have a stock discussion topic ready as a standby. For example, "OK, we seem to have talked ourselves out

> **LifeRing Convenor Adam H.:**
> When I am convening I note what people are saying during How Was Your Week and use the common themes as suggestions for the topic portion of the meeting.

about current events. How about we have a tool-sharing session? Let's talk about how to recognize cravings and urges, and what can we do when we have one?" Or, "How can we recognize when we seem to be in relapse mode?"

The *Recovery by Choice* workbook is a gold mine for topics. Filling the time after the check-in is one of the many areas for convenor creativity and innovation.

3.12.3: "Quaker Meeting" Mode

A third option is for the convenor to say nothing and let the silence reign. Silence can be a creative force. It is the sound of people searching their minds to find something meaningful to say – always a good exercise.

Eventually someone will be moved to speak and the silence will be over. Keeping quiet and letting silence happen may not be easy for an inexperienced convenor the first time, but it's a perfectly valid move at LifeRing meetings; it displays a lot of strength and confidence.

> **LifeRing Convenor Chet G.:**
>
> I get uncomfortable in meetings where the convenor thinks that she/he must say something at EVERY person who speaks – like some kind of overbearing Guru. It always seemed detrimental to some of the shyer attendees whose body language and foot tapping made it obvious to me that they'd like to say something but the constant torrent of talk and advice from the Chair wouldn't allow a word in edgewise.
>
> That's one of those things that "dead air" is for – there are times when some amazing wisdom comes from a 20 or 40 or 50 second pause broken by a member of the group who seldom speaks. And what's wrong with a pause for folks to take in and process all that led up to it?
>
> Sometimes, just for grins, I'd time the pause and I NEVER saw one last more than a minute and a half – someone ALWAYS breaks the silence.

Sometimes in the silence people do bring out deep concerns that would not have surfaced otherwise, and the best part of the meeting follows.

Dead airtime is rare at LifeRing meetings once people get into the groove. In evening meetings in a residential facility where people have no transportation issues and nothing else to do until bedtime, it's common for the LifeRing meetings to run overtime.

Week after week we've sat glued to our chairs in this meeting talking way past the hour, hardly conscious of the people in the hallway passing by our open door coming from the twelve-step meeting. Their faces say, "What's so fascinating in there?" It's the LifeRing meeting format: personal narrative combined with friendly feedback in a down-to-earth sober atmosphere.

3.13: How Much Should the Convenor Talk?

Eventually each convenor will develop a personal style that feels comfortable and works for them. There's usually more than one valid way to deal with any given issue that comes up in a meeting. The method that best suits the convenor's personality and recovery needs is probably the right one.

One of the issues that convenors usually face as they get more deeply into the role is how much to talk as convenor. The convenor needs to find a personal comfort zone somewhere in between talking too much and not talking at all.

• Talking too much. In a meeting with a stable membership, convenors who talk a lot after the opening statement, and who interject a comment during and after each and every member's share, and who talk a lot more at the end of the meeting, are probably talking too much. They may be trying to control the meeting where it doesn't need control. They may be turning the meeting into a process that is mainly about them, rather than about others connecting with each other. Convenors who are know-it-alls, who have answers for everybody even for questions they didn't ask, who persistently give unsolicited advice, will drive people away and kill meetings.

• Talking too little. On the other hand, convenors who only say "How Was Your Week?" and then not another word, may not be talking enough. There may be newcomers who have questions about LifeRing and this convenor doesn't answer them. Some members may talk too long or monopolize the crosstalk, and this convenor doesn't move the meeting along. Some members may lead the discussion way off topic, or talk in an uncivil fashion, and this convenor doesn't restore the meeting's focus. This convenor isn't exercising control where control is required. Convenors who consistently fail to speak when words are necessary will also drive people away and kill meetings.

Deciding when and how much to talk also depends on the maturity of the meeting and the number of newcomers present in a given session.

When many participants are at their first LifeRing meeting, the convenor has to give more of an introductory presentation. This is particularly important in meetings at rehabs with a rapidly rotating client census. In this setting, the convenor may work up a standard ten or fifteen minute informational talk about LifeRing. This is also a good time to pass out copies of the local meeting schedule.

In meetings with a more stable membership, once everyone is in the groove, the convenor may need to say very little as convenor.

Developing a personal style in the comfort zone between talking too much and too little takes time and experience. Meetings are usually quite tolerant with convenors – convenors, after all, are ordinary people, peers – and allow plenty of slack for making mistakes.

Meetings tend to be appreciative of convenors who bring thoughtfulness and creativity to their effort. For example, one convenor I know sometimes brings a guitar to the meeting and plays a tune or two; another writes poems and reads them aloud. Why not?

It's helpful if a convenor can relax and experiment with different approaches, rather than clinging for dear life to one particular routine. It may be helpful just to ask people in the meeting for their opinions about the way the meeting is going.

One useful function of convenor workshops and of the Annual Meeting is to allow different convenors to share their personal approaches to convening, so that every convenor can add more options to their personal convenor toolbox.

Some convenors make a practice of attending other meetings to learn from what other convenors do. The *liferingconvenor* email list, accessible via *lifering.org*, is a valuable resource for connecting with other convenors. Whatever your question or concern, very likely there are others on that list who can respond.

3.14: When the Convenor Must Speak

Most of the time, the convenor's role as convenor is to listen attentively. The convenor will participate in the check-in and in crosstalk like every other member. In a meeting that is running well, the convenor will have little occasion to speak as convenor apart from a few words at the opening and closing.

Some garden-variety situations where the convenor probably will want to intervene have been covered above. In addition, there are some other situations where the convenor must speak up. These are extraordinary, but it is well for the convenor to be mentally prepared. For example:

- Incivility. The convenor must speak if someone in the meeting makes racist or sexist remarks, or attacks or insults another member, or otherwise seriously oversteps the bounds of civility. We're not a Sunday school meeting and we don't flinch at earthy language and colorful expressions, but we always try to remember that the point of the meeting is to bring people together in recovery.

• Intoxication. Convenors need to speak up if a participant attacks the sobriety foundations of the meeting. If an individual who is currently under the influence is trying to speak or disrupt, or if someone advocates drinking or drug use, the convenor needs to take control and ask the participant to maintain silence or leave.

• Politics. The convenor has to step in if the discussion turns to politics. It is fine for LifeRing members to be passionately active in political arenas, but LifeRing meetings are not a political arena and political argument does not belong there.

• Theology. No less divisive than politics is discussion of religion or theological issues. It is fine for LifeRing members to have passionate theological beliefs and to be active members of their churches, synagogues, temples, ashrams, atheist or agnostic clubs, or whatever. But LifeRing meetings are not the place for theological discussion.

• Breach of confidentiality. The convenor has to step in if someone is violating someone else's confidentiality. Who is present and who says what at a meeting is supposed to stay at that meeting. This ground rule is essential to give members a feeling of safety, and the convenor has to enforce it.

• Bashing other programs. Sometimes people come to LifeRing straight out of intense twelve-step involvement with the sense that they have escaped programming by a cult. (See, for example, Bufe 1998). The convenor may let them vent briefly, but if this becomes the person's main topic or if the person invites other people to develop the theme, the convenor has to step in. People with cult deprogramming issues should seek referral to specialists in that therapy. Criticism of other recovery programs is always Off Topic within the walls of LifeRing meetings.

• AA pushing. The flipside of AA-bashing is AA pushing. This usually happens out of ignorance. The meeting participant doesn't know the LifeRing ground rules, or doesn't even realize that this is not a twelve-step meeting, and comes out with a share about the step they're working, their issue with their sponsor, a particular AA meeting they found, and so forth. Or they inject some AA doctrine or slogan into the meeting. The convenor might say something along the lines of, "Thanks for sharing, but the place for talking about your AA work is in an AA meeting." (Similarly, AA meetings disallow sharing about "outside" recovery programs.) It's not uncommon for people to attend both LifeRing and AA meetings. To do that successfully they need to learn to keep these two overlapping worlds more or less neatly separated.

• Way Off Topic. Relevance to recovery is a rubber band that can be stretched quite a distance, but some people snap it. They vent personal fixations on some topic that hasn't the remotest connection to recovery. As they go on, the meeting loses focus and people's attention drifts away or turns hostile.

When a convenor has to interrupt, as a general guideline the best first move is to deflect and move forward. "OK, Marty, we heard you, that's enough, it's time to move on now. Pat, how was your week?"

LifeRing Convenor Mona H.:

We were so worried at Greenwich because we had patients from detox that would go back to the "unit" and report on our meeting when we were new. Often they were twelve-step people who had relapsed so we would be very careful to not have any program bashing. I did have a drunk person once. They just talked too much and I reminded them of our opening statement if we had been drinking etc... It all works out!

If that doesn't work, the next best move may be to share with the person how their words are affecting you personally. "Ronnie, what you're saying makes me feel really uncomfortable and I'm seeing people looking for the exit. Now I'd like to hear from Chris."

If that still doesn't work, the person is probably not just being insensitive or having a bad moment, but has come to the meeting in bad faith. If so, the convenor has to be firm and clear and ask the person to be quiet or leave the meeting.

Fortunately, instances of this kind are extremely rare in face meetings. In more than twenty years of attending, I have heard of only four cases of disruptive people. Two of these left immediately after the convenor calmly but firmly told them their conduct was inappropriate in our setting.

I have heard of only two situations in LifeRing meetings where it was necessary to call building security because of a disruptive, intoxicated visitor.

I have found it helpful to try to remember that the purpose of the meeting is to facilitate connections between the "sober selves," the "S" inside each participant. When the "S" is speaking, participants deserve the widest latitude and the utmost freedom.

But on rare occasions, the "A" inside one or several individuals at a meeting may surface and attempt to establish a connection with another "A", or to break up the connections between the "S" and the "S."

In those situations, the convenor's task is clear: shut down the "A" connections, re-establish the "S" connections.

Abstract principles such as "freedom of speech in general" are misplaced here. It is not the purpose of the meeting to provide a forum for addicted speech, but rather for sober speech, and sober speech only.

In all situations of this type, the convenor's personal style and social skills will play a role in shaping the outcome. Convenors with a relaxed, humorous style will often be able to defuse budding problem situations quickly with just a word or two before they get out of hand.

Convenors who lack assertiveness in the face of disruption may find that the meeting gets chaotic and turns into an uncomfortable experience for many of the participants – an experience that undermines rather than fortifying their sobriety.

Participants look to the convenor to take charge, and when that does not occur, tensions rise. Convenors may need to remind themselves that the interests of the meeting as a whole clearly outweigh the interest of a disruptive individual.

3.15: Threats of Harm

A difficult situation arises if a meeting participant discloses an intent to harm themselves. This has occurred a handful of times in LifeRing meetings, mainly online. Whether the person is "just talking" or seems to have a serious intent, the convenor can be helpful by referring the person to a suicide prevention hotline. There is a national suicide prevention hotline at 1-800-273-8255. Many communities also have local hotline numbers. The convenor and/or other meeting participants may also want to talk with the person after the meeting.

The convenor is not a counselor and does not have a legal obligation either to assist or to inform authorities if a suicide threat is made. But friends don't let friends talk about harming themselves without doing what they can to help out. In some cases, depending on the situation, that may in fact involve reporting the matter. If the meeting is on the premises of a treatment center, the report can be made to treatment staff. Otherwise, to police.

What if a meeting participant discloses what sounds like a plan to do serious physical harm to another person? This has never yet happened in a LifeRing meeting to my knowledge, but it has happened in older organizations and it is wise to be prepared. It is useful to know that the law does not honor our rule that "what plays in a meeting stays in the meeting." Any meeting participant can be compelled in court to testify about the threats of harm – or for that matter, confessions of harm committed in the past – that another participant uttered in the meeting. Therefore, if a meeting participant discloses what sounds like a serious intent to injure or kill another person, the wisest thing for the convenor to do is to inform them that, unless they retract the statement immediately, it will be reported to the police. We should never be placed in the role of accessories to murder by our silence.

When threats of harm to another are made online, the convenor often has no idea of the speaker's identity and no way to report them. In such a case, if the person persists in their threat, the best practice is to block and eject the person from the online venue immediately and permanently.

Threats of harm do not emanate from the sober self, and have no place in a recovery meeting. LifeRing meetings need to be places of safety and comfort so that the recovery process can unfold and flourish.

3.16: A Camaraderie Like No Other

A person usually comes to a recovery meeting after a considerable internal struggle. That struggle continues after they leave the room. The meeting is one episode, one battle, one hour. The war within goes on 24/7/365 until the sober side acquires a decisive superiority of forces.

Recovery, particularly early recovery, is a bit like doing construction in a war zone. What you build today is at risk of being bombed to pieces tomorrow.

The LifeRing meeting hour is like a council of review and planning that allows the sober builder within each person to do a damage assessment and to formulate a plan for repair, reinforcement, and expansion in the days ahead.

To the maximum extent possible, we try to leverage the work of the meeting hour so as to assist the person to retain and to gain sober territory during the time between meetings.

This means at the very least that the content of the meeting must be affirmative of sobriety and free of elements that trigger, activate, and energize the person's inner "A." It must be as free as possible of elements that paralyze and demoralize the person's sober self.

It means, further, that the content of the meeting needs to be helpful to each individual in responding to the specific, particular recovery challenges that face that individual during the intervals between the meeting hours. It needs to help them process their recent inputs, and pre-process their pending outputs, with sobriety as the priority.

As a convenor, you will have seen that the LifeRing meeting format is not designed like a church service or prayer meeting. It is not a lecture on abstract principles, like in a college classroom. It is not entertainment, like a freak show at a circus. It is not a revival meeting to save souls. It is not a promotional rally to win recruits for the organization. It is more like a tactical council of war during an ongoing campaign – a working session – having but one object: to serve each participant in winning their particular challenges, climbing their particular mountains, and fording their particular rivers, so that they can come back to the council next week still clean and sober.

This aspect of the meeting, as a council of war in a continuing campaign, also helps to shape a positive attitude between the participants. We may not each have the identical challenges, the same mountains and rivers each week. But we each know what the other is going through.

We can resonate, empathize, look the person in the eye on a level basis. Because it is built on the premise that we are all protagonists in a continuing war, the meeting builds a camaraderie like no other.

3.17: The Format in Perspective

The typical LifeRing meeting format described in this chapter is built from two culturally familiar modes of discourse: personal narrative and friendly conversation.

Personal narrative – this is what happened to me, this is what is going on with me – as a form is probably older than the written word, older than the *Odyssey* and the *Iliad*. Experience sharing has been part of American alcohol recovery meetings since at least the Washingtonians in the 1840s. (White 1998:9)

The LifeRing edition of this format puts the main focus on our current work-in-progress rather than on our past debaucheries. In so doing, we depart from the model of the Christian revival meeting. Our format more resembles a cooperative workshop where the participants are sharing a skill, such as repairing motorcycles or raising piglets or writing poetry, or helping one another with a shared burden such as surviving grief or going through divorce or parenting special children.

Friendly conversation as a form of discourse has been in decline since the rise of television, and some people have experienced it mainly on the screen, in scripted programs such as Cheers and Friends. Still, there seems to be enough sap left in the tree so that in a positive climate it readily sprouts again.

At the best sessions, there are moments when the protocol of taking turns and raising hands evaporates and the group catches fire, with many people spontaneously contributing, back and forth quickly but not chaotically, with high energy and focus, often ending in gales of laughter. Eventually it settles back into its circuit, with the participants' faces flushed with laughter and feelings of togetherness.

For more than a few participants, the LifeRing is the only gathering place where they can talk both honestly and safely. Here they can be themselves and be respected. Here they can see eye to eye with peers and feel connected. For some people the LifeRing is their sober family, or their family, period.

Because the format's building blocks are culturally familiar, people can feel comfortable participating in this recovery support group from day one. Most people participate (talk) at their first meeting, and do so regularly thereafter. It is rare for someone to pass. There are a number of benefits:

- Participation is powerful in facilitating self-knowledge and change. Oftentimes when people are going through passages in their life, they may not know what they are thinking until they hear themselves saying it. Sometimes people need to think out loud in order to work through some problem in which they feel stuck.

- Participation is a motivator. People tend to feel good about a meeting if they got a chance to talk. When people talk, they become more invested in the meeting because they helped to make it what it was. They gain self-respect as sober persons.

- Participation, especially in crosstalk, allows people not only to take support but also to give support to others. They come to see their personal sobriety as meaningful to others.

- Because the talk centers on current events in the members' lives, the meeting is an ever-changing river. One can attend for many years and always hear something new.

- "How Was Your Week" is an equal-opportunity format. It's democratic. If you've had a week, you can talk. Your week did not happen in someone else's book and you don't need to be learned or eloquent to talk about it.

• The current-events focus brings the hour of decision and the hour of consulting with a sober group close together, and makes it more likely that the group process will play a role in the individual's decision making.

• The reporting format encourages people to take charge of their recovery course, plan for contingencies in advance, and report the results back to their sober reference group.

• The current-events format is likely to help people carry the meeting with them in their minds during the week. "I went down the wine aisle of the supermarket but I wasn't even tempted because I imagined I had you all walking with me!"

In a nutshell, the combination of tool-sharing and supportive conversation exercises and reinforces the sober impulse inherent within recovering people. The reporting and tool-sharing work tends on the average to fortify the more analytical and intellectual side, and the supportive conversational atmosphere tends by and large to supply more emotional sustenance.

The combination of the two functions facilitates the all-around growth and competence of the sober self within the recovering person. As the person repeatedly works through the processes comprised within the LifeRing meeting format, they become more confident and capable – in short, empowered – as persons who live clean and sober lives.

3.18: Lifetime Recovery Agendas

The two major components within the LifeRing format lend themselves to different lifetime recovery agendas.

• Some rely on LifeRing mainly as a tool-sharing and pro- gram-building workshop early on, and gradually transition to participation in LifeRing-as-extended-family over a longer term of years, or life-long.

• Some people rely on LifeRing mainly as a workshop for the tools they need to get started; they then rely mainly on other support systems, such as their significant other, family, peer group at work, church, sports team, social club, and the like, for motivation to stay sober long term.

• Some come to LifeRing with their sobriety already well in hand, but they want a congenial long-term sober support environment.

• Still others use LifeRing initially as a kind of artificial womb; and only later start taking advantage of it as an educational cooperative and tool-sharing workshop.

The LifeRing format can readily accommodate each of these different patterns of utilization and personal recovery agendas.

As will become more clear from the chapter on Self-Help, the issue of how long to participate in LifeRing meetings is entirely up to the individual; it is one of the many questions that the person in recovery answers in the process of constructing their personal recovery program.

3.19: Partners and Loved Ones

Parents, relatives, partners and loved ones of persons in recovery are almost universally welcome to attend LifeRing meetings. It's educational for the loved ones to hear about the recovering person's struggles, and it's equally educational for the recovering person to hear the concerns and struggles of their loved ones. In almost every case, the involvement of loved ones promotes healing and recovery. "Very cathartic all around," said one convenor after a session that included spouses.

There are exceptions. In one meeting I convened, the two partners were in the process of breaking up, and could not refrain from using the hour as a platform for badmouthing the other. That, of course, is totally inappropriate. The point of the meeting is to offer support and to build stronger connections, not to vent one's venom when a relationship goes south.

There have been some efforts to start up a separate LifeRing Loved Ones or LifeRing Partners group. However, as with any other project, starting up a new group requires a small group of passionately dedicated and tenacious individuals, and so far, that has not materialized. If you are interested in moving this project forward, please contact the LifeRing Service Center.

3.20: Variations on the Theme

The process-centered format described in this chapter is the usual pattern seen in the typical LifeRing meeting in the regions where LifeRing has achieved its greatest development at the time this book is written.

LifeRing Convenor Cindy K.:

In Connecticut we held a family and friends meeting where everyone was offered the opportunity to bring someone, though not required. We had three spouses attend, along with several of our regulars without spouses/friends. It went very well and we plan to make it a regularly occurring occasion – at least once per month if not more. It wouldn't surprise me if the spouses/friends didn't start planning connections on their own..

Prior to trying it we polled our members several meetings in advance asking how they felt about it, and reiterating that it is "our" meeting and we don't want to lose our focus. All were in support of the idea, with no issues or potential issues raised. At the meeting, our "regular" members say they got a lot out of it as well the spouses. There was great crosstalk among all participants. Those not present look forward to future meetings of this nature.

While this doesn't fully answer the need for a regular/consistent support group that is non twelve-step, it is working as a first step for us.

By no means is this format an iron mold. Convenors and members are free to innovate, improvise, and adapt the format to suit the needs of their particular time and place. The basic guideline for modifying the meeting format is the sobriety needs of the people who are participating there and then. For example, meetings in special settings and meetings online may use significantly different formats, discussed later in this book.

Even in regular face meetings, variations are common and beneficial.

• For example, some convenors like to read a motivational passage at the outset.

• Some organize a special session periodically where people bring in and discuss their favorite current reading.

• Some invite a guest speaker (for example, an effective counselor), or arrange for a member to give a presentation on a favorite recovery topic, or go see a movie together.

• Some convenors experiment with ways to include the *Recovery by Choice* workbook in the meeting format.

• One convenor introduced breathing exercises at the start or end of the meeting, and this proved popular with the members of that group.

It is entirely possible that a more content-centered LifeRing meeting format will emerge alongside or within the process-centered format described in these pages.

Occasionally, where the meeting is small and everyone is familiar with everyone else's current issues, the talk is completely free-form and wanders wherever it will within the broad parameters of LifeRing philosophy. It is another hour well spent in sober company.

The LifeRing meeting format is a living thing in constant evolution. Convenors and members are busy all the time tweaking and pushing the envelope in small and large ways. Time and experience discard the changes that don't work and conserve the ones that do.

Chapter 4: Opening and Closing

4.1: About This Chapter

This chapter is about the opening ritual of LifeRing meetings, about the formulas and labels that participants use when they begin to speak, about the treatment of newcomers, and about the closing of the meeting.

4.2: Primacy, Latency, and Ritual

The beginning and the ending of a complex message tend to leave the deepest imprints in the mind. People's memory of the material in the middle is more selective.

This basic fact of human psychology, known as the principle of primacy and latency, is the reason why people who make their living communicating put extra effort into their openings and closings. (Chase 2001)

The openings and closings of regularly recurring group events tend to be repetitive, ritual exercises. Rituals can be entirely secular. Banging the gavel to open a courtroom session, cutting a ribbon to open a road, singing "Take Me Out To the Ballgame" at the seventh inning stretch, throwing out last year's calendars at New Year's, singing "Happy Birthday" and blowing out candles are a few among many examples of rituals having no religious content.

The opening and closing rituals of a meeting establish boundaries that let people know when it's time to focus, and when it's time to go. They establish a sense of familiarity and they bond people together. The closing rituals, in particular, leave an emotional imprint that people carry away with them, and that influences whether they will come again next week.

The convenor who wants the meeting to live long and prosper will pay attention to its opening and closing rituals.

In many of the best LifeRing meetings I have attended, there are definite opening and closing rituals. The content of the rituals expresses something vital about the LifeRing philosophy. In keeping with that philosophy, the duration of the rituals is brief. The formula for success with LifeRing rituals is: short and sweet.

4.3: The Opening Before the Opening Statement

Reading the opening statement is the spoken ritual that launches the meeting, but before that happens, there is a series of silent acts that have a ritual as well as a functional significance.

- Are the directional signs and the door sign up?
- Are the chairs arranged?
- Is the literature laid out?
- Is the convenor there?

The presence of these familiar tokens reassures the member that all is in order; their absence signals some kind of disturbance in the field. The chapter on Nuts and Bolts discusses these preparations in more detail.

The convenor's self-presentation also makes a first impression that forms part of the opening experience for new arrivals. The convenor is clean and sober. The convenor who is cheerful and who greets people agreeably as they arrive sends the message that being at the meeting is a Good Thing. The convenor who remembers names from last time earns points. Many convenors begin informal chatting with people as soon as they arrive, before the opening statement, and set the tone of the meeting before it formally begins.

4.4: Starting On Time

It is good practice to start meetings on time. If the convenor waits too long for stragglers before beginning, then the people who showed up promptly will feel that their time is being wasted, and will come later next time. A minute or two is enough time to allow for people's unsynchronized watches. Starting on time sends the positive message that there is much to do and little time to do it in. Beginning promptly is a part of the ritual and will, with repetition, become part of the meeting's expected format.

4.5: The Opening Statement

The opening statement is the vocal ritual that signals the formal beginning of the meeting. It stops the informal chatting and focuses people's attention. It informs newcomers and reminds old-timers of the basic philosophy of the group. It alerts new arrivals that they're in the wrong meeting if they were looking for something with a different approach. It outlines the format and ground rules. After a few meetings, reading of the statement becomes familiar and puts people at ease.

Here is a "boilerplate" opening statement that many meetings use. It probably isn't the best statement that could be written, but it has the essential stuff and it's short.

Welcome to LifeRing.

LifeRing is a self-help support group for all people who want to get and stay clean and sober.

We feel that in order to remain in recovery, we have to make sobriety the top priority in our lives. By sobriety, we mean complete abstinence from alcohol and other addictive drugs.

Out of respect for people of all faiths and none, we conduct our meetings in a secular way, which means that, during this hour, we do not use prayer or talk about religion. We rely in our recovery on our own efforts and on the help of the group members and other friends.

Everything that we share at this meeting is completely confidential and stays in this room. If you are under the influence of alcohol or drugs now, we ask that you maintain silence at this meeting. You may speak with members afterward.

The meeting format is flexible. We generally begin by checking in and talking about our past week in recovery. Next we focus on what we plan to do to stay clean and sober in the coming week. Please introduce yourself by your first name. If you would like, also tell us how long you have been in recovery.

We encourage crosstalk throughout the meeting. By crosstalk we mean questions and positive, supportive feedback. Positive experiences from your own recovery are welcome. Please allow enough time for everyone to participate by limiting your speaking time.

The meeting convenor may read the statement or may ask a volunteer to do the honor. Some readers paraphrase, modify, or ad lib parts of the opening statement so as to freshen it up, add emphasis, or give it a personal touch. If a volunteer reads the statement, it's good manners for the convenor to thank them when finished.

Each meeting is free to compose its own opening statement, provided the contents are consistent with the basic LifeRing philosophy. That means, generally, the following three points.

• The meeting is dedicated to abstinence from alcohol and other drugs.

• The meeting is secular.

- The meeting is based on self-help.

The way in which these three points are phrased may vary. A more detailed discussion of these points is in the chapters on the "Three S" philosophy in Part Two of this book.

The opening statement also needs to remind people that the contents of the meeting and the identities of the people present are confidential; that supportive crosstalk is welcome; that a person who is currently under the influence needs to maintain silence during the meeting; that people should be respectful of others' time by not monopolizing the floor; and that LifeRing literature is available for those who want to know more.

It is important that the opening statement not go on too long. One or two minutes is about right. This is particularly important in a meeting with a fairly regular, stable membership. In such a

---

LifeRing Convenor Chet G.:

IMHO, the most important part of being a convenor is setting the tone.

Making it clear that it's not a hierarchy, that the convenor is not the leader or owner of the group.

Making it clear that we should speak from the "I" perspective – I did, I felt, I accomplished this by doing that.

Making it clear that the meeting is for everyone present – that everyone gets time to speak but that no one person can monopolize the time.

Making it clear that the purpose of the meeting is for everyone to receive support in their sobriety.

Making it clear that the meeting must remain positive and proactive.

By making all of this clear with the convenor's own mood, body language, voice, presence.

The opening statement is a serious document – it should set the tone and make all of the above clear.

It's amazing how few "tricky moments" one encounters when one does the above.

setting, newcomers who want to know more about LifeRing than can be told in a brief opening statement should be referred to our literature, or invited to stay and chat afterward.

The situation is different in a meeting with a high turnover, such as at a rehab where the average client may be gone in less than two weeks. Here, after the opening statement or as a continuation of it, the convenor would do well to provide the participants with a more extended explanation of what LifeRing is, what it does, how it works, etc., and to answer questions.

If there are announcements of upcoming events or other business, most convenors put them immediately after the opening statement. Some convenors also use this opportunity to pass out the current issue of the LifeRing Newsletter, as well as current meeting schedules and flyers about new meetings or other events, if available. This may also be a good time to ask if anyone has urgent issues or emergencies they need to talk about right away.

Most LifeRing meetings proceed directly thereafter into the main body of the meeting. Practices such as asking people to raise hands to indicate how much sobriety time they have, giving out chips, and the like, are at this time rarely if ever seen in LifeRing meetings. There is no rule against such practices; there simply has not been much membership demand to have them.

LifeRing Convenor Mona H.:

I just wanted to mention, we have added a sentence to the opening statement that reads;

"In the spirit that we believe there are many paths to recovery, we refrain from any negative talk of any other recovery groups during this meeting."

We've found in Greenwich Connecticut group this at least curbs the "I hate AA" comments. We have quite a few AA people that flow thru the hospital rehab that come to our meeting and many people who do both AA and LifeRing together...

The practice of asking people about their sober time, in particular, can be punitive for people who have come back to the meeting after a recent relapse. People who come back into recovery after a relapse deserve extra praise and encouragement for returning.

4.6: Personal Talking Rituals

Meetings not only have collective rituals such as the opening and closing, they generally set up models that people are expected to follow in talking, and these models contain ritual beginnings. So, for example, many people who learned their talking format in twelve-step meetings begin with a phrase such as "I'm Joe, alcoholic." Many treatment centers train people to add their "drugs of choice" and their clean and sober time: "I'm Jane, cocaine, 14 days."

LifeRing members at this time have not reached consensus about the utility of this kind of personal talking ritual. Stating one's first name is clearly useful; that helps people to get to know one another. Most variations of the opening statement ask people to say their first names. But the rest of it is strictly optional. Some people say more, some people don't. There's no pressure to go one way or the other.

Most LifeRing participants I've met keep track of their clean and sober time. If they mention their clean and sober time at a meeting, many meetings will give them a round of applause. It's generally up to the convenor whether to initiate this custom.

I personally favor giving people a hand for their sober time in meetings where there are a lot of people in their early days. It's a good, quick and strong way to express group support for their individual success at a time when every little bit helps.

I watch the faces of people when we applaud them and they usually show a genuine happy smile. Their sober self is getting reinforcement. Sometimes as convenor I'll ask a group to clap harder for people with the fewest days, because the person in their first few days is probably doing the hardest work and deserves the most credit. After a while it gets almost effortless most of the time.

If people don't keep exact count of their clean and sober days, or don't mention it, that's fine also. It's a legitimate question to ask people in crosstalk, but it would be heavy-handed to pressure people to include this in their personal talking format if they don't want to.

4.6.1: Label or Not?

There are good arguments on both sides of the question whether to call yourself "alcoholic" and/or "addict."

• People who label themselves "alcoholic" and/or "addict" generally believe that doing so helps them overcome denial. They use the phrase as a reminder that they cannot drink or use the way "normal people" can. They believe that labeling themselves in this way keeps them honest and committed to their sobriety program.

• People who do not use these labels generally believe that the labels shortchange who they are. They are not "just" alcoholics or addicts, they are also worthwhile people with many positive qualities and estimable roles. They see the labels as a way of shaming oneself, which can undermine one's sober confidence and promote relapse. They feel stronger in their abstinence if they don't use the labels.

That's the upside of the reasoning on both sides. But there's also a downside to each of the arguments:

• For some people, the "alcoholic/addict" label turns into a slippery slope to relapse. Since alcoholism is defined as a progressive, fatal, relapsing disease, they come to believe that they will very probably relapse, or even that relapse is inevitable.

Most clinicians have seen people in advanced stages of alcoholism who say that they relapse frequently because they are alcoholics and relapsing is what alcoholics do.

• For some people, avoiding the "alcoholic/addict" label also turns into a slippery slope. After a time they may forget why they are not drinking or using, and begin to believe they can have "just one" or "just a few now and then," and that usually leads back into the toxic soup out of which they had laboriously raised themselves.

To complicate the picture further, there are people who wear the "alcoholic/addict" label to fit in with the crowd, but who don't really believe it in their hearts. Others believe it secretly but can't bring themselves to say it out loud. If you ask people what the labels actually mean to them, you may get a jumble of concepts. The label issue is a mess.

The street-corner workshops where new language is coined have not yet come up with a phrase or an image that everyone can wear and that has no downside. In this linguistic vacuum, people experiment with hybrid formulas such as "I'm an alcoholic in recovery" or "I'm a sobrietist," or "I'm a recovered alcoholic/addict" or "I'm a good mother and a competent systems analyst who has the disease of alcoholism" and many other variations. Some people go back and forth, using the ritual labels on Tuesdays and Saturdays but not on Wednesdays or Sundays.

The good news is that, on the whole and on the average, it makes no difference how or whether people label themselves.

Research suggests no strong relationship between self-labeling and outcome. Many treatment failures are quite willing to accept the label 'alcoholic,' and many people respond favorably to treatment without ever calling themselves alcoholic. (Hester & Miller 1996:95)

Therefore, the ritual use of labels when individuals open their statements at meetings is likely to remain optional in LifeRing.

Convenors who have strong preferences for one formula or another need to allow space for the strong feelings that run the other way, and for the ambivalence of the undecided. Either approach is valid if it works as a recovery tool at that moment for the person using it.

It isn't necessary to accept a personal diagnosis of alcoholism or addiction in order to participate in LifeRing. The label "alcoholic" or "addict" is not part of our organizational name. Our bond of unity is not acceptance of a label, but practice of a behavior – abstinence, which means living free of alcohol and other drugs. If people are successful at remaining free of alcohol and drugs, who cares what label they wear on their foreheads? People can very well learn to stop drinking and using first, and then worry about the label afterward. LifeRing will not try to force a label on people for the sake of ritual, or otherwise.

4.7: Closing the Meeting

The meeting's closing ritual is the last impression it leaves as a group on the individual. The closing forms an emotional imprint that remains latent in the individual's memory long after much else has faded, and its quality may tip the scales in their decision whether to return next week.

Most LifeRing meetings at this time close by the participants giving each other a round of applause. This is a simple, positive, upbeat ritual that packs a profound message. The unspoken message goes more or less like this:

> The outside world little understands or appreciates our recovery journey. They tend to believe that we can 'just say no' and be done with it. But we who fight this battle every day know the inner struggles we go through and the work that's involved in rebuilding our lives. We appreciate the courage that it takes to be here. We know the sweetness of the victory that each sober day signifies. We applaud one another, and ourselves, for our success in being here clean

and sober today. If someone among us has tripped and fallen, we applaud them all the more strongly for coming back. We applaud to express our confidence that we can meet our challenges in the coming week. Recovery is an estimable project, and we have earned the self-esteem that we feel today. We are heroes and winners in each other's eyes.

From time to time, as the situation allows, the convenor may want to say a few words along those lines to explain the significance of the closing ritual. "Let's give each other a hand for being clean and sober today" is one good shorthand formula. The main point is to close on a strong upbeat note, and the practice of clapping hands together with a loud approving noise meets that requirement perfectly.

Perhaps as the sound of the applause reverberates in people's memories, they will gradually shed the hang-dog attitude that so many bring in with them. Many first-timers have been taught that participating in a recovery meeting is a punishment. They feel that being in these rooms is a sign of how low they have sunk. They slink in as if expecting to receive a beating. How can they ever become free with such an upside-down attitude?

Those who remain in the cave of drinking and drugging are the ones receiving punishment. Those who are still drinking/using are the ones who have sunk low and are sinking still lower. Those who are too deep in their addiction to pick themselves up and begin attending recovery meetings are the true prisoners in shackles.

Participating in a LifeRing recovery meeting is a privilege and a mark of self-respect. Being here is a sign of how high you have risen. You are entitled to walk in with your head held upright, as a free person. Society ought to shower people in recovery with respect and honors. Until society wakes up to the contribution that people in recovery make to the world, simply by making their recoveries, we will have to be content with respecting and honoring one another.

4.8: Everyone Here Is Above Average

In the thousands of LifeRing meetings I have attended, I have never seen a participant brought in chained, wrapped and gagged like a prisoner into Guantanamo. Without exception, they all walked in on their own feet or their own prostheses, or rolled in on their own wheelchairs.

Even if their family, employer, court, doctor, or other authority figure confronted them with a stern-faced "either-or," they made a choice that at least for this hour, their family, job, health, freedom, or parole status were more important to them than their drink or other drug.

They could have said, "Screw it, I'd rather drink/drug than have a family, job, health, freedom, or parole." Many do. We hardly ever see those at meetings. They don't get it together to come. Those are the powerless ones whose life has become unmanageable.

The ones we see at meetings already have the power to make sobriety their priority, at least for right now. They made the decision and they managed to carry it out. The proof of their strength is that they are here. Sometimes that was far from easy. Their presence deserves respect.

Sometimes I see newcomers slinking into the meeting with a hangdog expression, as if there were something to be ashamed of. They look as if they had been bad children and expected a whipping. They say things such as, "Alcohol brought me here," with a tone that says, "I never thought I'd sink so low as to be at a meeting like this."

I want to say to them: "Look around. Where are you? Are you passed out on your floor? Are you kneeling before your toilet? Are you brawling and pissing in a bar? Are you in court? Are you in the emergency room? Are you in the 51-50 lockup? Behind bars?

Wearing a toe tag? Those are the kinds of places where alcohol brings people.

"I have never heard of alcohol bringing a person to a meeting dedicated to stop using alcohol. No, my friend, what brought you here was your determination to be free of alcohol. Pick up your spirits. You came on the 'S' train. You deserve a pat on the back, not a whipping."

Another frequently-heard expression that needs to go back to the drawing board is "My best thinking got me here," said with a sarcastic sneer. The sarcasm is misplaced. My worst thinking kept me drinking. My best thinking led me to stop drinking and come to the meeting.

Because people who come to the meeting are winners, we do not waste their time with tedious, empty rituals. We try to make the meeting experience a reward, rather than a punishment. We try to acknowledge rather than to insult their intelligence. We invite them to speak and to participate actively in the conversation from the first day, and we structure our format to make participation possible for everyone.

Even the person who has been clean and sober only one day has something precious and important to share: how they did that. They have an achievement that thousands of others can only envy.

The person who comes back to a meeting after a relapse demonstrates extraordinary reserves of strength. They have climbed out of a pit in order to be present. The average person did not have so far to climb. They deserve recognition for that achievement.

Many people come to meetings or enter treatment after achieving a string of clean and sober days (sometimes years!) entirely on their own, or at least without any organized recovery support. We should applaud them for it, and ask them to share how they did it. Their achievement is evidence that the power to be clean and sober is strong within them.

People do not come to recovery meetings because they are unable to help themselves. If they were unable to help themselves, they would not be able to come to meetings.

People come to recovery meetings because they can and they want to. They find that doing self-help in company is more rewarding, more likely to work for them, more interesting, and more fun.

Like many other kinds of projects – playing the guitar, raising piglets, doing carpentry, riding motorcycles, learning computer graphics, learning Japanese, doing creative writing, flying drones, and many others – you can get started by yourself, maybe you might even excel at it by yourself (who knows?), but doing it with other people who share your interest makes you feel good, leverages your strength, provides you with new challenges, raises your level, sustains your motivation, expands your consciousness and your circle of friends. Working together with others makes the work lighter and the time pass more quickly.

All help is ultimately self-help. We can yank people forcibly out of the water and pump them dry, but if their will to survive doesn't kick in, we'll lose them again. Without self-help, life is over; all that's left is life support.

When people hit a bottom, they will just lie there and bleed unless a spark of self-help inside of them ignites a flame of motivation to pick themselves up.

That's why in LifeRing we usually say "get the wake-up call" instead of "hit bottom" to describe the experience that turns a person around. "Getting the wake-up call" (or a similar up-button metaphor) means that their inner drive for self-preservation has become active as a motivating power.

They have stopped trying to destroy themselves. They have begun to help themselves.

There are moments of decision in life when we are completely alone with our inner monsters. Groups, friends, counselors, and all the rest of our external support network are tucked in their beds somewhere, and God is busy with the flood in Bangladesh or the earthquake in Nepal. Self-help is the only help immediately available.

Those are the moments when relapse steals as silently as a fog into the control room of the sober mind that believes itself powerless.

At pivotal moments like these it makes all the difference to know that the strength to win lies inside of us. We are not one hundred per cent zero. We are better than that. We are sober at the core. We can block this subtle bandit and retain control of our lives.

Our usual closing ritual, giving one another a round of applause, is consistent with the reality that the people who come to meetings, like the children of Lake Wobegon, are all above average.

By coming here we have demonstrated sober strength, management ability, motivation, and intelligence, and we deserve every appropriate measure of recognition and credit.

4.9: After the Meeting

In a growing number of cases, convenors can offer the meeting participants a way to stretch the togetherness into a social event. After the meeting, people go out for coffee, pizza, Chinese food, whatever.

LifeRing Convenor Tom S.:

Our Friday night meeting here is ninety minutes.... Most often we have a lively and informative discussion and will extend the meeting for fifteen or twenty minutes just to fit everyone in. Even more, we will spend another half hour outside, in the parking lot, talking and a bunch of us will go to a local pizza joint for another hour (or two) talk more.

A lot of people love it when convenors can put together special events like potluck barbecues in the park, sober dance parties, walks or runs, dog walks, and other social occasions. The twelve-step organizations, much older and bigger, are still way ahead of LifeRing in the variety of social gatherings they offer, but as we grow, we are better able to serve the desire of some of our members to have more of a social life with LifeRing friends.

We should make clear that it is not the intent of LifeRing to envelop the recovering person 24/7/365 in the recovery bubble. On the contrary, the objective of empowering the sober self is to enable the recovering person to participate fully and soberly in all the social, cultural, athletic, political and other activities available in their community. But sometimes special bonds of friendship develop between people traveling the recovery passage together, and convenors would be performing a service to facilitate sober social activities outside the meeting walls wherever possible.

Chapter 5: Newcomers

5.1: About this Chapter

This chapter touches on one of the convenor's most important concerns: welcoming newcomers.

5.2: Newcomers

Some years ago one of the cult-watcher sites on the Internet listed our predecessor organization as a cult. Gales of laughter followed, and the site quickly retracted the listing. Cults have elaborate systems for seducing and engulfing newcomers. Cults assign teams of recruiters to each newcomer, find out everything about them, surround them with overt and covert cult friends, teach them to speak the cult language, think cult thoughts, feel cult emotions, read cult books, eat cult foods, live in cult housing, sleep with cult lovers, work cult jobs, and give their money to the cult, all of it.

Groucho Marx once said that he wouldn't join a club that would have him as a member. Some of our predecessor groups had the flip side of that attitude: we wouldn't admit anyone who wanted to belong to us. It's difficult to think of an organization that was less cult-like in its approach to newcomers. We either ignored them until they went away, or we made them the focus of the entire meeting until they squirmed and ran like ants under a magnifying glass on a sunny day. If they hung around despite this treatment, it meant they had to be really deranged desperate misfits, and that finally made them OK to join our club.

Somehow those meetings didn't grow much.

The collective mood in LifeRing has brightened since those very early days, but there remains much room for convenors to improve the treatment of newcomers. For example:

• The convenor can be sure that each newcomer gets the LifeRing handouts and the LifeRing meeting schedule, so that they don't leave empty-handed.

• The convenor can be sure that each newcomer knows that they can phone or send emails to anyone who signs in on the meeting's sign-in sheet.

• The convenor can take a few minutes before or after the meeting to chat with a newcomer and take an interest in their particular situation and concerns.

• The convenor can refer the newcomer to members or to third persons who have similar interests, or who live near the newcomer and could share transportation.

• If the newcomer is online, the convenor can refer the newcomer to the online resources of LifeRing beginning at *lifering. org*, so that the newcomer can hook up with LifeRing online support between face meetings.

These and similar small gestures send the newcomer the message that they are welcome and we want to see them again. More importantly, they send the meta-message that we think highly enough of our group to want to see it have a future.

In extending oneself to welcome the newcomer, the convenor also follows a personal agenda that dovetails with the organization's. Today's newcomer, half a year from now, may become the next convenor.

5.3: Offering Direction

The newcomer whose only experience with LifeRing is the How Was Your Week format may find it entirely satisfying. Or not.

Some people, for a variety of reasons, expect a more directed and structured approach. The experienced convenor will be sure to point them toward the *Recovery by Choice* workbook. This book contains a structured approach (the nine domains) toward the same goal as the How Was Your Week format, namely empowerment of the sober self.

Of course, simply handing the newcomer this 300-page volume with best wishes may not be enough. It may be more helpful to open the book and suggest that the newcomer might, for example, work the exercises in the first domain, or some other part of the book that's relevant to an issue the newcomer shared during the meeting.

The convenor who is personally familiar with the workbook can weave references to the book into the meeting's dialogue to acquaint participants with it. The book is also a deep resource for conversation topics.

Some people thrive in the How Was Your Week format like fish in water, and need nothing else. Others want more structure. LifeRing provides both. The convenor who has absorbed the range of material available in LifeRing will rarely stand before a newcomer empty-handed.

LifeRing Convenor Carola Z.:
I am very opposed to any sponsorship or mentorship in Lifering. That's what Lifering is all about as far as I'm concerned – no sponsor, no steps, no higher power. We are the people who don't want to be told what to do and we don't take people by the hand to lead them through their recovery process. If we try to copy other organizations, then where would people like me go?

5.4: Sponsorship?

People frequently ask whether LifeRing has sponsors, as in AA. AA literature in its early years made no mention of sponsors. When the sponsor role first made its appearance, it had to do with bringing a person to a meeting and introducing them, nothing more. Only in fairly recent years has the sponsor role taken on the dimension of comprehensive mentorship. Today's AA sponsor has two main functions. They meet with the sponsee one-on-one between meetings, and they lead the sponsee through the twelve steps. "Get a sponsor, work the steps" is a common AA slogan directed at the newcomer.

LifeRing values sober-to-sober social connections in meetings and also between meetings. The signup sheets at meetings provide the participant with a list of contacts with whom they can connect between meetings, by phone, email, or in person. In that sense, LifeRing participants can have several or even many sponsors, not just one. Every meeting participant can be the "sponsor" of every other.

As for working steps, LifeRing participants build personal recovery programs (PRP). As Chapter Fourteen explains, the *Recovery by Choice* workbook does not contain a generic program; it is a tool for building individual programs. Since there is no standard

---

LifeRing Convenor Pernille F.:

If a newcomer comes to enough meetings they will get all the 'sponsors' they need: the whole group. And if they keep coming and stick around before and after meetings too they will find all the one-on-one potential they need. It can grow like all other relationships do.

I think a better strategy ... would be for the convener or some other member to lead the way to the nearest coffee shop after each meeting. The occasional party or pot-luck dinner or visit to a restaurant might help too:-) And I suspect 'old-timers' will still give their phone number to newcomers, even though it's not AA. I certainly would.

factory program that everyone has to work, there is no role for a mentor to guide the newcomer through it. Apart from abstinence, which is the foundation of everyone's program, a mentor's personal recovery program may be very different than what the newcomer needs.

It is fine if people pair up, or form small groups, to support each other's work in the *Recovery by Choice* workbook, for example, but it has to be clearly understood that there is no authority to tell a person whether they are doing it right or wrong. If they stay sober, they are doing it right.

People are encouraged to pick the brains of someone in the meeting whose recovery they greatly admire, but no member is a recovery boss over any other member, no matter how much sober time they may have accumulated.

The very limited research on sponsorship in AA appears to demonstrate that this form of service is beneficial to the sponsor, but

---

LifeRing Convenor Mary A.:

In LifeRing, I like the idea of supportive friendships that are mutual, reciprocal and equal.

One or two comments on the notion of 'sponsorship' – [here] in South Africa it is common enough in AA groups in larger urban centres but often discouraged in smaller places because of the problems with fostering an unhealthy dependency. Many black women in recovery find patronising overtones in the idea of being 'mentored' or 'sponsored' and point out that the original 1940s AA pamphlet on sponsorship simply refers to the practice of introducing those who want to get sober to a meeting, nothing more. We're not social workers, counselors, therapists or experts in recovery just because we've stayed sober a few months or years longer than a newcomer.

In the last year a number of AA meetings out here have closed down because of incidents of sexual harassment associated with 'sponsorship' schemes, especially those involving teenagers or young gay men preyed on by older members. The idea of intimate private 'mentoring' is problematic and lends itself to abusive or predatory behavior. Who is able to monitor such relationships?

the evidence of its helpfulness to the sponsee is not so clear. Anecdotally, some AA participants credit their sponsors with saving their lives. But more than one sponsor has relapsed, taking their sponsees down with them.

The mentorship power of the modern AA sponsor often exceeds that of physicians or addiction treatment professionals, but without any training, examination, licensure, insurance, code of ethics, or accountability. There are anecdotes of abuse – emotional, financial, sexual, even physical. We are not comfortable with endowing any LifeRing member with that degree of power over any other. Fortunately, our strategy of building personal recovery programs does not require such an institution.

Another, closely related reason for our decision not to have sponsorship is that there is virtually zero demand for it among newcomers at our meetings. One of our groups experimented with a mentorship program some years ago, and a number of longer-time members signed up for it, but, reports LifeRing convenor Mary S.,

> Not one newcomer or struggling person has ever taken advantage of it. Why? I can only guess it's because folks who are attracted to LifeRing aren't interested in this type of involvement. We do not see ourselves as powerless, and do not look to external sources for 'redemption.'

LifeRing Convenor Chet G.:

In the early days before LifeRing was well known there, when we presented LifeRing to the clients at the Oakland CDRP and the subject of sponsorship came up, as it did in that AA-infused place (back then), we'd answer that 'we're the one step program; "Don't Drink or Use No Matter What!" and what part of "Don't Drink or Use No Matter What!" do you need a "sponsor" to explain to you?'

Personally, I consider the "sponsor" one of the most perfidious negative aspects of AA. To not only allow but PROMOTE or DEMAND that self-appointed, untrained, (essentially ignorant), lay drunks/addicts micro-manage another addict's life is not only dangerous but in most cases counter-productive....

Occasionally, a treatment program requires a client to "get a sponsor and work the steps" in order to participate in its aftercare program. The underlying intent, insofar as it isn't simply parochial, is to have the client commit to a sustained recovery effort.

In one program, we were able to satisfy this perfectly legitimate wish by substituting "work the *Recovery by Choice* workbook." There's certainly enough material there for sustained engagement with recovery issues. The recovering person could demonstrate progress by completing the partial recovery plans at the end of each of the nine domains. Although this arrangement has a flavor of compulsion to it – it isn't entirely "by choice" – it may be a price the recovering person is willing to pay in order to stay connected with the given rehab's aftercare program.

5.5: E-Pals

People who find LifeRing online, as many do, may benefit from an online connection with an individual LifeRing participant. This system is called E-Pals, modeled on the traditional pen pal relationship. LifeRing convenor Craig W., who initiated and manages it, explains:

> For several years, LifeRing has offered an opportunity to be connected by email with one of our volunteers for one-to-one support, information and friendship. A newcomer sees it listed as an online option and writes me – I pass on the request to the group of volunteers and one of them offers to respond.
>
> It can be frustrating for our volunteers – the newcomer is often very tentative about the whole recovery process and the disappearance rate is high, which leaves our volunteer thinking they somehow drove the person away.
>
> But for some people, it works very well – people who are reluctant to join a group of any kind or who feel particularly vulnerable and fragile. And, of course, for people who know pretty much nothing about LifeRing and are just exploring.

I've been working on ways to expand the concept by reaching out to website commenters and book purchasers. I view this sort of one-to-one outreach as very important – certainly for the newcomer who is drawn in to recovery and also for our volunteer who, when it works, gains a great deal of satisfaction. Also for LifeRing, as we spread the message around the country and world.

As I mentioned, it can be frustrating for the volunteer, and obviously we don't have a mechanism for 'matching' the volunteer with the newcomer very scientifically. But it works often enough to make it very worthwhile, in my opinion.

I strongly feel there's a need for this sort of program to be expanded to include more people. It does require a commitment from the volunteer, though, of time and emotional energy, so it's not easy to find people to handle more than one person. It's incredibly rewarding, though, when it works well.

LifeRing Convenor Tim R.:

The E-Pal program works quite well in many situations. I am "three for four" in my E-Pal efforts. Some people just seem more comfortable with that sort of written interaction (as do I). So for me it is a perfect fit.

The E-Pal program has bearing on the "sponsorship" issue: I am always very careful to make it clear that this is a "pal" program and that I am not a mentor or sponsor in any way. If more than a couple of e-mail letters are exchanged, and with some judgment on my part, I start signing the letters as "your pal." or "your friend" to make that point perfectly clear. In one particular situation, my E-Pal and I have actually become good friends and we plan to meet "face to face" sometime in the fall.

Anthony N.:

I am one of those who benefited from the E-Pal program. In the beginning, I was reluctant to join a group and if it was not for the E-Pal program and Craig's support in particular, I would not be one year and eight months sober today, for which I am very grateful. I have still not managed to convene a group, but I am very willing and happy to sign up as a volunteer to help just as I was helped.

Chapter 6: Nuts and Bolts

6.1: About This Chapter

This chapter deals with the tangible tools of the meeting convenor's role: signs, chairs, books, clipboard, the room, furniture, etc., and how to use them. In a pinch, a LifeRing meeting can happen without any of these items. All it really takes is two people supporting one another's sobriety here-and-now in a down-to-earth way and with a self-help attitude.

The convenor's intangible tools – the attitudes and skills necessary to lead people in having a productive recovery meeting – are far more vital than the tangible tools, and can't be put into a box. But the tangible nuts and bolts also make important contributions to everyone's meeting experience.

6.2: The Message of the Chairs: Circle Format

A few years ago, there was a scheduling mix-up and we had to end one of our LifeRing meetings a bit early. As we were filtering out we watched the setup people for the next meeting (a different kind of group) hurriedly rearrange the chairs.

Where we had set them up in a circle, the other group needed the chairs in classroom format: most of the seats in rows facing forward, with a few chairs in front facing rearward.

Chair arrangement serves meeting structure and, to a great extent, influences meeting process and content. Chairs set up classroom style (also called auditorium or theater style) assume a division of the group into two uneven parts: a small number of teachers (or presenters, speakers or performers) and a comparatively larger number of students or audience members.

This arrangement, in general, says that the minority will be active or productive and that the majority will be passive, receptive, or reactive. This is an oversimplification, but it is true enough.

Such an arrangement would not serve the LifeRing recovery meeting process, as we now practice it. We use classroom seating on special occasions, such as lectures and presentations at our annual meetings, but for our everyday recovery meetings we use circular seating. We aren't called "life *ring*" for nothing.

The message of the chairs-in-a-circle is that we are all equals and that we are all equally active participants. The ring pattern allows each person to see each other person's face and make eye contact.

What we have in mind by "bringing people together" is to create multilateral connections. We can imagine each person in a ring connecting with each other person, so that the network of lines between them forms a dense web. See Diagrams A and B in the second chapter.

The roundness also seems to send a meta-message of togetherness that facilitates bonding and conflict resolution, a point often observed in the design of tables for diplomatic conferences.

That's why the LifeRing meeting convenor, before the room fills up, has seen to it that the chairs are in circle format.

6.3: Table or Not?

Convenors rarely have the choice whether to use tables or not; the available space and furniture usually decides. But where there is a choice, many convenors prefer to do without the table.

The table cuts people off at the waist visually and may block out useful messages from the lower half of participants' bodies, particularly the feet.

When someone has been speaking too long, or the topic is uncomfortable, or there is some other anxiety, people often signal it unconsciously by wiggling, tapping, or straining their feet. The experienced convenor reads the feet.

Nevertheless, a room with a table is vastly superior to no room at all, and I have attended wonderful meetings in grim hospital conference room settings where the furniture and the whole physical environment became irrelevant, and all that anyone noticed was the voices and faces and experiences and the support.

6.4: When We Outgrow the Room

The LifeRing preference for circular seating, or rather for the format that circular seating serves, necessarily puts an upper limit

---

LifeRing Convenor Betsy Y.:

I have been convening a LifeRing meeting at Mills Hospital in San Mateo for almost two years now from 12 to 1 pm. When I first started convening the group, it was very small. There were never more than 3 or 4 people. During this time our meeting has become quite well known and growing rapidly. We now have the patients from detox join us every Saturday which can be anywhere from 2 to 5 people. The outpatient unit has also referred their patients to us and many people who have graduated from outpatient continue to come because they really benefit from our meeting. I love convening very much and love the fact that our group has grown.

I am now very concerned with my group as it has grown to 20 plus people and today we had an additional new group of 7 people anxious to join our group.

I would very much appreciate some advice as to how to manage a group of this size. Does anyone else have a large group that can give me some input?

on meeting attendance. This format works best when the group size is small.

When meetings regularly exceed the size at which general participation is practical, convenors need to be prepared to split the meeting.

We have accumulated considerable experience doing this on Saturday mornings at the LifeRing meeting at the Kaiser Permanente Chemical Dependency Recovery Program (CDRP) in Oakland, CA, and the convenors there have worked out a routine for the process. It takes two rooms, two convenors, two signup sheets, two baskets, two sets of literature, and a few extra minutes of time. Everyone concerned agrees that it's worth it.

There is no hard and fast rule about the break point at which splitting is advisable, but think about the clock. If the meeting is sixty minutes and there are twenty people present, that makes an average of three minutes each. I've seen and led many a good LifeRing meeting including crosstalk with as many as 24 people in a room. However, it's difficult to go into much detail in that amount of time.

One LifeRing meeting needing to split, and having about equal numbers of men and women, arranged the split by gender. According to the convenor in the women's room, the conversation there was considerably more lively and participation was greater

---

LifeRing Convenor John O.:

If the convenor is prepared for it: (1) has a qualified person lined up in advance to handle the second group, (2) has a nearby room identified, with the second convenor aware of where it is and how to get there, (3) has duplicate materials [opening statement, pens/pencils, sign-in sheet, clipboard, basket etc.] immediately available for the second convenor [a pre-packed "second group" folder in the meeting box can be helpful], and (4) both convenors work together to get the splitting activity underway as soon as possible, it isn't all that difficult to accomplish. Two of us used to do this frequently and we saved far more time than was lost in executing the split.

than it usually was in the mixed-gender meeting. I didn't have a report from the convenor on the male side to see if that was true there, also.

I once visited a LifeRing meeting, also at the Oakland CDRP, with 45 participants, completely filling the room and spilling out into the hallway. Each person got to announce their first name, their sober time, and – in 25 words or less – the main issues in their recovery during the week. After each share, there was loud applause from the group. It was so loud that you could hear it down the hall. There wasn't time to get into much detail, nor much crosstalk. But everyone got a chance to check in and get applause, and the room was full of energy and enthusiasm. This format was a creative way of dealing with a situation where the resources for splitting into two rooms were missing.

Some convenors prefer a maximum of fifteen participants. Some feel that the ideal LifeRing meeting size is about eight or ten people. It's up to the convenors to make the call, based on the resources available.

It's a fact that if LifeRing ever becomes wildly popular, the flood of members will put severe strains on our participatory meeting format. We'll need lots more rooms and lots more convenors, or we'll have to turn people away. Those are bridges we'll have to cross when we come to them.

6.5: The Box and Where to Keep It

The clipboard, the opening statement, the blank signup sheets or meeting logs, the directional signs, the door sign, the tape, the stamp, the pens, the meeting schedules, brochures, the books, the basket, and other sundries (but never cash!) are most conveniently kept in a box or briefcase.

A cardboard file box (sometimes called "banker's box") works fine for this purpose, at least for a few months. A plastic portable file box with a handle on top, available at most office supply stores, is a step up. You can put hanging file folders inside to hold blank signup sheets, the opening statement, the signs, and other tools of the trade.

Convenors also use briefcases, salesmen's sample cases, small wheeled airporter suitcases, backpacks, gym bags, and the like. Mark the container prominently: "LifeRing."

Once you have a box, where do you keep it?

If the convenor takes the box home after each meeting, the meeting will have a problem on the inevitable occasions when the convenor is late or absent. By Murphy's Law, newcomers always show up in force on such occasions, and form their first (and usually last) impression of LifeRing from the spectacle of a handful of regulars patching together a Frankenstein version of the opening statement from memory, making lame excuses when asked for meeting schedules and LifeRing literature, and not having paper and pen to write down the newcomers' email addresses.

Solution: keep the box on the meeting premises. If you can store the box at the premises in a secure location, that's wonderful. If not, store it at the premises anyway. Unless it contains money, the box is an unlikely target for petty crime. Addicts are not going to lurk on street corners flashing stolen workbooks under their coat flaps – "Psst!"

Store the box under the sink, under the stairs, behind the door, in the reception booth, projection booth, janitor's closet, equipment room, ladies' room, behind the potted plant, wherever. Label the box prominently as LifeRing stuff. Let everyone in the

LifeRing Convenor Susan K.:
I thought I might mention my meeting last week here in Victoria had 20 people! The biggest group I have facilitated. It was really good though. There was enough time for everyone to check in and a shortish talk. I would say, though, that was really a comfortable maximum!

meeting know where it's kept and how to access it. That way, if some night you the convenor are late or absent, the meeting can have its materials.

P.S. NEVER keep money in the box.

6.6: Door Signs and Directional Signs

The meeting won't have much growth if newcomers can't find it. Somehow many of our meetings end up on the twelfth floor of a hospital annex on a weekend when the main entrance is closed and you have to make a quarter-mile detour through the catacombs. Or in the garret of a haunted mansion accessible only via a secret passage and a spiral staircase. Or in the basement of a conference center on floor A-2 accessible only via Elevator Z, and if you miss the turn you're in the boiler room.

To let people find you in challenging environments like these, you need to have directional signs. More important, you need to post the signs before the meeting, and then you need to take them down again afterward. You may come to refer to them as "those damn signs."

Getting and making the signs is the easy part. Sign templates are posted on *www.lifering.org*. You download them as PDF files. You can choose signs with arrows pointing left, right, up, or down. You can add legends, such as "Take Elevator Z to Floor A-2 and exit via rear door."

You may curse the signs, or look on them as an exercise opportunity, because of the running. Before the meeting, you have to go to the meeting room, get the signs out of the box, retrace your route to the main entrance, post the signs, and return to the meeting room. When the meeting is over you have to hike back to the main entrance, collect all your signs, bring them back to the meeting room and put them back in the box. By then, everyone you wanted to socialize with after the meeting is probably long gone.

Of course you could take the signs home, instead of keeping them in the box, so that you post them as you enter and collect them as you leave. But then comes the inevitable day when you arrive at the meeting having forgotten to bring the things, or when you're late or absent.

Some convenors keep a duplicate set of signs, one set in the box, one set to take home. Inevitably the sets get mixed up and both sets end up in the box or at home. You could try deputizing another member as assistant in charge of the signs. You could try leaving the signs posted up permanently. You could try to find a storage place for the signs near the main entrance.

Lucky is the convenor whose meeting room is within eyeball range of the main door, so that hanging up and taking down the door sign is the extent of their sign-posting chore.

The early symptoms of convenor burnout in LifeRing aren't bags under the eyes, snapping at people, and lack of concentration. Regulars can tell that the convenor has lost it when they come to the meeting and the usual signs aren't up. Those damn signs have worn out another perfectly good convenor.

6.7: Attendance Slips

Judges, parole officers, substance abuse case managers, and other authorities can be a distrustful lot when it comes to people who get in trouble for drinking and/or drugging. When they require such a person to attend a given number of meetings, they want documentary evidence that the person complied. This evidence is the attendance slip. It's a simple form, usually smaller than a letter-sized sheet, with a space for a date, time, place, and signature. The person carries the form and gives it to the convenor at each meeting to fill in and sign. The convenor does so and gives the slip back. Eventually, the person turns in the full slip to their case manager as proof of compliance over time.

The argument has been made that recovery meeting leaders should refuse to sign attendance slips as a protest against forced meeting attendance. This argument arises from scenes where a bus pulls up and unloads thirty resentful Drug War parolees who sit in the back of the meeting with their hoods up, never speak, put no money in the basket, and leave as soon as their attendance slip gets signed. Refusing to sign the slips is a way of sending the message that this type of conscript visitor is not welcome. If they can't get their slips signed, they won't come.

So far, such a scenario has not played at LifeRing meetings very often. When it has, the results have usually been disruptive, but sometimes brilliant. The key issue is whether the participants have come to the LifeRing meeting by choice, or whether their rehab has just crammed them into a bus and dumped them without asking.

All kinds of people come with attendance slips they need signed, but they exercised a free choice to come to this meeting rather than any number of others. They come in manageable numbers, they participate earnestly, they are civil, they put what they can in the basket, and it's a pleasure to have them. Accordingly, there is little resistance currently among LifeRing convenors to signing attendance slips. It's a distraction, at best, but with a little practice it's quickly dispatched.

The usual system is for the person to hand their slip to the convenor (or deposit it in the money basket next to the convenor) as they come in. If there's time before the meeting starts, the convenor might fill the slip out right away and hand it back. Otherwise, the convenor fills in the accumulated batch of slips in idle moments during the meeting, and whenever that's done, sends the finished batch around the circle, with each person claiming their own. Sometimes convenors use the money basket to return the completed slips; the basket goes out filled with slips and comes back filled with dollar bills. If there's no time during the meeting for the convenor to sign the slips, people just have to wait until the end.

A LifeRing rubber stamp can speed the convenor's chore. If the meeting consistently has many people who need slips signed, the convenor might also speed things up by having a signature stamp made, and ask attendees to fill in the date themselves. You can also get a small self-inking date stamp. There's no good reason for the convenor to develop writer's cramp or take major focus away

---

LifeRing Convenor Byron K.:

Last night an unfortunate incident occurred at the Kaiser CDRP LifeRing meeting in Santa Rosa, CA. DAAC, the county treatment contractor, arbitrarily chose to begin forced busing of their Turning Point residents to the Kaiser LifeRing meeting. Approximately ten additional attendees showed up at meeting time with no advance notification. That's OK.

What occurred next is disturbing. Almost immediately after the Opening Statement was read, several of the Turning Point residents (5-6) walked out of the room into the corridor and rest rooms without returning. There was almost obviously dealing, using, and sex taking place. This is a three-story building with multiple tenants, rest rooms, and open vacant rooms. Some of the Turning Point residents that remained in the room were continually disruptive. No DAAC supervision was in attendance.

I emailed the director of the program this morning explaining that I will not be responsible for the conduct of DAAC clients while they attend meetings on private property. Meetings for people in residential treatment facilities should take place at the treatment facility or outside attendance should be supervised. The simplest solution to this issue is for DAAC to allow LifeRing to convene meetings at their facility which would easily solve these problems. DAAC has refused to allow LifeRing to convene meetings on site.

from the meeting to fill out paperwork. The convenor is a facilitator, not a bureaucrat.

It is OK in the current climate for convenors to sign and return slips at the start of a meeting, even if this occasionally means that the slip owner leaves immediately. It is not OK in my opinion for a convenor to sign a slip for someone who did not show up at all. That usually gets back to the case manager and brings heat on the meeting. If the authorities get too pushy about slips, convenors are likely to opt out of the system. Most convenors are happy to do a little paperwork as a service to other people in recovery, but few are willing to act as unpaid parole officers.

If I have a lot of attendance slips to process, I'll usually ask someone else to "run the meeting for a few minutes" while I have my head down. This is a good way for others to get their feet wet in the convenor role.

LifeRing Convenor Byron K.:

Three weeks ago I was complaining about the county contractor busing its treatment residents to an LSR meeting unsupervised.

Last night, many of the same residents contributed to one of the best LifeRing meetings in which I have ever participated.

Because the treatment residents do some form of check-in at least twice a day, the How Was Your Week format isn't always appropriate. Last night I used a topic meeting format suggested in the *Empowering Your Sober Self* book. The topic was paraphrased from an Albert Schweitzer quote. The topic was, "What does your inner doctor tell you regarding your using/drinking?" Many of these attendees are street hardened and prison hardened. Their contributions to the discussion were brilliant. Some of their statements were absolutely profound.

I am writing to the DAAC director this morning to thank her for the contributions of her residents.

6.8: The Clipboard

Most LifeRing meetings use a signup sheet, and this requires a clipboard and a pen. The clipboard becomes an emblem of the convenor's role. If you want to know who the convenor is, it's the person who keeps the clipboard.

Pre-printed signup sheets are available for download from the lifering.org website. They aren't mandatory and some meetings don't bother with them. A "meeting log" that's just a blank sheet of paper with spaces for names and contact info would serve as well for most purposes. Signing the sheet is always optional. Sheets can serve useful social functions, such as:

• When you put your name, email address and/or phone number on the sheet, you are giving permission to other members to contact you between meetings in case they need to hear a sober voice or see some sober mail in their inbox.

• When you put your email address on the sheet, you are giving permission to the convenor to put you on the local email list, if there is one.

• The sheet helps people learn each other's names.

• Signing the sheet is a symbolic way of affirming your commitment to sobriety.

• The convenor uses the sheet to keep track of basket donations and book sales.

• The sheet serves as a running count of how many people attended.

• If someone needs proof their attendance but did not carry an attendance slip, or lost the attendance slip, the signup sheet is a backup.

• In case of emergency, the convenor can look at the information on the signup sheet to try to contact a person.

• At the annual LifeRing Congress, in the event there are questions about a delegate's credentials, the sign-in sheet can serve as validation of the meeting's existence.

Some convenors make a brief announcement before circulating the signup sheet or meeting log to be sure that members understand its voluntary nature and its purposes.

Convenors generally do not use the signup sheets to conduct telephone surveys of past meeting participants, or to check up on members to find out why they were absent from a meeting, or for any similar non-emergency reason.

Signup sheets are not disclosed to outsiders. The fact that you attended a meeting is confidential unless you give permission to disclose it.

As a general practice the meeting convenor puts filled-in signup sheets back in the box. To date, no privacy concerns have arisen over this custom. The convenor could also take the sheets home, keep them in a safe place as long as seems reasonable, and then send them to the LifeRing Service Center or destroy them. The LifeRing Service Center collects filled-in signup sheets for statistical and historical purposes. Eventually they go into the shredder.

When a meeting is on the mandatory list of a treatment center, the convenor may circulate two clipboards with two signup sheets, one for LifeRing and the other for the treatment center.

For example, at the Kaiser treatment facility in Oakland, patients in the Saturday morning program get an hour during which they have to attend a support group meeting. AA, NA, LifeRing and sometimes Al-Anon all meet in different rooms on the premises during this hour. It's the patient's choice which one they attend.

At this session, which is consistently one of the biggest LifeRing meetings in the area, the convenor has to deal with three signup papers: the Kaiser sheet, our sheet, and the attendance slips of people from other programs. Despite all the paperwork, these are great recovery support meetings.

Choosing the right moment in the meeting to pass the clipboard(s) is a convenor's judgment call. See the "Basket" section below for a discussion.

6.9: Books and Handouts

Laying out display copies of LifeRing literature is part of the convenor's room setup routine. If there's a side table or a coffee table, the literature can be arranged for display there. If the meeting convenes around a standard height table, the books can be laid out in the middle.

If the room only has chairs, the literature can be laid out on the floor in front of the convenor, with the titles facing toward the center.

Some convenors circulate display copies of the LifeRing Press books during the meeting so that people can get their hands on them and scan through them. It's always appropriate to pass a bundle of handouts around for those who don't already have them.

• The main handouts form a trilogy that explains the basic Three-S philosophy of LifeRing: "Sobriety Is Our Priority" (green), "Secular Is Our Middle Name" (gray), and "Self-Help Is What We Do" (pink). The convenor will have fewer complications in keeping the meeting focused if all participants have already familiarized themselves with these introductory brochures. Passing them around at the start of the meeting is a surer way to get them into people's hands than leaving them on a table.

• The *Recovery by Choice* workbook is a tool for self-help based on the LifeRing philosophy of constructing one's individual tailor-made recovery program. The book presents the recovering person with a set of the most common issues that tend to come up in recovery, organized into nine domains. The book allows the person to make the choices that will work best for their personal situation. It's a structured method of empowering the sober self. The format works well for individual self-study at home, and can be adapted for group settings. A number of treatment programs purchase *Recovery By Choice* in quantity for patients/clients who request an alternative to "Big Book" study.

• *How Was Your Week?*, the present book, is of course a convenor's book. But it is normal and healthy for members to want to know everything that convenors know. Encouraging every interested member to become familiar with a convenor's handbook is a way to prepare members to step into the convenor role as soon as they are ready.

• *Empowering Your Sober Self: The LifeRing Approach to Addiction Recovery* is a 275-page introduction to LifeRing written for the person in recovery and for treatment professionals. It outlines the reasons why an alternative such as LifeRing needs to exist. The basic principles of the LifeRing approach are explained here, with frequent references to the scientific literature. The book is currently in its second edition.

• The *Bylaws* text, available on *lifering.org*, and easily printed out, is just what its name states: the exact text of the LifeRing "constitution," adopted by the founding Congress in Brooksville, Florida in 2001, as amended by the annual Congresses since then.

By the time you read this, the selection of LifeRing brochures and LifeRing Press books may have changed. You can always get the catalogue of current offerings on the Internet at *www.lifering.org*.

In addition to the printed materials available from the Press and the Service Center, some convenors also download selected articles from *www.lifering.org*, print them on their computer printer, make some photocopies, and lay them out for the taking. In a pinch, you can also download PDF copies of the three principal brochures from *www.lifering.org*, and print and fold them yourself.

A good role for a member who is an avid reader and wants to become more involved is Bookperson or Librarian for the meeting. This volunteer can take over the purchase, setup, display, distribution and sale of LifeRing and other literature from the meeting facilitator.

Meetings may also want to experiment with operating a lending library that includes not only LifeRing Press books but also a selection from among the many other recovery titles that may be of interest to LifeRing members and friends.

6.10: Literature Racks and Bulletin Boards

Many institutions that provide space for LifeRing meetings have literature racks, or places where you can set up a rack, and they have bulletin boards.

Where do you get these racks? Contact the LifeRing Service Center, *service@lifering.org*.

Keeping the current meeting schedule in the racks and posted on the boards, and keeping the racks supplied with handouts, are small services that send a big message: we are here, we are alive, and we want to see you.

If the racks are empty or contain long outdated materials, they send a negative message. Convenors may want to check the rack and the board as a regular part of their setup routine, or may want to recruit a volunteer to do it.

Bulletin boards and literature racks also exist in chemical dependency treatment facilities and other high-traffic locations that do not have LifeRing meetings on the premises. A convenor who can place LifeRing materials in these sites will help bring more newcomers to the meeting.

It goes without saying that convenors need to get permission from the host institution before using its rack spaces and before placing a rack of our own. Some facilities also have rules about who can post what and when on their bulletin boards. Observance of these rules promotes good relations with the space provider.

6.11: The Basket

At some point, it may be helpful to remind meeting participants of how much money they may have spent feeding their addiction. Although sobriety is much cheaper, it costs money to keep a support group network afloat and this deserves their generous support.

Passing the basket is a traditional routine at self-help recovery meetings, and LifeRing is no different in this respect. There is never an admissions charge at LifeRing recovery meetings, but there is almost always a basket. The exception is venues where meeting participants aren't allowed to possess money: locked psychiatric wards, some inpatient treatment programs, and the like.

"Basket," actually, covers a wide range of different containers. I have seen meetings use a wicker basket, a plastic basket, a file card box, a big floppy inter-office envelope, a regular No. 10 envelope, a paper hat, all kinds of real hats, a sock, a scarf, a saucer, a paper plate, a salad bowl, a coffee mug, and a Chinese food takeout box.

The most ingenious basket I have seen was a java jacket – a bottomless cardboard sleeve that serves as an insulating handle for hot paper cups. The java jacket worked fine for paper money. It couldn't hold coins, but that was good news from the standpoint of the person responsible for counting the collection – coins are a bookkeeper's headache.

One meeting I know doesn't pass a container at all. They put the cardboard file box that holds the books and signs in the middle of the room. As people stand up to leave they throw their donations into the box.

At another meeting, they pass the basket before reading the opening statement.

Choosing the right moment to start the basket going around, same as with the clipboard(s), if you use them, is a convenor's judgment call. If you pass them right at the opening, you will miss the people who come in late. If you wait until just before the closing, you will miss the people who leave a little early.

Passing the basket and/or the clipboard just before the closing also raises other issues. A person can't handle the basket or the clipboard and join in the closing round of applause at the same time. Having a money basket circulating while people are getting up and leaving the room can also lead to problems.

Many convenors start both the basket and the clipboard(s) going round at some point in the middle of the meeting when everyone who is going to come has arrived and everyone who will

---

LifeRing Convenor Craig W.:

LifeRing is not exactly rolling in cash these days. In fact, we're looking for ways to either increase our income or decrease our expenses. Convenors can help with this task, as Gloria C., convenor of the Saturday morning Oakland CDRP has demonstrated. For the past few weeks Gloria has simply pointed out that a) we depend on donations and b) there has been a good deal of inflation since a dollar became embedded in all of our minds as the "standard" donation. Without pushing at all, she simply mentioned that maybe $2 would be more appropriate. The basket came back with twice the average level of contributions.

How about giving this a try at your meeting?

leave early is still there. They can be launched in the same or in opposite directions. The basket or board may pause momentarily when they come to the person who is currently talking, then resume their course. The ongoing talk is usually captivating enough that the clipboard and basket complete their circuits without a ripple.

In meetings with a lot of unknown first-timers, the convenor may want to keep an eye on the basket as it makes its rounds.

Whichever system you the convenor choose, it helps the members if you establish and hold to a regular pattern, so that a certain way of dealing with the basket and the clipboard becomes part of the meeting's familiar rituals.

If you store your meeting's materials box on the meeting premises, don't leave money in the box between meetings. That's like leaving honey in your tent in bear country while you're off hiking. Once money is found in your box, your box may be subject to constant disturbance.

A more detailed how-to guide for the meeting's Money Person is in the next chapter.

Chapter 7: The Meeting's Money

7.1: About This Chapter

This chapter is about the money that meetings collect when they pass the basket: how to keep track of it and what to do with it.

7.2: The Three B's

For the person who handles the meeting's money, the basic tools are the three B's: the Basket, the Book, and the Bucks.

The "basket" and when to pass it is discussed in the Nuts and Bolts chapter, above. When the meeting is over, the meeting's Money Person or Treasurer counts the basket collection. If there's more than a few dollars, it may be good practice to ask a second person to count it again so as to verify and witness the amount. The Money Person then writes the amount collected in the basket in the lower right corner of the meeting's signup sheet or meeting log in the "Basket $" line. Money received for books sold is tallied separately on the "Book sale $" line.

Treasurers of meetings that pay no rent and have essentially no expenses have the easiest job. Treasurers can simply put the basket money collected at each meeting, plus the money from book sales, totaled separately, into an envelope showing the date and amounts. The Service Center supplies preprinted little brown envelopes for the purpose.

The convenor can write a personal check for the amount and mail it to the Service Center (LifeRing Service Center, 1440 Broadway Suite 400, Oakland CA 94612). The Service Center will supply SASEs for the purpose.

PayPal is a payment method that is becoming more popular with convenors for sending money to the Service Center. It does away with paperwork, postage, and delay. Contact *service@lifering.org* for PayPal payment details.

The Service Center will deposit the funds received in the bank and will record meeting money and book sales separately into the accounting system as appropriate. Written reports can be generated at any time for review by the convenor.

It's helpful but not essential if the person forwarding the money will tally the amounts by date. That way the convenor (and the Service Center) can get a historical overview of the meeting's development.

In case of a question anywhere along the line, the receipts can be compared with the amounts on the money envelopes and on the signup sheets, and everything should balance. There is so little work involved in this arrangement that the convenor often handles it personally and a separate Treasurer may not be necessary.

Basket money and book sales money always needs to be tallied separately for tax purposes.

If the meeting also has expenses, notably rent, the Treasurer's job becomes immediately more complicated. The Treasurer in such a case will almost certainly want to keep an account book. This "book" can be as informal as the back of an envelope or as formal as a computer spreadsheet.

Some meeting keep their money records on a Google Docs spreadsheet that can be viewed by anyone with Internet access and the link.

Whatever its form, the Treasurer's account book usually moves about with the Treasurer, and does not usually stay in the meeting's box on the premises.

Recording the amounts of money collected in at least two places, on the signup sheet or meeting log (which normally stays in the box at the meeting site) and again in the Treasurer's own account book, is very useful in the event one set of records becomes lost. It happens.

The meeting Treasurer's own account book is the place to record all of the meeting's expenses. Rent, obviously. Purchases of books and other literature from LifeRing Press. Incidental expenses for refreshments, flyers, mailings, stamps, etc. Expenses related to the annual LifeRing Congress. And so forth. The Treasurer will want to keep track of all the meeting's intake and outgo in the Treasurer's book.

Meetings that pay rent and have other expenses will want to hear periodic financial reports from their Money Person. The Treasurer's account book will provide the basis for these reports. The convenor might call for a short business meeting after the regular meeting, or set aside time at the beginning of the meeting, to hear the Treasurer's report.

7.3: Book Sales

A basic element of the meeting is having LifeRing books available. But how to get the books, how to pay for them, and how to resell them?

Different meetings use different methods. Brand new meetings and big established meetings have different needs.

For brand new meetings in virgin territory, the Service Center can put together a "convenor kit"consisting of starter quantities of the key literature. The convenor can use the provided books as samples or loaners. People can then order books for themselves online from *lifering.org*. LifeRing Press ships books promptly – more promptly than *amazon.com*, because amazon has to order the books from LifeRing before shipping them to its customers.

Established meetings in settings where lots of people don't have online access may want to set up an account with LifeRing Press. This is a good subject for a phone or email chat with the LifeRing Service Center (1-800-811-4142, *service@lifering.org*). LifeRing Press offers quantity discounts.

Some meetings also find it useful to donate LifeRing books to local centers where recovering people may be found.

The *liferingconvenor* email list, linked on the *lifering.org* website, is also a good resource for different book handling options.

7.4: Shoe box or Checkbook?

Treasurers have the option of running the meeting's finances on the shoe box system, or through a checking account. "Shoe box system" means that the Treasurer keeps the bills and coins collected at the meeting segregated from all other money, for example in a shoe box or a money pouch.

When it comes time to pay the rent or other expenses, or to make a contribution to the Service Center, they take the money out of the shoe box. They pay out the same bills and coins that came in.

The "shoe box" or other cash repository should never be kept in the meeting box on the meeting premises.

Some Treasurers find the shoe box system cumbersome, and prefer to handle the meeting's finances through their personal checking account. After carefully noting the amounts received in at least two places (the signup sheet and their own account book) they commingle the meeting's bills and coins with their personal currency.

When it comes time to pay the meeting's rent or other meeting expenses, they write a personal check. They also use a personal check to mail the meeting's surplus funds to the LifeRing Service Center, along with a note that breaks down how much is from the basket and how much is from book sales. Or they use PayPal to do the same thing.

As mentioned earlier, the Service Center will issue reports and email them to the Treasurer, so that in case of question there is an audit trail. The Service Center stores each transaction on a computer so that, if necessary, the transaction history can be reviewed.

So long as the meeting Treasurer keeps an accurate account book with back-ups, and is a financially responsible person, there is nothing improper about handling the meeting's money through the Treasurer's personal checking account. The sums involved are usually small and below the radar for purposes of the Treasurer's personal income tax return.

If a meeting develops a larger financial volume than can be comfortably handled with this homespun setup, then it's time for the meeting to set up a business checking account. The account needs to be in the name of the local LifeRing group, for example Ourtown LifeRing, organized as an unincorporated association. As a general practice, two signatures should be required on a check.

Meeting Treasurers who come to this bridge may find it helpful to consult with the LifeRing CFO at the Service Center, *service@lifering.org*.

When selecting a Money Person, it is wise to choose someone who is financially responsible and stable in their recovery. Know where to find your Treasurer! It is also a good policy to keep the meeting's cash reserve down to the necessary minimum – two months' rent is a ballpark figure – and avoid the accumulation of large surpluses.

7.5: The Meeting's Surplus

Each LifeRing meeting is a financially independent entity. It keeps its own books and makes its own decisions how to spend its money. The LifeRing Bylaws say that meetings are bound to support the national organization "to the extent the Meeting sees fit." (Article 11, LifeRing Meeting Charter.)

At this time, many meetings have no rent to pay and no other significant expenses, and these contribute practically their entire basket collection to the LifeRing Service Center. Some meetings contribute practically their entire revenue above their rent. Some meetings contribute a set amount each month. Some meetings contribute little or nothing. This is a common pattern in organizations such as LifeRing that lack a compulsory dues structure.

The entire financial structure of LifeRing is based at this time on volunteerism. Every LifeRing convenor from the meeting level down to the directors and officers serves without pay or reimbursement of expenses.

At this time, the national organization's regular business expenses are modest and consist of items such as office help (a part-time office administrator), office rent, Internet costs, telephone lines, postage, supplies, printing costs, and the like; see the annual Financial Report to the LifeRing Congress for details.

Given the voluntary, meeting-focused financial structure of LifeRing, the center needs to continually justify its existence and its good works to the meetings if it hopes to have their financial support.

This means on the one hand that meetings have no cause to complain that the national organization is squeezing or bleeding them for funds.

It means on the other hand that some meetings get the benefit of the Service Center's efforts without contributing to its support.

So far, this arrangement has worked with relatively little friction. However, as the organization grows, as the founding generation ages, and as the Center faces new demands for its services, it is quite likely that something resembling a dues structure similar to that in the twelve-step groups may become necessary.

The power to make changes in the LifeRing financial structure is in the hands of the LifeRing Congress.

Chapter 8: Online Meetings

8.1: About This Chapter

This chapter focuses on LifeRing meetings on the Internet. It discusses the benefits and limitations of the online medium and some of the noteworthy opportunities and challenges that face convenors of online LifeRing meetings.

8.2: Online Recovery Support Works

The Internet is a great boon to recovering people. The stock of recovery information and support available in your locality no longer limits you. Do you live in a remote outpost without human neighbors? With a few clicks you can access the resources of the wide world. Don't care for Brand A recovery? In a few minutes online you can access the available alternatives. Are the logistics or membership of your local gathering awkward for you? Online you can converse about anything any time with anyone, all the time.

The dream of recovery support how you want it, when you want it, as much as you want, is very nearly a reality. If you have an Internet connection, you need never again be alone with your inner monsters. Support is always there.

Although technical progress has made voice and video linkups much more widely available, many people value text-only communication as their primary recovery linkup. The fact that the other person cannot see them and does not know who they are provides them with a vital margin of comfort.

Before the Internet, people in prominent roles who feared their enemies, people who were painfully shy, ashamed, embarrassed, or afraid, were cut off, and many no doubt succumbed in isolation. Now they can get and give support online; they can be connected with other sober people.

Online support works for many people. We have a considerable base of experience on this point. I have seen people achieve many years of continuous clean and sober time with no other support system than the online communities. It does not work for everyone, but then nothing works for everyone. It works for enough people to remove any doubt about its usefulness as one recovery tool among others.

Online support is here to stay. The concept of "online meeting," considered something of an oxymoron a decade or two ago, is now a familiar one, and is enshrined in the LifeRing Bylaws. (LifeRing Bylaws, Art. 4.2: "A meeting may come together either face-to-face or via electronic communication ... ") Along with online meetings, we now have a growing cadre of online convenors.

The online convenor needs to have Internet access as well as the computer skills required for the particular online medium: email list, bulletin board, chat room, or social media. In text chat meetings, it is very helpful to be a fast typist. In other online venues, the ability to write clearly and thoughtfully is prized. Teaching computer skills is beyond the scope of this book, but there are many tech-savvy individuals online in LifeRing who will cheerfully extend themselves to help people get up to speed online.

8.3: The Varieties of LifeRing Online

From a basic email list begun by Florida convenor Tom Shelley in 1995, the LifeRing online presence has bloomed and spread. As of 2015, an inventory of LifeRing online includes the following:

• The **www.lifering.org** website. This is the main LifeRing website and is the portal for finding all the rest. It contains a comprehensive, up to date list of all face-to-face and online meetings, among many other resources. It contains the **LifeRing blog** and links to other LifeRing websites. You can also get **LifeRing Press** publications here, and make online **donations**. This is also the place to download an online copy of the **LifeRing Newsletter**.

• The **LifeRing chat room**. This offers not only old-fashioned real-time text chat but also several options for voice meetings and video meetings.

• **LifeRing E-Pals** is a service to connect newcomers online with a veteran LifeRing participant for purposes of orientation, and to provide one-on-one support and information. There is more about it in the chapter on Newcomers.

• **Email Lists**. About a dozen email groups exist to serve a wide range of users. Email groups function as a sort of slow motion meeting, running 24/7. Members write in to the group with a problem or a question and other members respond with positive, supportive messages drawing on their own experiences. All members can read all the posts but they are invisible to search engines or non-members. Email groups range from general sobriety support to more specialized topics. For example:

• **LSRmail**: The original online group, unmoderated, available 24/7.

• **LSRsafe**: open to all, lightly moderated to minimize disruptions.

- **LSRbody**: for people concerned with weight loss, exercise, body image.

- **LifeRing Sober Living**: for people sober a year or longer and concerned with life choices and the challenges of longer-term recovery.

- **LifeRing Dual Recovery**: for people dealing with concurrent disorders.

- **LSR-LO**: for family members and friends of Loved Ones who are still in addiction.

- **Workbook Study**: for working the *Recovery By Choice* Workbook.

- **LifeRingBOD**: for LifeRing convenors, Board members, and others interested in organizational issues.

- **LifeRing Convenors**: for LifeRing participants convening face-to-face meetings or considering becoming convenors. Much of the content of this book is based on the postings to the *liferingconvenor* email list.

- **LifeRing Online Convenors**: for LifeRing participants who convene online meetings or are interested in doing that.

- **LGBTQ Portal**: A Google group for people in recovery who identify as Lesbian, Gay, Bisexual, Transgender, or Questioning.

- **Sober Coffeehouse**: Wide open discussion of topics too remote from addiction recovery to run comfortably on the other lists.

There are also locality-based lists for people in the San Francisco Bay Area, the UK, Ireland, and Scandinavia.

- The **Ning** social network is a simplified version of Facebook that's limited to LifeRing participants and people interested in LifeRing.

- The **LifeRing Forum on Delphi** is an active bulletin board with an archive approaching 100,000 messages. The Forum is visible to search engines, unlike email lists, so personal identification information should be avoided.

- And of course, LifeRing has a presence on **Facebook, Google+,** and **Twitter**. Professionals can now also connect with LifeRing on **LinkedIn**.

Links to access all of the above are on the **lifering.org** website. (*Lifering.org* is the successor to the *unhooked.com* website, launched in 1996.)

8.4: Issues with Narrow Bandwidth

The LifeRing chat room now offers voice and video meetings in addition to text. Participants can also set up their own voice and video meetings via Skype or as Google hangouts. These broadband media go some distance toward including the nonverbal communication signals that are central to face-to-face conversations. But most online participants at this time still use channels limited to text: text chat, email lists, and the social platforms.

Text-only communication has powerful positives. It strips away attributes such as gender, age, ethnic background, nationality, accent, disability, weight, appearance, and other features that might be obstacles to empathy. The narrow bandwidth of text is a radical leveler.

At the same time, the anonymity of narrow bandwidth filters out civil inhibitions usually present in face-to-face conversation. People don't see the hurt in our face from their words. Habitual haters can vent their bile without fearing consequences. Even ordinary nice people sometimes behave online in ways that sober people rarely do when face to face.

Most online meetings most of the time are friendly, sober, and supportive, but the chat convenor will need to be quick on the keyboard and have good communications skills if disruptive users appear.

Fortunately the online media also supply tools that match their challenges. In the text chat room, for example, the convenor can filter a given speaker out so that their posts cannot be seen by others, although they can see other people's posts. The chat convenor can have a completely private conversation with someone in the room while the meeting is going on. This is very useful for welcoming and orienting newcomers. Most online convenors have tools for ejecting a persistently disruptive person (a "troll") from the venue if necessary.

It should go without saying that online convenors have to be role models in online civility. A person who indulges in vulgarity, personal or professional attacks, grandstanding, theatrics, sarcasm and similar troll-like behavior drives people away from LifeRing and cannot be recognized as a LifeRing convenor. Conversely, a person who is patient, kind, unruffled, and unfailingly civil with every online participant will bring credit to the LifeRing network and will gather a wide circle of friends online.

8.5: Online Format Issues

The format of online meetings other than the chat room is unstructured. There's one continuous 24/7 meeting with unlimited crosstalk. If there is an opening statement, it's provided to new members when they join and rarely referred to thereafter. There's no set topic, and discussion may range from trivia about the local weather to intense discussion of a member's difficulties.

In email groups, a number of topics ("threads") are open at the same time. They may begin with a descriptive subject line on the original email, but often veer off in several directions.

At the Delphi Forum, messages are divided by topic so that posts are better organized, but even there, considerable meandering occurs. At the Ning site, as at Facebook and Google+, the structure is wide open. Basically, anyone can say anything at any time.

Chat room meetings can also be unstructured. The chat room often serves as an informal hangout with no set format or topic. But online chat takes place in real time. This advantage gives the chat meeting convenor the opportunity to create something resembling an orderly face-to-face meeting.

The peg on which the format hangs is the user list shown on the side of the chat window. Each user sees the same list, and it is in alphabetical order. The convenor can ask the participants to take turns doing "How Was Your Week" as in a face-to-face meeting by beginning at the top of the user list and proceeding down the list in sequence, as if the participants happened to be sitting in a room together in alphabetical order. Crosstalk is encouraged in the same way as in a face meeting.

This structured chat format tends to keep the conversation on recovery and ensures that even the shy and the slow typists get a turn at reporting on their recovery work. Once the meeting clicks together, it can be a beautiful and profoundly moving experience. Sharing recovery support simultaneously with peers from all over the world is a memorable uplift.

A member who finds chat room discussion not their cup of tea can participate instead in the social platforms or the email lists, where messages can be as long and thoughtful as essays, and where flying fingers are not necessary.

The newcomer may find the format of these groups chaotic at first, but the names of frequent posters and the topics of urgent concern quickly become familiar. New names and new topics generally receive a warm welcome. The unstructured format allows for a safe, comfortable, relaxed and easy-entry environment.

There is no online basket to pass, but automatic "bot" messages go out to the chat room from time to time to suggest donations and to encourage participants to take a turn at being convenors. LifeRing has to pay for many of the online venues, beginning with the website, and online users who recognize this point and go to *lifering.org* with their credit cards and make a monetary contribution are much appreciated.

8.6: Proof of Attendance Online

Online chat meetings are slowly gaining acceptance as accredited meetings by some treatment centers, parole authorities, and others who mandate meeting attendance. The chat convenor has available a verification system for attendees needing proof of attendance. On request, a standard confirmation email goes out to verified online meeting participants. This is the online equivalent of the paper attendance chits that convenors routinely fill out on request in face-to-face meetings.

8.7: Conclusion

The Internet involves a balance between access and bandwidth. You get a tremendous expansion of access to recovery resources wherever and whenever you want them. Without the Internet you would probably never connect with people across the many social and geographic boundaries that tend to keep people apart. The price is a loss in the harmonics of communication – the facial expressions, tone of voice, body language, social identity, look, warmth, and touch that we take for granted when we meet face

---

LifeRing Convenor Bob O.:

I got sober thru online stuff here at LifeRing, hated F2F meetings of any kind, but when the only LifeRing meeting in my area needed someone to keep it going because the convenor had to take a leave of absence I said I would help. It was then that I saw the magic of a LifeRing meeting by convening. Its a win/win, help yourself while helping others. It may just be the best thing you can do for your long term sobriety.

to face. Although bandwidth is bound to improve, you'll never be able to shake someone's hand, smell their breath, or give them a hug except face to face.

It's also important to keep in mind that there are recovering people who are not online. The economics of the Internet exclude a substantial portion of the population of this country and of the world; they live on the far side of the digital divide.

The future lies in learning to combine the online and the face-to-face modes of support in the most productive way. In Life-Ring, the roles that face-to-face meetings and online meetings play are both independent and mutually complementary. The online channels help people find existing face-to-face meetings and form new ones; they are incubators. The online venue frees people from the time constraints that can limit their participation in the larger face-to-face meetings. The face-to-face meetings send people to the chat rooms and other online venues; they are conveyor belts. Content perpetually circulates and synchronizes between them.

The natural tendency for people who have only met online is to want to meet face to face. The natural tendency for people who have met face to face is to continue the conversation online.

Both types of meetings rest on the same philosophical foundations, live within the same organizational network, and have the same mission.

Chapter 9: Meetings in Special Settings

9.1: About This Chapter

This chapter is about convening LifeRing meetings in chemical dependency treatment programs, mental health clinics or hospitals, halfway houses, homeless shelters, prisons, and other special-purpose environments. It discusses the convenor's basic approach and goals, the adjustments that may need to be made in the typical meeting format, and the rewards that come from convening in these settings.

9.2: Introduction

The heavy use of alcohol and/or other drugs has a tendency to yank a person out of their usual environment and land them in special settings. Chemical dependency treatment programs nationwide count a rotating enrollment of more than a million people. Addiction is a co-occurring disorder in a wide range of mental health treatment settings. Institutions in practically every branch of the social services, from child protection to homelessness to health care, regularly encounter clients for whom alcohol and other drug use are important issues. Alcohol and other drug use is a factor in a large proportion of arrests for a variety of crimes, and people convicted of drug possession form the major bulge in the U.S. prison population.

In all or most of these special settings, a number of patients as well as clinical professionals are looking for recovery choices. Simply as a practical matter, without ideological agendas, it has become clear to a growing number of people active in these settings that "we need something more." There is, therefore, a field of opportunity and, many feel, a social duty, to bring LifeRing into these settings. In the past two decades, many institutional doors that were once barred to options like LifeRing have opened up. The LifeRing Service Center regularly receives invitations from professionals in institutional settings to start LifeRing meetings.

As of this writing, LifeRing convenors have thousands of combined person-hours convening meetings on the premises of outpatient chemical dependency treatment programs such as those offered by the Kaiser Permanente health maintenance organization. LifeRing convenors also have a substantial experience base convening meetings on the premises of residential treatment programs such as the Merritt-Peralta Institute (MPI) in Oakland and others. Some LifeRing convenors have more than a decade of experience convening LifeRing meetings in a locked psychiatric ward for patients in acute crisis involving drugs/alcohol, and in similar mental healthcare settings. There is also the beginning of an experience base with LifeRing in a variety of prison settings.

Although we still have much to learn, certain basic points have become clear:

 • The LifeRing approach is viable in all of these settings. Our message resonates with a significant proportion of people in these institutions and assists them in helping themselves in ways that are noticeable to them, to their peers, and to clinical staff.

 • Convening LifeRing meetings in these settings requires convenors to become aware of and to respect the policies of the host institution. The convenor will benefit from good two-way communication with professional staff.

- Convenors active in special settings need to adjust the meeting format and tailor their own role to meet the particular needs of the population in the host facility.

- Convening LifeRing meetings in special settings is among the most rewarding experiences available in recovery. LifeRing convenors providing these services not only get to feel good as human beings, they also tend to develop their convenor skills rapidly and to a high degree of proficiency.

The number of LifeRing convenors who have experience in special settings is substantial and growing. This chapter attempts to pull together what we have learned so far, as a foundation for further progress in this area.

9.3: The Variety of Special Settings

All LifeRing meetings take place in settings that are special for those who participate. The fact that the meeting may take place on the premises of an institution such as a hospital does not, by itself, make it a special setting within the meaning of this chapter. The hospital may simply be acting as a premises host or landlord in the same way that a public library, a church, a community center, or a coffee shop does. A meeting takes place in a special setting for the purposes of this chapter when (a) the setting filters the people who may participate in the meeting and (b) the setting has policies and professional staff that play a role, however peripheral, in the conduct of the meeting.

9.3.1: Settings that Filter the People

The most obvious kind of people filter is a locked door. In the psychiatric ward, the convenor has to pass through a security gate in order to enter, and the patients are not free to leave. Residential rehab programs also frequently disallow (or selectively allow) outside visitors at LifeRing meetings, even though residents aren't locked in.

Outpatient programs generally don't limit outside visitors to meetings on their premises, but the institutional setting tends to repel the shy and insecure.

Community centers for LGBTQ people make a point of welcoming everyone, but some individuals are afraid to be seen there.

People with comfortable housing may be reluctant to attend meetings in homeless shelters.

Some people are uncomfortable in churches with in-your-face religious artwork, or churches of any kind, and won't go there.

And, of course, every setting tends to filter out people by its geographical location.

The convenor in every kind of setting will want to be aware of the filters that come with the territory.

In most cases, the situation won't require significant adjustments in the meeting format described in the previous chapters.

However, the convenor will find that certain adjustments are necessary where the setting's filters fill the room with people whose functioning is impaired, or whose recent life experiences include serious trauma.

Adjustments may also be necessary in settings with normal functioning but with very high turnover, such as in rehabs that discharge their clients after a few days or weeks. There's more about these issues below.

9.3.2: The Institution's Policy and Staff

A setting is "special" within the meaning of this chapter when it filters the people who participate *and* when the conduct of the meeting is contingent on compliance with an institution's policies and approval by its staff.

For example, when the psychiatrist in charge of the crisis intervention unit at a local hospital interviewed me in response to my request to start a LifeRing meeting there, almost his first question was what was our policy toward psychiatric medications. I told him our two-part test, described in the chapter on Sobriety, namely that if the patient has been honest with the physician and the physician is competent in addiction medicine, then we support the patient in taking the medication exactly as prescribed. In no case do we interfere with the physician-patient relationship.

That answer met with his strong approval. He volunteered that he was "sick and tired" of certain twelve-step sponsors who pushed his patients to stop taking their medications. LifeRing received clearance to start the meeting, and with some interruptions and changes of venue this meeting has run for more than a decade.

Another example. When I was the CEO of LifeRing, I received a confidential phone call from a staff member of a nearby outpatient treatment center where LifeRing had and has a number of meetings. He said he had reason to believe that the convenor of one of our meetings had relapsed and was currently using. The implication was clear that if this was true and we did not replace the convenor, the meeting would be closed. Without going into details, I promptly took care of the problem. The point is that permission to hold the LifeRing meeting in that setting was contingent on compliance with the institution's policy and approval of its staff. The LifeRing policy in this case was identical to the institution's, so we were not bent out of shape.

Once a LifeRing meeting is established, compliance and approval are rarely in question. The institution's policy and LifeRing's own policy are usually in synch, as in these two examples. But getting in the door in the first place, and handling the issues that come up in the ever-changing institutional landscape, are issues that may challenge the convenor and provide opportunities to raise our game to a higher level. More on that below.

9.4: LifeRing in the Psychiatric Crisis Setting

Just as a desert or a hurricane or a frozen mountaintop provides a testing ground for the fitness and equipment of an outdoors person, holding meetings in a psychiatric crisis ward is a proving ground for the basic ideas of LifeRing. The number of convenors who have ventured into this challenge is still quite small. I hope that after reading this chapter, more will rise to it.

9.4.1: Struggling to Find Level Ground

I remember the cold fear that I felt when I first stepped into the dual-diagnosis crisis intervention ward at a local hospital and saw the doors lock behind me. The physician in charge had advised me that most of the patients had been brought there by police on a "51-50" – they had tried to kill themselves, or someone else, or had been found wandering naked in the street.

In my fear, I struggled to find ground on which to stand. At moments I pictured myself on a mountaintop, looking down on the rabble from my bastion of sanity and sobriety. At other times I wanted to crawl into a mouse hole and scurry away. I had no competence to deal with these people, and they would quickly see me as a fraud and hoot me out of the room. I had to struggle to find level ground. Other convenors have had similar experiences.

As usual, the anticipation was worse than the reality. Once I got settled in the room, said a few words, and got people talking, it began to dawn on me how much we had in common. That man over there with a bandage around his neck, who drank a fifth of bourbon and then picked up a kitchen knife and slashed his throat – I've felt like doing that myself. That nice-looking young man over there with a triple diagnosis (addiction, depression, HIV+)

– that could have been me. That scholarly-looking woman sitting all slumped over and struggling for words – that could have been a fellow-student from graduate school. That distraught-looking woman with the sunken eyes seeing visions – that could have been my grandmother.

The longer I listened, the more I saw that there is no great chasm that separates people in this setting from those on the outside. It is more a matter of degrees and situations and luck, rather than a separation of kind. After one spends some time listening, the people with special challenges that one meets in these settings come to seem like friends and family, and sometimes they *are* friends and family.

Finding level ground does not mean having identical diagnoses. I do not need to have slashed my own throat or experienced clinical depression or had psychotic episodes or a murder conviction in order to relate as a peer to the people I find in special settings. It does mean, I believe, having had some experience in life where one falls into the abyss, loses one's bearings, abandons all pretense, looks death in the face, but survives and recovers.

The late historian of AA, Ernest Kurtz, refers to such experiences as "kenosis" – literally, emptying out, figuratively a dark night of the soul, a visit to the abyss. (See White 1998:333) Nearly every person who has followed the call of alcohol/drugs for some considerable distance in life has had such experiences.

Achieving "authenticity of emotional contact" (White's phrase) with people in such settings is a two-way process. People in this setting tend to have low expectations of the people who come in from outside to see them. They may expect to be judged and preached at, or pitied and held in contempt. When someone makes an effort to meet them on level ground they tend to react with pleasant surprise. They will teach patiently, if the convenor is willing to learn. The convenor's evident desire to establish a level relationship goes a long way toward achieving success.

It is helpful if the convenor begins the meeting by clarifying the convenor's role. In the locked psychiatric crisis ward, for example, I usually begin by saying that I am not a doctor or other clinical professional, I am not employed by the hospital or otherwise paid for being here, I have no particular credentials in psychology, and my only qualification for being here is that I used to do alcohol and drugs a lot but have now been clean and sober for a period of time, and I want to share the insights and methods of the group in which I am doing my recovery.

That's a legitimate reason for being present, and rarely is there any objection. On this footing, the convenor can be firm about asking people to participate in our process. We are present without pretense or apology. We stand on level ground.

9.4.2: A Focus Group Like No Other

In the typical meeting in the crisis ward, a few of the participants are sedated and barely awake. Most of the rest range from tired and bored to relaxed and curious. A handful are hyper-aware, borderline paranoid, keenly attuned to any false note. It's a focus group like no other. The situation calls for a bit of an introduction explaining why you're there and what you want to do. If you're boring, the low ones will drift off. If you shovel any kind of BS, the high ones will catch you and skewer you.

It was in this setting that I gradually developed the "How Life-Ring Works" presentation, using the A v. S diagrams with circles and arrows, described in Chapter Two. I've repeated that talk, usually with a whiteboard, hundreds of times with a wide range of audiences. This presentation was developed and field-tested on the toughest audience of all – the people inside the psychiatric crisis ward.

9.4.3: Topics for Minds in Turmoil

In the acute psychiatric setting, the usual "How Was Your Week" format that we use in community meetings runs into limits. Prescribed medications severely constrict the horizon of some participants' recent memory. Others have the requisite horizon, but spent their previous week ramping up to and then performing the attempted suicide, homicide, or breakdown that got them into the institution.

There is generally no compelling reason for us to elicit the patients' "How I got into the ward" stories. They may excite our morbid curiosity or educate us but they serve little recovery purpose. They may even cause harm by reawakening sensations of trauma that had best be allowed to sleep a while.

In our usual community meetings, the point of talking about events of the week is that the person is engaged in an ongoing life-weaving project called recovery, and the meeting is an opportunity to share the current status of that work-in-progress.

In the acute psychiatric ward, many people don't yet define themselves as in recovery; they have not yet become proactive and got busy at the loom of their lives. The objective is to help them move toward that starting point.

For that reason, LifeRing convenors who work in this kind of setting generally ignore the patients' immediate histories and utilize a topic format. After the introduction, we ask people to talk about a broad, positive topic such as:

- Is there a clean and sober place inside of me, and if so, what does it look like?
- A clean and sober dream or vision I have for my life
- A clean and sober memory that I have
- A good time that I have spent with clean and sober friends
- People I know who love me as a clean and sober person

- If I were my own doctor, what treatment would I prescribe for myself?

Most of these topics were developed by LifeRing convenor Marjorie Jones. The point of these topics is to focus mental effort and social energy on affirming something positive and recovery-related within the person – some clean and sober identity, vision, memory, or friend.

Of these topics, I've had a particularly good response with the "sober dream" theme. I ask them if they know about the Rev. Martin Luther King's "I Have a Dream" speech. (They all have at least a general idea about it.)

Now, I suggest, suppose you are Martin Luther King and you are giving a speech about the dream you have for yourself. A dream of the clean and sober you. What would you say? What is your dream for yourself?

These can be moving sessions. Revisiting better times, reclaiming a better self, reaffirming a better vision for one's life can help people whose minds are in turmoil gain a few moments of comfort and a little boost of energy to pick themselves up and start over.

The convenor doesn't need a long list of such topics; there is high patient turnover and this handful of tested topics goes a long way.

9.4.4: Crosstalk in a Psychiatric Setting

Crosstalk (feedback, conversation) in the acute psychiatric setting can work wonders. To see patients engage with one another in a positive, supportive, sobriety-affirming manner is almost like watching miracles of healing happen before one's eyes.

Some patients can talk quite sanely and insightfully about their insanity, just as addicted persons can speak soberly and truthfully about their addiction. Patients can help each other recover in ways that may be quite difficult for physicians. When patients recognize one another as valid, worthwhile people, you can sometimes see their whole demeanor improve from one moment to the next. In my experience, peer-to-peer conversation can be even more effective in the acute crisis setting than in the ordinary community-based recovery meeting.

But – and it is an important proviso – crosstalk must be explicitly consensual. In the psychiatric setting, LifeRing convenors always ask the participant whether they want to have feedback, and get a clear "yes," before inviting others to respond. By contrast to the community meeting, crosstalk in the psychiatric setting is off by default, and each patient is empowered to turn it on if they want it. The convenor also must be on the alert for the usual snags that may come up in the crosstalk process, discussed in Chapter Three.

9.4.5: The LifeRing Uplift

In special settings no less than in ordinary community-based meetings, the convenor's role is to bring people together in recovery. But in order to come together with others, people have to believe in themselves, and the convenor has to believe in them. The quality of emotional resonance, of relating to people on level ground, communicates a belief in the potential for recovery. You wouldn't talk level with people if you didn't have respect for them.

This attitude resonates positively with some of the hardest of hard cases: the alcoholics/addicts who have attempted suicide. These make up the majority in the locked acute psychiatric crisis ward.

• They don't need to hear that their life is unmanageable; they know that, that's why they tried to end it. Even their death was unmanageable.

• They don't need to hear that alcohol and drugs are very bad and may kill them; that's what they were trying to accomplish.

- They don't need to hear that their characters are defective; they already feel like double failures – failed at living and failed at dying.

- They don't need promises that God will pull them out; if they still had faith in those promises, they would not have tried to kill themselves in the first place.

What they do need to hear is that there is something valid within them to build on. When we come in with the attitude that there is something good within them as they are, they tend to pick up their spirits. When we assume that there is the capacity within them to recover, they tend to come out of their paralysis and to validate our assumption. When we tell them that success depends on their own efforts, they tend to start connecting with others and entering into networks of support.

Many patients come out of the LifeRing meeting in the institution with a positive attitude, and some begin to take up their own recoveries. People rise to our level of expectation.

The LifeRing uplift in the psychiatric crisis setting has not gone unnoticed by facility staff. After LifeRing meetings had been going on there weekly for nearly two years, the Patient Care Manager of one such unit wrote:

> We have found that this [LifeRing] approach encourages patients to begin to think positively about themselves and to find a reason to live productively. This approach resonates with the significant portion of our patients [...] who have received little or no benefit from past 12-Step involvement. [...] Our treatment team believes that there are many viable paths to recovery, LifeRing being one very positive adjunct to our traditional offerings. The LifeRing meeting is a bright spot in the patients' week, and staff find that participation in the meeting enhances patients' motivation to get well.

(See full letter on next page.) Not only the patient but the convenor comes out of this process with a positive feeling and with motivation to continue.

9.5: Meetings in High Turnover Settings

The stay in the classical addiction rehab is supposed to last 28 days. The 28 days has become synonymous with this kind of program in the popular mind. In reality, however, patients in these programs are typically gone long before Day 28. In one well-known 28-day residential rehab, staff told me that the actual average patient stay is just twelve days. This is not uncommon in the industry.

Alta Bates

A SUTTER HEALTH AFFILIATE

April 5, 2000

To Whom It May Concern:

We are writing this letter to describe the invaluable work that Mr. Martin Nicolaus has done at Alta Bates Medical Center on 4 North Herrick, the Dual Diagnosis Unit. As a dual diagnosis crisis intervention facility, our patient population consists largely of persons who are suffering from psychiatric and mental health problems combined with a variety of substance abuse disorders. The majority of our patients arrive here against their will, having been placed on an involuntary psychiatric hold for observation and treatment because their psychiatric condition has caused them to be dangerous to themselves, or others, or gravely disabled and unable to care for themselves.

Since late 1998, Mr. Nicolaus has volunteered to lead a one hour weekly meeting of Life Ring Secular Recovery (formerly SOS) with our patients. Mr. Nicolaus brings to this group his personal life experience as an alcoholic in recovery. Much like the members of Alcoholics Anonymous and Narcotics Anonymous, he shares his own story of recovery, modeling a message of strength, hope and recovery for our despairing patients. As a volunteer, and a non-professional, Mr. Nicolaus also brings a model of self-help through community support to our patients.

The LifeRing group approach encourages patients to look within themselves and to each other for the strength to achieve abstinence and a healthier life style. Unlike the more traditional Alcoholics Anonymous approach, Life Ring does not use the concept "Higher Power" or the "12 Steps of Alcoholic's Anonymous." The philosophy and methods of LifeRing were developed as an alternative to AA for those people who need tools for recovery but have personal difficulty embracing the concept of "Higher Power." We have found that this approach encourages patients to begin to think positively about themselves and to find a reason to live productively. This approach resonates with the significant portion of our patients on 4 North who have received little or no benefit from past 12-Step involvement.

Although the Life Ring group's philosophy is different from the 12-Step model, we have not experienced any friction or strife as a result of adding the LifeRing meeting. We also offer AA to our patients . Our treatment team believes that there are many viable paths to recovery, LifeRing being one very positive adjunct to our traditional offerings. The LifeRing meeting is a bright spot in the patients' week ,and staff find that participation in the meeting enhances patients' motivation to get well.

Based on our experiences at this facility over the past two years, on behalf of the treatment team on 4 North, we would recommend similar LifeRing meetings to other facilities interested in expanding the range of their patient services.

Sincerely Yours,

Jane Haggstrom RN, PhD

Jane Haggstrom, R.N., Ph.D.
Patient Care Manager
4 North Herrick
Telephone: 510-204-4339

Alta Bates Medical Center
Herrick Campus, 2001 Dwight Way, Berkeley, CA 94704
Tel 510.204.4444

The reason is insurance. Under the Managed Care regime, most insurance coverage for chemical dependency treatment goes day-to-day. Programs have to employ full-time staff whose sole job is to report the patient's status to the insurance adjuster nightly. The adjuster decides when to pull the financial plug. It's not uncommon for clients in such a program to have no idea whether they'll still be there tomorrow. Clients with long-term insurance or with private means may be the exception.

In such a setting, the LifeRing convenor may find a room full of people who have never heard of LifeRing and have no idea what it's about. Moreover, many of them will not be there next week. This meeting may be the convenor's first and only chance to acquaint the participants with the LifeRing approach.

9.5.1: Working up a LifeRing Intro

Merely reciting the stock opening statement used in LifeRing community meetings isn't enough in a high-turnover setting. In order to have a productive hour, the convenor may have to begin with a bit of an informational talk about LifeRing.

How much and what kind of an informational talk is appropriate depends on the situation. I always have good luck with the "How LifeRing Works" talk, using diagrams like those in Chapter Two of this book. I can deliver this with a whiteboard in anywhere from five to 12 minutes. (An online version in the form of a Flash video takes just two and a half minutes; it's posted on *www.lifering.org*.) This little talk implicitly conveys two fundamental points of the LifeRing approach: (1) That the potential for getting clean and sober is within us – the "S," and (2) that empowerment of the sober self comes via human relationships.

Once the audience is on board with these two points, the rest flows naturally. But that's my personal preference; it suits my style.

Each convenor will benefit by working up a bit of a LifeRing talk that helps the audience understand what LifeRing is about, and that the convenor feels comfortable repeating whenever needed.

In some sessions, after the little introductory talk the participants will have questions about LifeRing. If the questions seem argumentative, the convenor will probably want to defer the response "until after the meeting," which means in effect forever. But if the questions seem sincere and well-intentioned, the convenor may open the floor to an extended Q&A session.

Sometimes this occupies the whole hour. That's fine if that's what the meeting participants wanted to do at that time. They were hungry for knowledge and entitled to be served. At other times, a few sentences of amplification on the introductory talk will be enough.

The convenor needs to play it by ear. The priority is to keep the participants engaged and participating. All other things being equal, I strive for a 1:4, 1:3 or 1:2 ratio between explaining LifeRing and doing LifeRing. So, in a one-hour session, we may spend 12 to 20 minutes discussing LifeRing concepts, and the remainder of the hour having a LifeRing meeting.

In some settings, the convenor will face the competing demands of people who are new and want explanations, vs. people

---

LifeRing Convenor David R.:

In short-term treatment programs we see any given attendee once, twice, maybe 4 times tops. On a "first-impression" basis, a strictly How Was Your Week format probably isn't going to do as much to engage that person's interest (or help their sobriety) as would a more "Intro to LifeRing" approach to the meeting format.

That is, we answer their questions about LifeRing as fully as possible, let them know what they can expect in regular "real life" meetings, and make sure to connect them with those meetings. If there's time left after that (and there often will be), you can do what you feel is best- go for a quick HWYW-type check in, discuss a particular topic that's come up, pick a new topic that might be relevant for the group as a whole... you'll get the feel for it.

who heard the explanation last week or the week before, and want to have the actual How Was Your Week meeting. One effective device in this situation is to ask the veterans, who heard the explanation last week, to act as presenters for the newcomers. LifeRing convenor Robbin L. introduced this method. This approach has multiple benefits. The presenters deepen their own understanding, on the principle that one way to learn something is to teach it. The presenters are also more likely than the convenor to be on the same wavelength as the newcomers in that setting, and their words may be more immediately accessible. Finally, the convenor can measure the effectiveness of last week's explanation by listening to its echo this week, and can make the appropriate adjustments.

High-turnover settings also challenge the convenor to come armed with LifeRing literature, particularly handouts and meeting schedules, and to keep the host institution's literature racks filled at all times.

The convenor's Rule One – train your successor – can't be applied in the usual way in high-turnover settings. A core group of regulars cannot form there. Instead, the convenor will need to recruit a successor from meetings in community settings. How-

---

LifeRing Convenor John B.:

I do a Detox meeting in Victoria. I explain that we usually start off with how was your week at the usual meetings but acknowledge the fact that their past week probably hasn't been all that great. We try to focus on the positive.

We do a check-in and sometimes the subject will be what does sobriety mean to you or what are your plans when you leave, etc. This works well at getting people sharing the different types of recovery and resources available. I've learned a lot from these meetings myself.

Last night the convenor did the usual how was your week and it turned out fine. The relaxed atmosphere of a LifeRing meeting seems to loosen people up and they'll start talking.

ever, some of the clients in rehab settings this week may start participating in LifeRing meetings in the community next week.

As graduates of the rehab where they first heard about LifeRing, they may in time return to that rehab to become highly effective convenors of the LifeRing meeting there.

9.5.2: "Talked Out" Settings

A different kind of challenge faces the LifeRing convenor in some residential facilities where the population is engaged in a constant round of other meetings. Here, the convenor may find that the participants feel "talked out." The conventional opening, "How Was Your Week?" may bring responses such as "We already talked about that in community meeting this morning."

It may be worth moving ahead with the How Was Your Week format nevertheless. I have led LifeRing evening meetings with resident patient groups who have spent almost all their waking hours in meetings, but where the LifeRing process elicited feelings, ideas, insights and self-revelations that had not occurred to the patients – or that they had not dared express – in their other encounters. Despite the fact they had been talking all day, they talked way past the closing time, and I had to eventually disengage myself.

There are meetings and meetings. In many treatment environments, and outside as well, meetings tend to be staged and scripted events at which most attendees are passive spectators. Even the so-called "process meetings" in treatment programs – sessions that on their face bear the nearest clinical resemblance to LifeRing meetings – can be stylized affairs, where people have to grovel and speak in formulas.

The down-to earth atmosphere (the secularism) of the LifeRing format often gives people permission to let their hair down and speak their real feelings without having to fit into some Sunday School formula.

The LifeRing spirit, which sees the recovering person as pro-active, can motivate people to hold their heads up straight and look monsters in the eye that they would otherwise believe themselves too weak to challenge.

The encouragement of feedback and conversation ("crosstalk") builds an embracing sense of community. The open architecture of the LifeRing approach may get people thinking realistically and optimistically about their own forward path.

In short, as they become comfortable with the LifeRing format, people may come to realize that although they had been moving their lips all day, they have not really talked at all.

I have seen counselors in the hallway outside our door scratch their heads wondering what in the world the patients found to talk about after a full day of meetings. The LifeRing difference is not necessarily in what we talk about, but in how we talk.

However, if the convenor senses terminal process fatigue in the room, there is always the option of switching to a topic format. The *Recovery by Choice* workbook is a gold mine of discussion topics. The resourceful convenor will keep a copy always handy You can open the book almost at random and find a topic that can keep a meeting focused for an hour or more.

9.5.3: The "LifeRing College"

In one residential rehab, the administration decided that the How Was Your Week format was not a good fit for their program (for whatever reason) and that the LifeRing meeting time should be devoted to information about LifeRing. As it happened, I was the convenor. Since I had considerable experience making informational presentations, the new format was not a big problem.

We evolved a "LifeRing College" format consisting of a rotating series of five sessions, covering the usual meeting format, the

Three-S philosophy, and the first five domains of the *Recovery by Choice* workbook.

The LifeRing content is highly scalable; it can be presented in a 30-second elevator version or in a week-long seminar, if necessary.

9.6: Professionals in the Room

In many special settings, program staff stay out of the room when LifeRing meets, and the convenor interfaces with the clients on the same peer-to-peer basis as in a community meeting. This is the LifeRing ideal. We are a mutual aid group, which means peers aiding peers. Convenors, as has been made amply clear in a previous chapter, are not professionals and always remain peers.

But in other special settings, program staff sit in on the Life-Ring meeting. The program administration requires it. There is nothing that LifeRing can do about it. The question is whether LifeRing should flex and adapt to the situation, or stick to a pure-peer model and withdraw from the institution.

My view is, it depends.

9.6.1: Professional Backups

When I first started convening LifeRing in the acute crisis psychiatric ward, I was grateful to have a licensed psychiatric social worker in the room with me as a backup. There were moments when my experience base in regular LifeRing meetings just wasn't tall enough to handle some of the challenges that some patients in the room presented. On a few occasions, the presence of an authority figure in the room who could get a patient to be quiet or to leave the room saved the meeting.

Even a decade later in a different venue and with a higher functioning patient group, the mandatory professional in the room is still a definite asset. The staff member frames LifeRing for the patients as a valid option, puts LifeRing literature on the table, introduces the convenor in a respectful way, and acts as a resource when patients have questions about their treatment.

In a certain residential rehab, a counselor always sits in, but after taking roll at the start of the meeting he remains in the background, and participants appear to ignore him. He has never interfered with the LifeRing process.

When I'm convening in this kind of setting, I'm not only providing mutual aid to the patients or clients, I'm also educating the staff member about LifeRing. From time to time, staff from neighboring wards, or the chaplain, or students from a nearby college visit and sit in on the meeting. As convenor, I'm spreading the message of LifeRing to their institutions. Later, when they get their professional licenses, they will already have had a personal experience with LifeRing which, hopefully, will lead to wider acceptance in the healing professions.

Professional visits can go too far. Occasionally the visiting staff and students in the psychiatric ward outnumber the patients, like a tribal village where the anthropologists outnumber the indigenous.

Most annoying in this kind of setting are the interruptions by doctors or other clinical staff who barge into the room and yank out one or another patient for a consult. They have no respect for the meeting's process.

I can imagine professionals in the room who take over the meeting, lean forward with their positions of authority, and turn the encounter into a group therapy session that has nothing in common with the LifeRing approach. However, I have never seen that happen, yet.

My experience with professionals in the room has been overwhelmingly positive. True, the professional in the room is a fly in the doctrinal ointment of pure peer leadership. That is a negative.

But by flexing and adapting to this setting, LifeRing reaches people suffering from addiction whom it would never otherwise see, and who in many cases benefit greatly from our presence.

Moreover, LifeRing becomes an accepted and valued part of the institution and of the healing professions who make it run.

Those are powerful positives. These positives translate into more doors opening for LifeRing in the institutions and more referrals from professionals to LifeRing meetings in the community.

Referrals from professionals, a LifeRing survey showed, is the Number One source of new members to LifeRing meetings. The good opinion of professionals is far from a trivial matter for the growth of this organization.

9.6.2: Professionals as Convenors

What about professionals leading LifeRing meetings in the absence of a regular LifeRing convenor?

One Christmas Day I arrived a few minutes early at a residential rehab where I regularly convened an 8 p.m. meeting. Instead of the usual throng of clients milling in the hallways, there was silence. I proceeded to the meeting room and found, to my total surprise, the LifeRing meeting in full swing. Because of the holiday the facility had moved the meeting time up to 7:30. A counselor was present and acted as convenor, moving the check-in along. I found a seat and participated. I was thrilled. There's no stronger proof of a meeting's vitality than its continuation in the absence of its usual leadership.

That, of course, was an exceptional situation. Or was it?

I once sat as visitor in a LifeRing meeting in a county-run rehab about 50 miles outside the San Francisco Bay Area. About 20 clients of the facility filled the room. The convenor used the How Was Your Week format. There was active participation and plenty of positive crosstalk. LifeRing literature was on the table.

It was one of the better LifeRing meetings I've seen, and it was a regular part of the program's weekly schedule. The convenor had a light touch, spoke to the participants like a real person, and was obviously well liked. But she wasn't a person in recovery from addiction. She was a full-time paid staff member of the institution.

This was not a peer-led meeting in the plain meaning of the word, yet it was a successful LifeRing meeting. Some professionals, whether they have a recovery history or not, enjoy an exceptional peer-like rapport with their clients, and are able to facilitate LifeRing meetings that are indistinguishable from any other.

There was at the time no regular LifeRing convenor in that area who could have led that meeting. The choice was either a good LifeRing meeting led by a professional or no LifeRing meeting at all. A few years later, incidentally, regular peer-led LifeRing meetings sprouted in this community by the dozen.

Every startup, as it grows, encounters challenges where it either compromises or it dies.

As LifeRing becomes better known and as the demand for Life-Ring in institutional settings takes off, there will be more and more situations where a regular LifeRing convenor is simply not available to start the meetings that the program wants to start.

In fact, unless a LifeRing meeting gets started in that location, a convenor may never emerge there, because convenors don't usually fall from the sky, they mostly arise out of existing meetings.

If we want to grow, we have to make allowances for LifeRing meetings that are led, at least for an initial startup period, by staff members of the institution.

We will need to ask the staff members in these settings to become thoroughly familiar with the LifeRing convenor role and with the LifeRing approach generally. We will need to keep an eye on these meetings to make sure that the professionals are fostering the development of peer convenors.

We will need to decide whether or how such meetings are to be included in LifeRing's democratic internal process. These are good problems to have – much better than the problems we had twenty years ago, when the doors of institutions were dogmatically slammed in our faces.

9.7: Professionals and the *Recovery by Choice* Workbook

The role of professionals is an emerging issue not only with LifeRing meetings based on the How Was Your Week format, but also in regard to the *Recovery by Choice* workbook. The workbook is designed to be used by individuals as bibliotherapy. It can very well be used by individuals while enrolled in treatment programs.

A growing number of programs even now are ordering the workbook in quantity and distributing it to their clients as guidelines for their recovery work during their stay. One such program gives clients the following choices for its long-term outpatient program: Either get a sponsor and work the steps, or work the *Recovery by Choice* workbook.

In these and other ways the workbook becomes part of the clinical interface between the client and the program's professional staff.

One of the projects currently under consideration is the publication of a manual for professionals using the LifeRing approach as the framework for their treatment program.

Currently, the recovering person enrolled in treatment often encounters LifeRing only for an hour or so during a week dominated by twelve-step facilitation therapy. The trend is toward the expansion of the LifeRing presence from the margins toward the middle.

One day, perhaps not so far in the future, there will be treatment programs centered on the LifeRing approach. It goes without saying that treatment professionals will play a key role in realizing this vision.

9.8: Sticking Together On The Inside

This section was contributed by LifeRing convenor Patrick Brown. After the experience he relates in this section, Patrick successfully completed his parole and received a B.A. in psychology and a Master's in Vocational Rehabilitation Counseling at the University of Texas in Austin. He worked for three years for the State of Texas as a Vocational Rehabilitation counselor, then toured the world for three years as a performer in Arcattack. He is currently Manager of Product Development at a corporation developing coating technology. He is also a very active volunteer coordinator at Burners Without Borders, Corpus Christi, Texas, cleaning up local beaches.

Hello, my name is Patrick Brown, and this is the story of my experiences in the Texas Department of Criminal Justice (TDCJ) system. I was sent to a rehab program as a stipulation of my parole. It is called a Substance Abuse Felony Punishment Facility, putting stress on punishment. I remember the day that we first pulled up to the gates and I saw the razor wire. I thought to myself, "This place doesn't look like much of a rehab to me." Little did I know.

The date was May 28th, 1999. The sun was beating down hard on the central Texas ground. Hondo, Texas would be my home for the next nine months, and I was anxious to get acclimated to my new surroundings. I had heard some horror stories while locked up in the county about the place that I was about to enter, but had no idea just how strange and twisted the place really was. If I were to be asked now to describe the facility, the first word that would pop into my mind would be "cult."

As soon as I was stripped of my street clothes and put into the TDCJ whites, I was led to a little room where they took all of my personal information and did paperwork. I was now classified as a "client" in a medical context, and with that I suddenly disappeared off the face of the earth. Anyone checking the TDCJ prisoner database would no longer find me.

When I first entered my building, they shaved my head completely bald to strip me of the last vestiges of my "street mentality." For the first 35 days, I was in the orientation phase of the program. I was not allowed to speak to any of the other "clients" and was only allowed to sit in a certain place in the day-room called "the box." I was segregated from all others, save for the few "clients" who happened to be in the orientation phase along with me. I was told that I was "toxic" and that I had not earned the privilege to speak with the "family members." But every night I was forced to attend AA meetings, and was not allowed to talk during them. I was not allowed to attend the secular meeting that was going on, even though I said that attending AA was offensive to me.

Our day began at 4 a.m., when we were awakened for breakfast, and we were not allowed to lie back down until 8 p.m. We were "programming" for the bulk of that time, having very little time for anything else. It was a constant round of seminars with a monotonous content. The main answer that one always received to every problem was "turn it over to God." We were forced to attend seminars on "Step Study," and we would receive strict punishment, including the threat of unsuccessful discharge or an extension of our term if we tried to buck the system. I believe that being subjected to AA indoctrination is a violation of my freedom of religion. When I confronted the counselors on this matter, they would not give me a straight answer. I had to keep attending their twelve-step seminars.

I dealt with this problem the only way that I knew how: by passive-aggressive behavior. Whenever they gave a seminar, I would interrupt with points of clarification, like, "When you say a power greater than myself, you mean God?" And they would give the typical sidestep answer, "A higher power can be anything." To which I would reply, "It couldn't be anything with a power less than mine, though, isn't that right?" We would go on and on like this, and they would always end up telling me, "Until you turn your life over to the care of God as you understand Him, then you are screwed. You will never be sober and you will always be a loser." That didn't make sense to me then and it still doesn't today.

As soon as I "got out of the box" i.e., became a "family member" (and my hair grew back out a little) I began to go to the secular meetings. I knew that I had found my answer when I first read Unhooked and saw the logic of this approach. It made sense and I knew that it would work, so I began to build it into my daily life as well as I was able.

At that time our group was ostracized by the other "clients" and we were branded as godless heathens. We were also slandered as racist, even though two of the original members of the group were minorities. We were not allowed the same privileges as were the other "clients" and we were not allowed to meet every day as were the twelve-step groups. They claimed that there was no room for us to have our own meetings, and so while the others were having their meetings, we would just have to sit on our bunks and read. We were okay with that, but then the others complained because it seemed a privilege to them. It turns out that they didn't really want to attend AA meetings after all! Go figure.

We ignored the name calling, stuck together, and just did our thing. We never quit asking questions in the mandatory twelve-step seminars. We used the LifeRing platform to get some pretty serious work done on ourselves and to really map out where our sobriety would take us. Our group remained small, averaging seven to nine people, for the first six months or so of my stay, but then matters improved. The private outside contractor who had been running the program changed, and there was a lot of hub-bub in the background about pay rates and contracts. When the dust settled, we were recognized as a "real" group at last and we were allowed to give seminars on the secular approach to sobriety.

We put together a quality seminar on the secular approach. Some of the counselors who had been the target of our questions in their twelve-step seminars tried to retaliate with sniping of their own, but we knew our stuff and could not be rattled. Grudging admission of the validity of the secular approach followed, and we were awarded an equal amount of meeting room space. I was named Liaison for our building and before I left (and passed on the torch) our numbers had swelled to equal AA and NA. We were finally getting the constitutional protection that we had fought so hard for.

There were two counselors who had a special hatred for our group. One of them told me to my face that I had no idea what sobriety was all about and that I would relapse as soon as I got home. The other used a mandatory meeting to deliver a church sermon complete with Bible quotes. He gave us all a handout with the scripture passages. I tried to mail it to the American Civil Liberties Union, but it disappeared from the prison's out basket. I hope that these counselors have grown in their sobriety as I have.

The scars that I received in that hellhole are fading with time. I now have more than fifteen years clean and sober. Drinking simply is not an option for me. It can be done. As a part of my Master's degree, I went on a tour of a SAFP-F and it was exactly the same as I remember. It was a strange experience, to be sure. Going back to that place as a visitor, to learn about what goes on in there. Now I am living my life and improving in some way every day. I am happy, finally. I took personal responsibility for my life and my sobriety, and I also take the credit for my success. I took my power back, and I feel good!

9.9: A Constitutional Right to Secular Support

In 2010, a California parolee named Barry Hazle adopted "passive aggressive" tactics in his mandatory twelve-step program similar to those that Patrick Brown describes above. Even though Hazle's disruption was done "in a congenial way," his parole officer had him recommitted to prison for an additional 100 days. Hazle brought suit, and after four years of litigation his case settled with a monetary award to Hazle of just under two million dollars.

The law is now quite clear that the government cannot lawfully coerce people into twelve-step programs when this is contrary to their religious beliefs. A prison – and allied parole and probation officials – must provide secular alternatives. There is more about this topic in the chapter on Starting a Meeting.

9.10: Corresponding with Prisoners

This section was contributed by Tim Reith, a LifeRing convenor in Arizona and currently the Secretary of LifeRing.

The letters I receive from prisoners are without exception handwritten (aka "snail mail") as none of them has access to a computer.

The turn-around-times for these exchanges are often two or three weeks, because all letters are read "going in" and all returning ones are read "coming out."

I have five prisoners that I am now writing to on a regular basis. Three are in California, one in Pennsylvania, and one in North Carolina.

Prisoners usually have no means of copying their letters before they send them. I always make two copies of their most recent letter and send one back with my next letter so they will have a record of what they wrote. Unlike me, they have no computer records. The other copy I keep in a safe place separate from the original.

I have found that most prisoners are lonely. Some have families but they are mostly forgotten or ignored. It's easy for me to write them a page or two. Some tell me I am the only one who even thinks about them. So sad for them and me, but it's rewarding to think I have helped out a little.

It's important to make my prisoner friends feel as though they are helping me, as I am helping them. I emphasize that our letters constitute "two-way streets" and indeed they do. I tell them stories about my personal struggles and some actually write back with advice.

Some LifeRing people use a PO box for a return address when writing to prisoners but I do not. I really don't think there is much danger in giving them my actual mailing address. I feel it engenders trust in them for me and sends a message of my respect to them.

One prisoner, upon his release, did not write for several weeks. Longer than usual. Just when I had about given up I received a "real e-mail" from him. He had spent those weeks learning how to use a computer so that he could write to me with something other than snail mail. He was rather proud.

It's important to assure each prisoner that our personal correspondences remain completely confidential. Accordingly I describe how I keep my letters to them (password protected computer folders) and their letters to me (scanned and placed in same folders). Trust is paramount in these conversations. In the comments that follow, in which I have used specific information about a particular person, I have their permission. One prisoner said I could use anything he might write and that his life was an "open book."

Many prisoners exhibit good intelligence in their letters. I have one prisoner friend who is exceptionally intelligent, and writes with particularly good insight. He was sentenced to 20 years to life. He killed a young man in a gang fight. He was tried as an adult even though only 16.

He is imprisoned in California where there is a new law passed last year (SB260) that allows consideration of such people for leniency. By virtue of this law he had a successful preliminary local board hearing and a recommendation for his parole was sent to the governor for final approval. (The governor must sign off on each person who may qualify for parole under the new law.) The governor signed the appeal (Jerry Brown.)

His release date has been set for December 20, 2015. We have been writing to each other since 2011 and have exchanged more than 60 letters (about 30 or 35 each way.) He calls me his "brother." We plan to get together upon his release.

9.10.1: Guidelines for Prisoner Correspondence

A few months ago Byron Kerr and I wrote the following guidelines for those LifeRing members corresponding or visiting with prisoners. They were also intended to act as reference tools for in-prison convenors.

• Exercise the LifeRing "Sobriety Priority" at all times. Sobriety issues are paramount.

• Correspondence will always remain safe and supportive.

• Care and caution are to be used when choosing wording. Offensive language should not be used. If offense is taken, apology must be swift.

• Avoid "you should" type statements or specific advice. Instead, use "I" language.

• Personal attacks, belligerent, or demeaning language are not allowed.

• Avoid all mention of guilt or innocence. Offer no advice regarding a person's specific case.

• Avoid asking the nature of a person's crime. If an individual volunteers information, that is their decision.

• Avoid mention of length of sentence and upcoming court issues including parole hearings unless volunteered by them.

• Encourage positive future activities for personal improvement: educational, vocational, and professional goals are good examples.

• Make no offers of financial assistance or gifts.

• There should be no communication to outside persons.

• Letters of support should be by request only.

• Confidentiality must always be respected.

• LifeRing's "Three 'S'" philosophy remains in place; sober, secular, and self-empowered.

9.10.2: Prison Visits

The Saguaro Correctional Center in Eloy Arizona unsolicitedly contacted the Service Center to have someone from LifeRing visit them to discuss LifeRing, and in particular how to "run" a meeting. Eloy is about one hour north of Tucson. I visited them in November 2014. I brought several copies of *Recovery By Choice, Empowering Your Sober Self, and How Was Your Week* books. I also brought "variety packs" of brochures to hand out.

I had a chart on the *Hazle v. Crofoot* case and started to briefly explain the lawsuit. Interestingly, I did not get too far. They seemed to quickly say that they were familiar with the issue and I did not need to go into the details. I'm wondering in retrospect if the word reached them that they had to offer a choice of recovery programs and this was the reason LifeRing was invited.

About 20 staff members attended and the interest and questions were good. They were most interested in the "Meeting Training" part of the discussion. I followed up a couple weeks later and they told me they had started one meeting with about 20 attendees.

In subsequent discussions they were not "generous" with their information, citing confidentiality reasons. They did not want any more books or other materials even though I explained our volume discount policy. There has been very little interaction with them since then.

9.10.3: Quotations

Several different prisoners wrote me after reading the *Recovery by Choice* workbook.

As adults there are no excuses. We may all have our strengths and weaknesses, but powerlessness is by choice.

On the third domain:

I think that this Domain serves to reminds us that we have all chosen life at last...The checklist means what it is to live. No longer can any of us choose to deaden our lives and claim ignorance...I love knowing that there is no going back after being enlightened in such a truthful way. I have chosen a life of sobriety, chosen to live. It is such a great feeling!

We must celebrate our successes in order to give value to our failures.

Most prisoners suffer terribly from the pain of guilt. These words were written by a man who many years ago killed another during an argument. He was a meth addict and remains in prison.

I've caused [victim's name] irreparable harm. Nothing I can do will ever be enough...But I cannot give up as this would completely dishonor his memory and his family...Ethically and morally the adult in me cannot justify it...My life will never completely be my own again. A piece of myself died that night too...I know that even on my deathbed I will know that I have not done enough...This is more than pain...My 20 years behind metal and concrete does not even come close...The crime that I committed is unatonable.

And from another:

I introduced my fiancée to heroin some years ago and she died of an overdose. I will always live with terrible guilt for the rest of my life. I have found a little star in the night sky and I pretend that it is her looking down upon me with forgiveness. I know this is not true, but I pretend it is because it lifts my burden a bit.

And finally, a sign posted on one high security prison wall:

Warning shots will not be fired.

9.11: Special Rewards

The LifeRing convenor in special settings gets to experience dimensions of life that are out of the ordinary. This line of service rightly attracts those who are hungry for a broader, deeper knowledge of reality, and who are not happy unless they are working at the cutting edge.

Special settings convenors display great emotional courage, resonating in empathy with fellow humans who are struggling through the most difficult passages.

Special settings convenors also display strong analytical powers when they apply general concepts creatively to a diversity of unforeseeable situations.

Many people in recovery don't feel challenged by what they are doing in life. They should become LifeRing convenors in special settings.

Special settings are excellent schools for the convenor. When it comes to presenting the LifeRing approach to audiences, there is no substitute for practice, practice, practice.

In the high-turnover setting, the convenor faces a constantly shifting stream of diverse minds, each with a certain interest in LifeRing and questions about it.

The convenor who listens to the questions and looks into the inquiring eyes will soon grow in ability as a presenter.

It is not only a matter of style, but of thinking hard about the questions people ask, and digging deep inside to find genuine ways of expressing the answer that engage people and lead to real understanding.

The convenor in conventional settings who is rarely challenged to say much beyond "How was your week?" might gain a great deal of depth and proficiency as convenor by taking a turn at leading a special settings meeting with a highly transient population.

Convenors in special settings perform a strategically important service for LifeRing and for society at large. One of the ignorant criticisms that is flung at us is that our approach won't work with hard cases. Convenors in special settings have the opportunity to demonstrate that the LifeRing approach can work quite well in locked wards with people who are suicidal, homicidal, or out of control, and behind bars with prisoners who are considered recalcitrant, rebellious, and unreachable.

Society has frequently hammered these populations with the twelve-step message twelve times over, and has given up on them because they do not respond. The LifeRing convenor does not come with a hammer but with a piece of string. We look for the good in bad people, no matter how tiny it may be, and we help them connect up that good with the good in others who are as bad as themselves, so that the goodness flows between them and grows stronger within them.

We do not stand as powers over them and we do not try to take their few remaining powers away from them; rather, we facilitate them to empower their better selves. In so doing, we are performing a service to the entire society.

It is gratifying that from time to time, LifeRing convenors receive recognition for the efficacy of this approach.

It almost goes without saying that the convenor in special settings receives a powerful personal sobriety boost from this service. Convening meetings in special settings yields emotional rewards out of the ordinary.

I do feel good at the end of our usual community meetings, but I have rarely felt such deep satisfaction as after leading a successful LifeRing meeting with people institutionalized in acute crisis. It's like the warm feeling you get when you have jumper cables and you stop and help a fellow motorist stranded with a dead battery on a freezing day – but better.

Why would you want to relapse when you can get this kind of all-around satisfaction in sobriety?

9.12: Delegates From Meetings in Special Settings

In regular LifeRing meetings, the convenor is not automatically the delegate to the annual LifeRing Congress. A delegate needs to be expressly elected as such.

In special settings as a general rule it is impractical or meaningless to hold an election. Where that is true, the convenor automatically becomes the meeting's Congress delegate. (LifeRing Bylaws, Sec. 5.4, as amended by the 2nd Congress, 2002.)

In the unusual situation where the convenor is not a peer but a paid staff member of the host institution, our Bylaws are silent and the issue will at some time need to be addressed.

Chapter 10: The Meeting of Meetings

10.1: About This Chapter

This chapter is about the connections between LifeRing meetings, particularly the LifeRing Annual Meeting and Congress. It discusses the nature and purposes of this event and outlines the key Bylaws provisions that govern selection and power of Congress delegates.

10.2: LifeRing Is a Network of Meetings

LifeRing is a network of meetings. The connection with other meetings is as vital to LifeRing as the connection with other sober people is vital to an individual in recovery. A meeting that is disconnected from other meetings is like an individual battling addiction in isolation.

The greatest sense of connectedness, the biggest radiation of warmth, and the greatest charge of energy, comes from the LifeRing Annual Meeting and Congress.

10.3: The Annual LifeRing Meeting and Congress

The LifeRing Annual Meeting and Congress is a face-to-face meeting. At this event, you can see and touch who you're dealing with. You can see their facial expressions, hear their tone of voice, take in their gestures and body language. You can see how they present themselves and how they react. You can tell if their feelings are hurt. You can see them laugh and cry. You can look into their eyes. You can smell them. You can hug them, pat them on the back, and shake their hands. Many of the preparations for the event take place online where you only see disembodied strings of typed words. But the annual event itself is an unlimited bandwidth experience.

The event usually takes place on a weekend, and consists of two main parts. Friday and Saturday are the Annual Meeting, which features socializing and education. Sunday is the Congress, LifeRing's self-government meeting.

• Socializing. This is the one chance of the year for most LifeRing people from different parts of the country and the world to actually meet each other. It's an informal talk-fest and hug-fest. It's a time to let one's hair down, get real with people, reaffirm old friendships and build new ones. It's a time for people who only knew one another online to meet in the flesh.

• Education. LifeRing Annual Meetings to varying extents have an educational component: workshops, seminars, lectures, slide shows, or guest speakers, to which the public may be invited. This part of the event shares our best practice, raises our consciousness, and can help LifeRing become better known in the recovery community.

• Self-Government. The heart of the event is the Assembly of Delegates or business meeting, generally known as the Congress. Here each delegate gives a report on the status and concerns of their particular meeting during the past year, followed by general discussion. The Executive Director presents an annual report. The Treasurer presents a financial report. The Secretary presents the minutes of the previous Congress. Delegates discuss and debate issues, and candidates for the Board of Directors state their views.

Voting on the issues and candidates used to take place at the Congress itself, but since a 2013 Bylaws amendment, voting takes place online by absentee ballot during the month after the Congress closes. Voting uses the instant runoff system so that there are no delays due to pluralities or ties.

Convenors can read the details of the LifeRing organizational structure and process in the Bylaws document posted on the *lifering.org* website. The drafting committee in 2001 went to great effort to keep the Bylaws short and in plain English so that the material would be transparent to every interested member. Inevitably, as the organization has grown, so has the number and complexity of the Bylaws.

10.4: Key Points in the Bylaws

What follows is a brief look at some of the main points of the Bylaws as they pertain to the Congress: who can attend, how voting is done, what is the organizational structure generally, and who has the power to do what.

• Delegate Selection. Any LifeRing member can attend the Congress, but only delegates may vote. Except in special settings, the meeting convenor is not automatically the delegate. There are various ways to become the meeting convenor, but to become the delegate there has to be a vote by the meeting's members. The delegate's role includes the express power to vote at the Congress, the implied duty to report to the Congress on the meeting's status, and the implied duty to report back to the meeting after the Congress.

• One member, one vote. A LifeRing participant may attend any number of online and face meetings, but can cast only one vote for delegate. It's the member's choice in which meeting they cast their vote.

• One meeting, one delegate, one vote. Each meeting is entitled to one and only one delegate. Each delegate is entitled to cast one and only one vote.

• Directors and officers. Any adult LifeRing participant who is in recovery from a substance addiction and has a minimum of two years' continuous abstinence can serve on the board of directors. Officers (Executive Director, Treasurer, and Secretary) need a minimum of one year. Officers' powers are minimal. Director terms are for three years. Relapse means automatic resignation. Directors and officers serve without pay or expenses.

• Powers of the board. The board is mandated generally to act as steward of the organization's resources and of its reputation. It audits the organization's finances, appoints and discharges the officers, and oversees the national operating entities (such as LifeRing Service Center, LifeRing Press), as well as the system of regional representatives.

• The Bylaws as of this writing (May 2015) make no mention of other specific powers that are either granted or denied to the Board. The exception is Section 6.4.2, which provides

> In order to protect the good name of the LifeRing organization, the Board shall have the power, subject to ratification at the next following Congress, to suspend or revoke any charter, or to refuse to issue a charter, in cases where a group persistently and substantially violates a fundamental principle of LifeRing, Inc. as to abstinence, secularity or self-help.

This provision is fundamentally necessary to provide an elementary measure of quality control for the LifeRing network. If a meeting were to deviate from the basic philosophy – for example, if it were to abandon abstinence or become religious –

it would drag down the entire network and bring the LifeRing name into disrepute. The Board has the responsibility and the power to take timely corrective action.

As the organization grows, it may well be necessary to fill in the blanks with a more detailed enumeration of powers granted and denied to the Board of Directors, and amendments to this effect are pending as this is written.

• Powers of the Congress. The Congress proper (the Delegates' Assembly) is the supreme legislative authority of Life-Ring. Via the online absentee ballot system, it decides all issues within its authority and elects the members of the board. However, the Congress may not amend or repeal the fundamental philosophy of LifeRing (sobriety, secularity, self-help).

The Congress is not answerable to any outside power. LifeRing has no financial sponsor and is no one's subsidiary. LifeRing is a free-standing, self-supporting, self-governed and self-managed organization.

10.5: Conclusion

The bottom line is that each LifeRing meeting is part of a larger network of meetings, which is ultimately an extended family of people. Like every organization, LifeRing has its business side and its internal politics. Whether a convenor chooses to become involved in LifeRing's business and organizational issues is, of course, up to the individual. But it is part of the convenor's role "to bring people together," and nowhere does this mission bring a higher, larger, and more satisfying result than in the Annual Life-Ring Meeting and Congress.

Chapter 11: Sobriety

11.1: About this Chapter

This chapter is the first of three that discusses the basic "Three S" LifeRing philosophy – Sobriety, Secularity, and Self-Help. This chapter discusses the meaning of the term "sobriety" in LifeRing.

11.2: Sobriety Is Our Priority

Sobriety is the most fundamental and most important principle in the LifeRing philosophy.

Sobriety is our reason to exist as an organization.

Sobriety, or the desire for it, is the only requirement for membership.

Sobriety support is the purpose of our meetings.

Sobriety is the objective of each member's work in building a personal recovery program.

All things individual and organizational in LifeRing start from and come back to sobriety.

We exist and we grow as an organization because and to the extent that our members, and especially our convenors, maintain sobriety. No one would pay any attention to any of our ideas except for the fact that they have helped us as individuals to stay sober and to accumulate significant amounts of sober time.

The "secret" of why the LifeRing network has achieved a certain amount of growth and stability in certain areas is simply that a core group of people in those areas emerged, identified as Life-Ring, and remained clean and sober for a sustained period of time.

Although we also need many other assets in order to grow as an organization, none of them can achieve the slightest traction without our sobriety. Sobriety, and the fact that we have it, is not only our most powerful message; it *is* the message.

Sobriety is the guiding principle of our meetings. We maximize participation (speaking) because that reinforces sobriety. We squelch war stories (drunkalogues and drugalogues) because they undermine sobriety. We encourage crosstalk because feedback is a powerful sobriety tool. Every element of the meeting format is designed with the sobriety priority in mind.

Sobriety is the essence of our program. Our approach is simple. Instead of a multitude of complicated stages that require a pilot to navigate, we urge one "prime directive": D.D.O.U.N.M.W. – Don't Drink Or Use No Matter What. Do whatever you must to achieve that; the rest will follow.

For individuals as well as for the LifeRing network, sobriety is the foundation of all else. If I have my sobriety, I can overcome all my demons; I can handle any adversity; I can realize whatever potential is within me. If I lose my sobriety, all the rest is lost as well.

11.3: Sobriety Means Abstinence

Sobriety in LifeRing always means abstinence. The word "sobriety" has had different meanings in different times, and some dictionaries give an alternate definition that equates sobriety with moderate or temperate use of spirits.

Those alternate definitions do not apply in LifeRing. In Life-Ring, sobriety always means zero consumption. Even a single drink or use is a breach of sobriety as we define it.

Occasionally, people who have vaguely heard that LifeRing is an alternative to twelve-step groups approach us with the expectation that LifeRing is a group that supports moderation or "controlled drinking."

Convenors and ordinary members alike inform them immediately that they are mistaken. Our position on this particular issue is the same as the twelve-step groups.

People whose concept of recovery consists of cutting down, having just a few, drinking/using more reasonably, switching from one drug to another, and so forth, will not find support in Life-Ring for such a program. That area lies outside our foundations. We will regretfully but firmly refer them out.

Moderation as a recovery strategy for heavy drinking has always been controversial, and a strong consensus of researchers and clinicians has always rejected it. (Roizen 1987) Large majorities of recovering people responding to surveys reject moderation and elect abstinence.

• More than 92 per cent of recovering people surveyed elected abstinence over moderation, including people who had no use for the disease concept, powerlessness, or other aspects of twelve-step doctrine. (Cloud & Granfield 2001)

• Out of 223 study subjects with successful recoveries interviewed by author Anne M. Fletcher – the majority of them not affiliated with twelve-step groups – only one elected moderation. (Fletcher 2001:21)

Nevertheless, moderation has often attracted positive press coverage out of all proportion to its merits, and it has had a camp of articulate defenders.

That camp took a body blow in January 2000, when Audrey Kishline, the founder and head of the Moderation Management group and author of its guiding treatise, resigned her position and abandoned the organization, admitting that she could no longer keep her drinking within moderate bounds.

Kishline then joined Alcoholics Anonymous and attempted abstinence, but it was apparently too late for her. On March 25, 2000, driving with a blood alcohol content of 0.26, more than three times the legal limit, and in an apparent blackout, she drove her pickup truck across the center divide of a rural Washington State freeway and collided head-on with another vehicle, killing the two occupants, a father and his twelve-year old daughter.

After serving a prison term of three and a half years for vehicular manslaughter, Kishline resumed drinking. She publicly admitted that her involvement with Moderation Management had been nothing but a pretext to keep drinking. She died in December 2014 at the age of 59 by hanging herself. (*http://www.thefix.com/content/remembering-audrey-kishline*)

If any individual had a vested interest in demonstrating the viability of moderation as a recovery strategy for heavy drinkers, it was Kishline. Her own admission that she could not practice what she preached – underscored by the highway carnage for which she was responsible – reinforces the thoughtful decision made by virtually all recovering people to maintain abstinence as their guiding principle.

LifeRing Convenor Chet G.:

I've convened groups that have had individuals who pay lip service to the desire [to abstain] but who obviously didn't take it seriously. In fact, one notable individual had a relapse story of the week to tell at every meeting – until he died. That much was a distraction to the group but everyone liked the old codger and the meeting was at a treatment facility so we had less leeway with anyone who was in the "program"...

Although LifeRing is an abstinence group and does not support moderation, this does not mean that we engage in a jihad against all other approaches. Addiction is a huge, many-headed monstrosity, and there are all kinds of warriors on many fronts attacking it with many different instruments.

As individual citizens, members of LifeRing may well choose to endorse non-abstinence policies such as clean needle programs and other harm reduction approaches. But LifeRing meetings do not distribute needles. We do not try to be all things to all people. While we can respect and appreciate other efforts, our own approach is different. Our section on the front line, our niche, what we do, is abstinence.

LifeRing is sometimes accused of being extremely hard-line on the abstinence question, and this is true. Alone among the alternative organizations that emerged from the 1980s, LifeRing has no taint of association with moderationism or controlled drinking. We have never had controlled-drinking advocates on our Board or distributed writings by moderationist authors.

LifeRing Convenor Peter H.:

I spent a long time trying to "moderate," and it just never happened. Every relapse I have ever had started out with the lie in my own mind that I would "only have a few drinks," and at the end of the night the bottle was always empty and I was blind drunk.

LifeRing, I think, is for people like me that KNOW moderate drinking is not an option, and that abstinence gives them a much better life than the attempts to moderate.... My brain is wired for "drink until you pass out" and I don't think a medication would change that.

So, abstinence may have been a "forced" choice at first, but after having a few years of sobriety, I can definitely say that it is a better life, even though I have days or evenings where I am in some kind of emotional turmoil and long for the oblivion of intoxication, but can easily "think the drink through" and realize where it will end up.

We are uncompromising on the abstinence issue because it is a question of life or death for so many of our members. Many of our members have flirted with the "Just One" genie and paid for it with a visit to the emergency room. Experience has burned into our brains the lesson that sobriety for us is digital, not analog. Zero is the portal to life. One is the runway to death. There is no inbetween.

The distinction between abstinence and moderation is fundamental to the LifeRing self-empowerment approach. Empowerment to moderate is an addict's delusion. Once an addicted person puts the substance into their body, control will go. One will lead to two and two to many.

Moderation is an unsustainable economy. It may happen instantly or it may happen gradually over months, but sooner or later control will go, struggle as you will. The brain circuits that would permit control simply aren't there. They may never have been present, or they may have been burned out from too much drinking/drugging.

Even faith in the Almighty does not appear to help here. It is surely no accident that there are no known alcoholics' recovery groups that rely on a Higher Power for support to moderate or

LifeRing Convenor Jeff K.:

I'm not sure how many people ponder their situation after their last drink, and commit to permanent abstinence. I certainly didn't think that way, it was more that I had exhausted all hope of being able to drink without the problems, and the only thing left was to try abstinence for as long as I was able to do it, or lose everything and die. I had drank myself into a deep hole chasing after "normal drinking", and it was clear I was never going to get there again.

It wasn't until later, not much later but weeks anyway, that I began to think longer term, and see abstinence as not just a forced choice but a superior choice, and later still before I seriously thought, why the hell did I keep drinking so long, this abstinence thing is great.

control their drinking. In that specific sense, a person addicted is genuinely powerless over alcohol and drugs.

Abstinence is a fundamentally different and doable challenge. The addicted person is not powerless to learn and maintain abstinence. We may have to struggle, but we can win. We may feel weak, but we are not paralyzed, and we will grow in strength with exercise. We have the brain circuits to do what we must in order not to pick up or use.

So long as we keep the substances out of our body, we can prevail over the cravings and the other lures that would pull us back into the pit. Zero is infinitely easier than "one," and is sustainable indefinitely.

Human beings can learn to do abstinence without supernatural assistance, and in fact many people do it even without formally organized human assistance every day.

Prof. George Vaillant of Harvard, a trustee of Alcoholics Anonymous, found in his research that about 60 per cent of alcoholics who remain abstinent long-term (more than five years) do it without AA. (Vaillant 2001)

Other students of the field cite higher proportions for non-AA recoveries. I have discussed this in more detail in the introduction to *Empowering Your Sober Self.* Sober self-empowerment on an abstinence foundation is a realistic and attainable goal.

Although LifeRing is uncompromising on the abstinence issue, we are generous and almost infinitely patient with people who

---

LifeRing Convenor Martin C.:

Lifering only works for people who have an abstinence goal. People who have a moderation goal might want to attend a few LR meetings, to see if they like the look of abstinence, but people who know that they are not up for abstinence have no place a Lifering. We cannot be all things for all people. It is not fair to the people at the meeting to encourage attendance by people who are not trying for abstinence.

struggle to get there. The requirement to belong is not sobriety itself, but the desire to achieve it.

Members may trip and fall many times, but so long as they keep getting up and trying again, they will always be included in the meeting's circle of support.

Some people contemplating or just beginning abstinence see it mainly in negative terms, as the absence of "fun" and other pleasures in life. As they get to know other people in recovery and participate in the How Was Your Week format, they will change their view.

The most convincing case for the joys of abstinence is the vitality, the health, the positive attitude, the compassion and the humor that sober people display.

11.4: Poly-Abstinence: One-Shop Stopping

In LifeRing, sobriety means abstinence not only from alcohol, but from all illicit or non-medically indicated drugs. We refer to this as across-the-board abstinence or poly-abstinence. In shorthand, sobriety in LifeRing means being both "clean" and "sober." This streetwise terminology doesn't please everyone, but the meaning is clear enough.

Our vision is to unite all recovering people into a single network of support regardless of "drug of choice." Therefore, if your problem is with alcohol, you are welcome. If it is heroin, you are welcome. If it is methamphetamine, powder cocaine, crack cocaine, marijuana, prescription drugs, ecstasy, nitrous oxide – whatever the addictive substance, you are equally welcome in LifeRing.

We do not segregate by "drug of choice." We are one family with one problem and one solution.

Our across-the-board abstinence policy is based in part on the widespread experience that the use of any addictive substance tends to open the door to use of others. People who attempt partial, single-drug abstinence are following a low-percentage, losing strategy. Generally, they are either led back to their original drug, or they end up substituting one drug addiction for another.

Our policy of poly-abstinence also reflects the needs of the typical modern person in recovery. Since the 1960s and 70s, the typical person in recovery has been poly-addicted – hooked on more than one addictive substance.

There is no sound reason to go to different support groups for your different drugs of addiction. You can work on all of them at the same time in LifeRing. We offer "one-shop stopping."

11.5: Quitting the Easy Ones

Poly-abstinence requires some participants to make adjustments that may seem obvious, but that nevertheless bear spelling out. Sobriety in LifeRing means quitting not only the drugs to which one is addicted – the hard ones – but also the easy ones, those to which one is not addicted.

Most people are addicted to more than one drug, but few people alive are actively addicted to literally all of them. For example, a person who is addicted to crack and meth may report occasionally drinking a beer or a glass of wine without harmful consequences. From time to time people with this type of pattern ask LifeRing for support to continue their non-addicted use.

The firm and clear answer that we have always given is, "No." In a poly-abstinence organization such as LifeRing, the member is expected to work at quitting not only the drug or drugs to which they are addicted, but also the drugs to which they are not addicted.

The "occasional beer or glass of wine" and the other non-addicted uses have to stop. Since the person says they are not addicted to these substances, letting go of them should be no problem at all. If letting go turns out to be a problem, could it be that there is a lurking addiction issue here after all? All the more urgent, then, to quit. Catch-22.

Sometimes people rail against this obvious necessity, and advance elaborate arguments why abstinence is not required from a substance where there is no addiction, no disease, no problem, no harmful consequences, etc.

They put up more argument over the "easy ones" than over the big ones. These arguments completely miss the point.

LifeRing does not require people to accept the diagnosis of addiction. Most people come to that conclusion on their own, but it's not a membership criterion.

LifeRing does not sit in judgment over the reasons why a person wants to stop drinking/using. The fact that they want to stop qualifies them for membership, period, no questions asked.

If they want to stop because they feel they have become addicted, fine. If they want to stop because they fear becoming addicted in the future, fine. If they want to stop because stopping feels better, fine. If they want to stop because they want to keep a job, a relationship, a driver's license, fine. If they want to stop because drinking/using is boring, fine.

Are there any bad reasons to stop putting drugs and alcohol into one's body?

The desire to stop, as evidenced by concrete efforts to quit and stay quit, is the golden bond that holds our community together. So, then, if someone does not want to stop drinking/drugging, why are they here?

A moment's reflection will show that a poly-abstinence organization that caved in on the issue of "non-addictive use" would quickly self-destruct. If we swept this under the rug, we would soon have a very lumpy rug.

If the group gave members tacit blessing to use drugs to which they are not addicted, before very long there would not be a single clean and sober person in the organization. There would be alcoholics smoking marijuana, marijuana addicts drinking alcohol, crack addicts snorting heroin, all kinds of people using all kinds of drugs – and the people who wanted to be clean and sober would be using the exit.

This is not a hypothetical scenario; I've seen it happen; see Chapter Sixteen. But not in LifeRing.

11.6: Take Your Medications

Many people in recovery today are dealing not only with substance addiction but also with a variety of mental health diagnoses, most prominently clinical depression.

Bipolar disorder (formerly known as manic depression), posttraumatic stress disorder, attention deficit disorder, obsessive-compulsive disorder, and borderline personality disorder are among the other diagnoses one encounters with some regularity in practically any substance addiction recovery setting.

The LifeRing meeting process evolved specifically to address recovery from substance addiction. It is oriented to the here-and-

---

LifeRing Convenor Dale B.:

When doing mailings to docs who prescribe opioid antagonists I actually staple a small addendum to my standard introduction letter that says:

Additional note for opioid antagonist prescribers:

Some members of twelve-step programs (such as AA & NA) can be antipathetic toward those using pharmacological means of assistance with their alcohol or drug problem.

In LifeRing Secular Recovery, we value all methods of combatting addiction and we do not interfere in the relationship between a participant and their health care provider.

Your patients utilizing medications to help overcome dependence are always welcome to participate fully in LifeRing provided their ultimate goal is complete abstinence.

now, it provides peer group feedback, it is supportive and positive, it is abstinent. It probably won't do any harm to persons with a mental health diagnosis.

However, no claim can be made that the LifeRing format has therapeutic benefits for mental illnesses, other than the usual lunacies that arise from alcohol and other drugs.

The recovering person with a diagnosis of mental illness would be well advised to supplement their LifeRing participation with other support groups and/or treatment specific to their diagnosis.

LifeRing respects the physician/patient relationship that is essential to the treatment of mental disorders. The LifeRing founding Congress specifically crafted the definition of abstinence so as not to obstruct patients and physicians in the use of prescription medications to treat mental disorders.

We are well aware that some addicts are artists at manipulating the clueless general practitioner to obtain drugs to feed their addiction.

To weed out abuses of this kind, we apply a two-part test.

(1) Has the patient been totally honest with the physician and made full disclosure of their past and current alcohol/drug use? And

(2) Is the physician competent in addiction medicine?

If the answer to both questions is "Yes," and the patient takes the medication as prescribed, then these medications are not a breach of sobriety. On the contrary, such medications can be valuable sobriety tools. The LifeRing sobriety message to the dually diagnosed recovering person under these circumstances is "Take Your Medications!"

LifeRing is open to and compatible with the use of prescribed medications targeted at substance use, such as Antabuse, Naltrexone, buprenorphine, and the like. In the appropriate case they can be useful sobriety tools. Of course LifeRing does not endorse any particular medication.

The LifeRing convenor's role does not include the practice of medicine. In the role of LifeRing convenor, we do not make medical or psychiatric diagnoses, we do not prescribe medications, and we do not attempt to override the diagnoses or countermand the prescriptions that physicians may have made.

We do generally encourage patients to become informed and proactive in their own health care, including mental health care and substance abuse treatment, and to exercise their rights as patients.

Disclosure of one's own mental health diagnosis and discussion of one's medications is not inappropriate in LifeRing meetings. Sharing experiences relative to different mental health and substance abuse prescriptions, providers, and facilities is a not uncommon topic of meeting conversation. There is an email list specifically for LifeRing participants with concurrent disorder issues.

11.7: Methadone

At this point, LifeRing has very little practical experience with methadone. The early joiners in LifeRing with heroin histories detoxified using buprenorphine and have not used methadone maintenance.

Methadone is a prescription medication that blocks the euphoric effects of heroin. It has been extensively studied and shown to be more effective when properly administered than any other known remedy for achieving abstinence from heroin. (Lowinson 1997:406, 411-412)

Persons on methadone maintenance who are taking it as prescribed, should be considered clean and sober in LifeRing.

However, the actual administration of methadone maintenance frequently falls short of the clinical ideal, and there are numerous instances of methadone abuse. For this reason, people using methadone as a recovery tool may encounter a certain amount of initial skepticism.

11.8: Support to Quit Nicotine

Scientific research and public opinion in the past thirty years have turned against the use of nicotine. Following a series of Surgeon General's reports, tobacco industry admissions, and an extensive medical research effort, nicotine is today recognized as an addictive drug whose use is not medically justifiable at any level.

The percentage of American adults who use nicotine has declined from about four in ten to about half that ratio, and surveys consistently indicate that a large majority of those who still smoke tobacco want to quit. (Robert Wood Johnson Foundation, 2001:40)

This turnabout in scientific and public opinion is making an impact on substance abuse treatment programs and recovery groups everywhere. (White 1998:309)

A few decades ago, nicotine use was an accepted practice in treatment programs and recovery support groups. Both of the co-founders of Alcoholics Anonymous were smokers, and both of them died of it.

Bill Wilson, a cigarette chain-smoker, stopped in the last year of his life but it was too late; he died of emphysema. Dr. Bob Smith, a cigar smoker, died of throat cancer. (White 1998:139-140; Order-Connors 1996).

The stereotypical AA meeting of that period was a smoke-filled room. Mental health and addiction treatment settings were little different.

Today, nicotine use in mental health and substance addiction recovery settings is in retreat. Research has established that nicotine use interferes with medications used in the treatment of mental illness, and is linked in complex ways with common mental disorders such as depression. (Lasser 2000; Resnick 1993)

The powerful links between nicotine addiction and addiction to alcohol and other drugs – some 90 per cent of active alcoholics are also smokers – have come under critical scrutiny.

The high death rate from smoking-related diseases among recovering alcoholics – it exceeds the death rate due to alcohol – has spurred reconsideration of the role of smoking in recovery. (Hurt 1996)

Alcoholics who quit drinking but keep smoking die just as prematurely as if they had kept drinking. (Vaillant 1995:209)

Many substance abuse treatment professionals today maintain that nicotine use in clinical settings undermines the facility's poly-abstinence message. A number of influential institutions in the field, including the American Cancer Society ("Nicotine Is a Drug Too") and the Robert Wood Johnson Foundation, among others, now define the target of substance abuse recovery efforts as ATOD: Alcohol, Tobacco, and Other Drugs.

There is an active movement among chemical dependency professionals to integrate nicotine cessation into alcohol and other drug addiction treatment. At least one state (New Jersey) has mandated nicotine cessation treatment in all licensed residential chemical dependency facilities.

Numerous chemical dependency treatment programs now treat nicotine addiction on a par with other substance addictions and maintain smoke-free facilities. A minority have not yet addressed the issue.

The nicotine issue was extensively debated in virtually every online forum within LifeRing for several years, and a consensus has emerged on the major issues, as follows.

At this time, LifeRing takes no position as an organization whether the use of nicotine is or is not "clean and sober." Life-

Ring as an organization does not say that people who use nicotine are not clean and sober.

Nor does LifeRing as an organization say that they are clean and sober. LifeRing leaves this decision up to each individual as part of constructing their personal recovery program.

People who still use nicotine, therefore, are welcome in Life-Ring. A desire to quit nicotine use is not a requirement for membership.

At the same time, LifeRing as an organization engages in support and education efforts to assist members to free themselves from nicotine addiction, if and when they wish. Members are free to ignore these support and education efforts. Quitting is voluntary.

Support and education for nicotine cessation means, in practice, mainly the following:

• It is appropriate for members to raise their issues and experiences with nicotine in any LifeRing meeting, face or online, on a par with their other substance issues.

• Members who plan to quit nicotine, have just quit, have a quit anniversary, or similar occasions, are entitled to demonstrations of support (applause, attaboys/attagirls) from their meeting on a par with the support members give each other in their battles with alcohol or any other addictive drug.

• Literature and web sites published under the LifeRing name will include educational materials about nicotine that relate to persons in recovery from alcohol and other drugs.

The LifeRing position of support and education for voluntary nicotine cessation should not be confused with a single-issue approach. LifeRing is not an appropriate setting for individuals who wish to quit nicotine but continue to use alcohol or other drugs. In LifeRing the voluntary nicotine effort is part of the integrated poly-abstinence approach described in an earlier section.

Revisiting this question, the LifeRing Board of Directors in August 2013 voted to support the creation of "special meetings," meaning particularly meetings devoted to smoking cessation for people who also intend to achieve abstinence from other addictive drugs.

It is my personal hope, which not all LifeRing members share, that our efforts of support and education for voluntary nicotine cessation will eventually prove universally successful, so that on some future date we will look around at our membership and realize that LifeRing has become a nicotine-free organization.

11.9: Medical Marijuana

LifeRing has not yet taken an official position on medical marijuana, but several encounters with the issue in individual LifeRing meetings suggest what that position will probably be.

On a couple of occasions, newcomers have come into a LifeRing meeting saying that they smoked marijuana on a prescription for stress. There was a lot of laughter and pushback. Members pointed out that everyone has stress, and that quack physicians handed out such prescriptions to anyone with fifty dollars. These newcomers were not made to feel welcome and ultimately left.

But if the newcomer had been a recovering cancer patient undergoing chemotherapy or radiation and taking marijuana to stimulate their appetite and promote weight gain, there would have been no objections.

LifeRing members in these meetings evaluated medical marijuana use by a kind of seat-of-the-pants yardstick: does this sound like a dodge, or is it medically legit? This standard follows from the basic definition that we stand for abstinence from drugs that are "not medically indicated."

11.10: Other Addictions

LifeRing convenors sometimes get inquiries from people whose issues are not with alcohol and other addictive drugs, but with food, sex, pornography, online games, gambling, and other behaviors that look and feel a lot like addiction. After extensive discussion, the LifeRing Board of Directors has decided that LifeRing, for the foreseeable future, will stay focused on the "chemical" or "substance" addictions, meaning alcohol and other medically non-indicated drugs.

If a person who wants to get free of their alcohol or other drug use also has an issue with food, sex, gambling or the like, they are welcome to participate in LifeRing and to discuss their other issues along with alcohol and other drugs. That has happened and generally works well. But LifeRing would not be an appropriate setting for someone who wants to, for example, overcome a harmful sex or gambling obsession but continue drinking or using other addictive drugs.

Food also presents the problem that LifeRing is dedicated to abstinence, and abstinence from food is a very bad idea. The person wanting to moderate their food intake in a non-religious environment should investigate WeightWatchers® or another of the commercially available lifestyle modification programs. A number of LifeRing members have participated in WeightWatchers and speak highly of it.

The general principles underlying LifeRing may very well be helpful to persons struggling with sex, gambling, food or similar problems. It's possible that independent support groups based on LifeRing principles but specializing in other issues may develop in the future.

11.11: Conclusion

The concept of sobriety is not a timeless absolute but an evolving historical construct. As LifeRing convenors, we are playing a role in shaping the present and future meaning of the term.

Our openness and inclusiveness as regards recovery from all the drugs of addiction, without segregation by drug of choice, places us in the front line among mutual aid organizations.

As LifeRing convenors, our commitment to sobriety is a settled and closed issue, beyond argument.

But this does not mean that there are no more problems to think about. The issues of methadone, medical marijuana, and nicotine – to name just three – are witness that the map of sobriety has not only a settled central plain but also a turbulent, changing frontier.

The turmoil and the occasional bloodshed on the frontier may be disturbing at times, but they are blessings in disguise: they stir the pot, force us to look again at our basic values, and keep the meaning of sobriety ever fresh in our minds.

Chapter 12: Secularity

12.1: About This Chapter

This chapter discusses the second "S" in the foundational philosophy of LifeRing. It explains the concept of secularity as it pertains to recovery.

12.2: Where Is Secularity?

The word "secular" is not a household word in the United States. Most people have never seen it in print and many can't pronounce it when they do. Many others think they know it, but confuse it with something else – social, circular, sexual.

Particularly widespread and frustrating is the confusion of "secular" with "sectarian." This occurs even in print; for example, a newspaper described us as a "non-secular group."

Right-wing Christian fundamentalists add to the confusion when they smear anything "secular" as homosexual communistic baby-killing Satanism. Only a relatively few college-educated people are familiar with the term.

The LifeRing convenor on the front lines of contact with the general public may well come to feel that the word "secular" is a marketing albatross. What people don't understand, they fear. To sidestep this obstacle if necessary, LifeRing convenors can and do use either "LifeRing Secular Recovery" or "LifeRing Recovery" in headlines of meeting announcements and other media.

Yet secularity is something thoroughly familiar that most Americans practice all day, every day. When you ride a bus, or drive on the street, or go to the supermarket or to the zoo, for example, you are on secular territory and operating by secular ground rules. The bus driver does not ask for your faith before allowing you to ride. The traffic light goes through its cycles without caring whether your car sports a Jesus fish, a Darwin footed fish, a gefilte fish, or no fish. The supermarket checker will cheerfully ring you up without prying into your beliefs. The scientist and the creationist can rub shoulders before the monkey cage in the zoo.

If someone on a bus, or on the highway, or in the market or at the zoo should approach you and try to convert you to religion, even to your own religion, you would probably feel that this was not the time or place.

There are no Faith Police here to arrest you if you do not conform to religious rules in the way you trim your beard or cover your face. Most of everyday life in this country is secular, and most Americans wouldn't have it any other way.

"Most Americans are religious in theory but secular in practice." (Lind 2001) Very high proportions of American consistently tell survey takers that they believe in God, an afterlife, angels, and so forth. But only a minority of Americans actually go to church, and attendance is declining. (Presser & Stinson 1998; Walsh 1998) The proportion of adult Americans who attend religious services or religious study meetings each and every day must be vanishingly small.

Thus, when we LifeRing convenors in the United States take our stand on secularity, our only real difficulty is the word. Once we get past the label, we stand in the mainstream. Secularity is the spirit of the infinitely great practical side of Americans, the side that gets things done, because "God helps those who help themselves."

12.3: Secularity is Trending

The interval between the publication of the first edition of this book and the current edition has seen a dramatic rise in the number of Americans who have no religious affiliation. The Pew Research Center (*www.pewforum.org*) conducts periodic large-scale studies of the religious landscape. Its most recent research found that "the percentage of Americans who are religiously unaffiliated – describing themselves as atheist, agnostic or 'nothing in particular' – has jumped more than six points, from 16.1% to 22.8%."

That's an increase of about 19 million people. Says the report:

> There are now approximately 56 million religiously unaffiliated adults in the U.S., and this group – sometimes called religious "nones" – is more numerous than either Catholics or mainline Protestants, according to the new survey. (Pew 2015)

Affiliation with "none" is particularly strong among the younger generations, the so-called Millennials.

> As the Millennial generation enters adulthood, its members display much lower levels of religious affiliation, including less connection with Christian churches, than older generations. Fully 36% of young Millennials (those between the ages of 18 and 24) are religiously unaffiliated, as are 34% of older Millennials (ages 25-33).

Disavowal of religious affiliation is also growing among older adults. Nearly one fourth of those born between 1965 and 1980 now say they have no particular religion or describe themselves as atheists or agnostics, up four points in seven years. Even Baby Boomers are more likely to identify as "none" in recent years.

People who identify as "none," says the report, are highly likely to remain that way, and their retention rate is increasing.

The trend away from religion exists both among the college educated and others, and among all income brackets, by similar ratios. It covers a broad demographic spread:

> Whether they are nearing retirement or just entering adult-hood, married or single, living in the West or the Bible Belt, Americans in virtually all demographic groups are significantly less likely to describe themselves as Christians and more likely to identify as religious "nones," compared with seven years ago.

The West has the largest proportion of the unaffiliated; "nones" are the biggest single group there with 28%, bigger than Catholics (23%), evangelicals (22%), and mainline Protestants (11%). But even in the South, the traditional Bible Belt, the percentage of "nones" has grown by six points, from 13% in 2007 to 19% in 2014.

What do these trends mean for LifeRing convenors? Strictly speaking, they're irrelevant, since LifeRing meetings are open to people of all faiths, as well as "nones." But as a practical matter, on the whole and on the average, research shows that people who identify

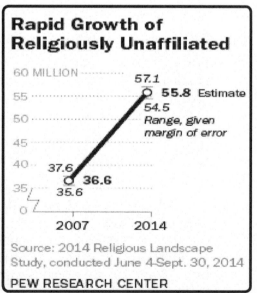

Rapid Growth of Religiously Unaffiliated

60 MILLION 57.1
55 .... ○ 55.8 Estimate
54.5
50 .... Range, given
margin of error
45 ....
40 .... 37.6
○ 36.6
35 .... 35.6
0

2007   2014

Source: 2014 Religious Landscape Study, conducted June 4-Sept. 30, 2014

PEW RESEARCH CENTER

with no particular religion are likely to feel more comfortable in a secular environment such as LifeRing (Atkins 2007).

LifeRing convenors are sometimes discouraged or intimidated by statistics showing that a majority of Americans are religious. Maybe so, but there is a sizeable and rapidly growing minority in all regions of the country that has no religious affiliation. That's about 56 million people, according to the Pew report, surely enough of a base from which to fill a room dedicated to secular recovery.

12.4: The Engine of Recovery is Secular

In Chapter 2, I sketched a vision of how the LifeRing meeting process works. The engine of recovery at work in our meetings is the cycle of reinforcing connections between the participants as sober persons. The flow of energy from "S" to "S" strengthens and empowers each of them.

This engine is secular. It does not require a "higher power." The flow of energy is not vertical but horizontal; not from something higher to something lower, but lateral from peer to peer. It does not matter whether the participants also maintain a relationship with their vision of a Superior Being. What counts is whether the participants are able to establish sober-to-sober communication with other ordinary beings like themselves. As we have seen, the How Was Your Week meeting format makes this kind of connection possible for virtually everyone from day one.

Because the axis of this engine is horizontal, LifeRing meetings are a venue where almost all kinds of believers and almost all kinds of nonbelievers can meet and work on their recoveries in complete comfort.

I say "almost" because there are some believers, and nonbelievers as well, who cannot refrain from "witnessing" or proselytizing even for an hour. Fortunately there are religious meetings, and also atheist-agnostic meetings, designed for people whose personal recovery agenda requires converting others to their cosmic vision. The LifeRing format is a live-and-let-live environment when it comes to theology. Like politics, theology in LifeRing meetings remains entirely a private affair.

12.5: Secularity Includes All Beliefs and None

One way to understand the meaning of secularity is to imagine that all the world's people are lined up side by side, grouped by their beliefs. So, for example, at one end you might have Judaism, then Christianity and Islam, and then Hinduism, Buddhism, and Confucianism, with agnosticism, and atheism at the opposite end of the range. The sector that includes Judaism, Christianity, and Islam has in common the belief in a single god. Hinduism includes believers and nonbelievers in a god or gods. Buddhism and Confucianism focus not on a god or gods but on virtuous behavior. Agnostics and atheists generally doubt or reject a god. There are many other groups that could be arrayed on this spectrum but these are enough to make the point.

There have been many efforts to bring the different religions together. For example, the movement to bring Jews, Muslims and Christians together is called ecumenism or interfaith. This spans

> **LifeRing Convenor Mary S.:**
>
> Secularity doesn't just protect us from proselytizing, it means that we don't use prayer or talk about religious matters. On one hand, we want to encourage people to talk about whatever is helpful to them; but on the other hand, statements about spiritual practices tend to promote one-upmanship by applying a very subtle pressure…"My religion is better/more enlightened than yours", which is frighteningly similar to "My higher power is better than yours."
>
> It has always pleased me to observe that even after knowing a lot about a person, having known them in meetings for several years, I do not know anything about their religious or political inclinations. I'd really like to keep it that way.

a wide range but leaves out a great many people – all the people who believe in different gods or no gods at all. The term that embraces the entire range from one end to the other – all kinds of believers and nonbelievers – is secularism. Another word for it is universalism.

Note that whenever two different groups are brought together, certain issues go Off Topic. For example, when Protestants and Catholics come together, the Pope becomes Off Topic. When Christians and Jews come together, the divinity of Jesus goes Off Topic. When Muslims come together, Muhammad's descendants are Off Topic. And so on.

When something is Off Topic, it means that people don't talk for it or against it. It becomes an issue like religion, politics, and maybe football at a big family reunion: nobody mentions it.

In a secular group, religion, pro or con, is Off Topic. If somebody at a LifeRing meeting says, "If you don't embrace Jesus you can't stay sober," that's Off Topic. If somebody says, "Religion is a crock, anybody who believes in it is a moron," that's Off Topic. Certain things have to stay Off Topic in order to hold the family together.

12.6: Keep Whatever You Believe

One of the great advantages of the secular approach to recovery is that it allows each participant to keep free enjoyment of whatever religious beliefs they may have or not have. Because we do not rely on religious concepts in our recovery toolkit and because we avoid religious practices in our meeting format, we are a safe environment for persons with every kind of religious belief or disbelief. You can probably do recovery in LifeRing, just as you can do laundry, ride a bicycle, or write software, without changing one hair of your theological belief system.

There is more than abstract virtue to this approach. Leaving issues of faith alone helps to focus one's energies on recovery. To attempt recovery with a program whose basic assumptions about God run counter to one's religious beliefs means having only part of one's energies available for recovery; the other part must guard the fortress of one's existing religious faith.

Those who believe in no kind of God are in the same situation in this respect as those who believe in a different kind of God. The faith-based approach saps the recovery energies of those whose specific belief or disbelief falls into the broad spectrum outside the program's required assumptions. Conserving and focusing energies in recovery may be vital.

A very wise counselor once told me, "Early recovery is hard work enough. When we ask people also to take on the issues of spirituality, oftentimes it's just too much for them."

LifeRing Convenor Njon W.:

I really enjoyed the [AA] agnostic meetings and met a lot of great people many of whom tried and stuck with LifeRing. The [AA agnostic] meetings here in San Francisco are topic discussion groups and it became really frustrating after some time listening to the same people relate their same sad drunken story to whatever the topic was that week.

At first, it was great to just be able to relate to folks. LifeRing quickly ruined it for me though, and I soon grew tired of hearing "Well, here's a LONG list of bad things I did, but now everything is GREAT!!!" without any specifics on progress or growth; the theory being,"I'm not using today, so things are perfect now, right?"

The groups also seemed much more focused on being atheist or agnostic than addiction support sources. LifeRing offered me the opportunity to get feedback on my current struggles and successes and pushed me way beyond abstinence and into personal growth. I really value the jumpstart experience I had with the agnostics but it did not serve my need in the long term. That said, it does appear to be a viable solution for many.

12.7: LifeRing Is Not an Atheist/Agnostic AA Meeting

One of the signs of ferment in the twelve-step world is the growth of atheist-agnostic meetings within AA (Agnostic AA or AAA). The literature of this tendency, generally speaking, rejects the "God" thread in the twelve steps and in the rest of the AA literature. Some AAA advocates have written trenchant critiques of AA's religiosity. They have clearly pointed out how the chapter "On Agnostics" in the AA Big Book treats atheists and agnostics with condescension. They have demonstrated in their own lives that the book is mistaken when it says that alcoholics cannot get sober until they find God.

AAA advocates have fought for decades to get their own literature approved by AA nationally, so far without success. In a number of regions, the local AA bodies even refuse to list AAA meetings.

LifeRing Convenor Rob M.:

Prior to Lifering starting in San Diego I was part of an effort to start a new Agnostics/Atheists/Freethinkers meeting, called 'We Are Not Saints.' Most of these meetings are called 'We Agnostics' or 'Freethinkers.'

From what I can glean these type of meetings are the fastest growing 'niche' in AA. I'm secretary for this new meeting, and we get 20-25 on a weekly basis, 50/50 male/female. The ladies seem even more interested and liberated by this approach. I'm also a regular at a more established meeting on Sunday mornings – my 'church.'

I find that it is a lot easier/more acceptable to mention LifeRing in that setting, or discuss it afterward. They are much more open to what LifeRing has to offer. So far, quite a few have come to a LifeRing meeting, love it, and now, like me, attend both.

So far, I have been able to successfully ride both ponies, and my shares at AA are not much different from those at LifeRing. I try to incorporate LifeRing principles whenever appropriate.

Hopefully there is something there for folks to build on.

One can certainly sympathize. The religiosity of AA (the "higher power" thing) has driven thousands away and remains one of the major obstacles that keeps newcomers from entering. AA arguably would be a larger, better, and more effective organization if it dropped the "higher power thing." But that isn't going to happen. "God" is at the core of the AA program. The legal structure of AA, outlined in the AA Service Manual, erects insuperable procedural obstacles to amendments of its program.

Agnostic AA meetings may feel like a safe harbor for people who believe that AA is the only road to recovery but are repelled by its religiosity. Meetings proceed without prayer or God-talk. But the meeting format remains AA: classroom seating, speakers who present variations on the same infomercial template, no crosstalk. There may be considerable atheist/agnostic advocacy. That's quite different from LifeRing meetings, which feature circle seating, How Was Your Week format, lots of crosstalk, no discussion of God issues pro or con.

LifeRing Convenor Greg H.:

I've been sober for over 12 years, but I never even heard of Life-Ring until a couple of months ago. Looking it up on the internet, I was delighted to find a meeting right here in San Diego. I was even more delighted to discover that it is totally in tune with my own perspective of total Abstinence, Secularity and Self-Help (ASS).

Lacking any more-appealing alternative (I tried and walked away from Smart Recovery first; and there is no SOS in town), I've been making an ASS out of myself in AA ever since my sobriety date in 2001. Having zero use for the 12 Steps, and needing to give myself a safe haven from the mainstream AA "Let go, let God" culture, I even started a couple of very unconventional AA meetings myself, never guessing that they were really just Life-Ring meetings that happen to be listed in the local AA schedule....

Anyway, the time has come for me to start yet another meeting; but this one will be listed in the LifeRing schedule. My long term goal is have at least one LifeRing meeting in San Diego every day of the week.

There's much ambivalence in the AAA trend about the twelve steps. Some AAA critiques go no deeper than "the God thing," and embrace the steps with that deletion. They don't have a problem with the powerless doctrine. They don't see the moralistic, negative, depressing, disempowering, relapse-engendering and even punitive slant of the whole approach. They don't see the hubris of the claim that this is a program that always works ("if you work it"). They don't understand that no single approach can be a good fit for a broad diversity of people. Even when individual AAA participants reject all twelve steps, bag and baggage, and throw out the Big Book in the bargain, they frequently still want to be considered part of the AA organization. They cling to the hope that if they beg AA to embrace them 1,000 times, they will get a different result than in the 999 previous attempts.

There's a conceptual vacuum at the heart of the AAA approach. How can recoveries happen if you take the "higher power" out of the twelve steps? What you have left in the steps, then, is only the demeaning, shaming, guilt-provoking gauntlet of negative emotions. The sole element that could (according to the theory) pull the alcoholic out of that hell is gone. The AA program, whatever else one may think of it, is a coherent whole. If you yank out one of its core elements, it can't work, and you need to supply an alternative explanation of how recoveries can happen.

LifeRing has a clear answer to that problem, summed up in the maxim, "Empower Your Sober Self." Our approach is not a partial erasure of the AA program. It rests on a fundamentally

> **LifeRing Convenor Robert M.:**
>
> Austin also has about 12 'Agnostic AA' meetings. These meetings are secular – no prayers, no God talk. In fact, they are similar to Lifering meetings, though they have the format of an AA meeting (topic, no crosstalk, etc)....
>
> Lifering fills a definite need in the recovering community. ... I know from personal experience that a good number of regular AA attendees are agnostic/atheist, but simply 'tough it out' in AA. Many of those would find the Lifering experience useful.

different model of human psychology, outlined in Chapter Two. It posits the recovering person not as powerless, but as the protagonist of their own recovery. The driving force of empowerment comes from human interaction, from social connectedness – the synergy of sober selves.

Certainly, Agnostic AA meetings are much closer to LifeRing than the traditional Bible Belt AA groups are. They may serve as a stepping stone to LifeRing for a number of individuals. But they may also serve as a substitute for the real thing.

AA in the past has usually managed to envelop and defang the oddball atheist and agnostic within its ranks, if only as a kind of bait to others. But will AA be able to digest a sizeable organized, self-conscious trend of member groups who reject the vital essence of its program? And how long will the organized atheist/agnostic participants tolerate their marginal, second-class existence inside AA?

Time will tell. While LifeRing convenors always respect the boundaries between different organizations, the close affinity of

---

LifeRing Convenor Mary S.:

Very few of our Albuquerque folks would ID themselves as agnostic or atheist. They seem to prefer LifeRing for so many other reasons. To name a few:

Dialogue vs. a succession of monologues

Not enduring unnecessary ego deflation

Emphasis on the present vs. endless repetition of war stories from decades ago

Emphasis on self-awareness vs. admission of defects of character that may not even be real

Finding their inner power vs. powerlessness

Emphasis on personal responsibility vs. reliance on and surrender to an external entity

I'm sure everyone on this list could point out additional reasons their group members prefer LifeRing over AA.

spirit between non-religious AA groups and LifeRing naturally opens doors of mutual communication and cooperation.

LifeRing meetings are different from atheist-agnostic AA meetings. They are not atheist-agnostic meetings at all. Although a good proportion of people in any given LifeRing meeting are not interested in religion and have no particular religious beliefs, there is no atheist/agnostic advocacy in LifeRing meetings, any more than there is religious "witnessing." LifeRing meetings are centered on support for staying clean and sober – on empowerment of the sober self – not on what you believe or disbelieve in matters of theology.

12.8: Secularity Lets People Come Together

The secular approach also has another virtue: it promotes peace in the social environment. The tremendously broad spectrum of religious beliefs and disbeliefs in the world contains numerous areas of bloody collision. There is endless theological strife, not only between major bodies such as Christians, Jews, and adherents of Islam, but between different factions and sub-factions within each of the major religions; between believers generally and unbelievers; and between different factions of agnostics and atheists.

It might seem that the secular format inherently favors the atheist and the agnostic, but a little reflection will show that this is not so. Advocacy of atheism or agnosticism is as much out of place at LifeRing meetings as proselytizing for Jesus, Yahweh, Allah, or Ganesh. Theology as a topic, one way or the other, is out of bounds.

What do people who have issues with drugs/alcohol feel like doing when stress levels rise and arguments break out? At the reunion of a big extended family, if we want peace and sobriety, we have to agree that we don't talk religion. Secularity is the only truly generic formula that can bring the entire spectrum of contentious, disputatious humanity together in one room for the purpose of recovery.

12.9: Secularity Lets People Relax and Be Real

Sunday School is an acquired taste. Few people enjoy a steady diet of it. Somehow, when the room begins to fill with God-talk, the atmosphere changes. People sit up stiffly. They peer over their shoulder before they speak to see if their parents are listening. The fluid motion of the conversation hardens into lime jello with mayonnaise.

LifeRing meetings are time-outs from the pressure to be spiritually correct and to say the right thing. In order to heal, people need to be real with themselves and with one another. It's hard to be real when you're censoring yourself. You don't want to let your hair down in a church service.

I've heard people say it time after time: the LifeRing meeting is the one time they feel free to be themselves, warts and all. People in residential treatment may go to meetings practically every waking hour, all of them run by the twelve-step book. You'd think they're completely talked out by the end of the week. Not so. In the LifeRing meeting, vital things come to the surface, like seals under ice, that could find a breathing hole nowhere else. People open up with themselves and with each other. People have meetings of the sober minds. People laugh deep, tension-releasing belly laughs. People talk way past the hour. All because there is safety and freedom in the secular atmosphere.

A few weeks ago, our Wednesday night meeting at the inpatient program had about half newcomers. The other half were people who had participated in LifeRing two or three times before. I asked these comparative veterans to explain to the first-timers what LifeRing was about.

"The atmosphere is positive. "

"You get to actually connect with people in the meeting."

"You build your own recovery plan."

Nobody mentioned the absence of god-talk. The secular atmosphere was so natural and fit so comfortably that it provoked no special notice. Yet, of course, secularity is the foundation on which the positive tone, the conversational atmosphere, and the freedom of building one's personal recovery plan are grounded. What these participants liked about LifeRing was, at bottom, its secularity.

12.10: Secularity is Research-Friendly

If I came to a physician with a medical condition such as diabetes, heart disease, or bipolar disorder and were told that my main hope was to say prayers and trust in God, I would draw one of two conclusions. Either that my condition was hopeless and that I should arrange my affairs and prepare to die. Or that my physician was a religious nut.

In these conclusions, phrased perhaps more diplomatically, I would enjoy the support not only of professional but of public opinion. A small margin of the American public outside of Christian Scientists would rely principally on faith for treatment of medical conditions, if given the choice.

Dr. Joseph Volpicelli, a pioneer in addictions research, writes in this respect:

> I have long been frustrated by the alcoholism and addiction field's reliance on miracle cures and horror stories, rather than on science, to guide patient care. After all, most Americans with diabetes or even an emotional problem such as depression wouldn't accept being told by a doctor that praying and 'turning your will and life over to the care of God as you understand Him,' as AA suggests, is the only treatment for their illness. Why shouldn't alcoholics and other addicts

get research-based medicine the way people do for any other disease? (Volpicelli & Szalavitz, 2000:4)

Mainstream common sense is stood on its head in the field of
substance addiction. Here great institutional forces bear down on
the patient to accept a God-based approach, and those who resist
are often marginalized. (Fransway 2000) If I accepted the priorities urged on the patient in much of what passes for mainstream
addiction recovery, and applied them to the rest of health care, I
would throw away my pills and crutches and give my money to
the preachers instead of the doctors.

The progress of addiction research is very gradually clearing the
ground of the old superstitions. It is too early to say that science
has solved all the riddles of substance addiction, but tremendous
progress has been made in recent years.

One day, hopefully soon, someone will earn a Nobel Prize for
pinning down the exact circuits and neurochemicals that make
addiction happen. Enough is known meanwhile to make it clear
that the core substance addiction is a physiological event at the
cellular level. Tens of thousands of mice and rats and other mammals have been teaching this fundamental lesson for the past few
decades. All that is necessary to turn them into addicts is to satu-
rate their bloodstreams with sustained high doses of the addictive substance for a period of time. (Gardner 1997:51) Defects
of character, immorality, weakness of will, spiritual alienation, or
other higher-level issues are redundant to the etiology.

We now also know from fifty years of psychometric studies on
humans that every kind of personality has an equal probability
of becoming addicted, and the notion of the "addictive personality" as a cause of substance addiction is a myth. (Hester & Miller
1996:90; Ketcham 200:65; Vaillant 1995)

Addiction research is also gradually shedding light on addiction
treatment and recovery issues. NIDA, the National Institute on
Drug Abuse, devotes extensive effort to bridging the huge gap

between research and clinical practice in chemical dependency treatment. The secular recovery approach welcomes the forward motion of addiction research and forms one of the channels through which research-based findings make their way into recovery practice.

12.11: Knowing Our Limits

The individuals who make up the LifeRing network form, collectively, a considerable database of expertise on the issue of how to get clean and sober and how to lead a clean and sober life.

> **LifeRing Convenor Jack M.:**
>
> Having been sober since first attending AA in 1952 ... I have had plenty of time to examine my own experiences. At times I still occasionally get nostalgic about AA and my participation in it because they were a large part of my life. I have lately thought of the 25th anniversary meeting of AA in Long Beach CA in 1960, which I attended. There were ten thousand people there to hear Bill W. and other early supporters of AA. Such events are not forgotten but they are also in the past to which one cannot return. My reason for supporting a secular program is because it is not faith based but is supported by increasing knowledge and information about addiction problems though fully understood as yet. I am not required to subscribe to notions that defy my credulity....
>
> So perhaps there are different objectives open to LifeRing members with the first being individual sobriety but a further one being the attempt to increase the acceptance by the general public of rational resolutions to drinking and drugging problems as opposed to so-called spiritual approaches.
>
> Don't see any easy solutions ... but would also venture that AA has plenty of its own difficulties unless it has radically changed since I departed the scene. The price of listening to much of the content became much greater than I was willing to pay for what I was experiencing. Bill W. himself, before he died, made the comment after some untoward incident involving AA that "unfortunately AA's reputation was much better than its actual character." Worth thinking about.

Compared to persons who are still drinking/drugging and who believe themselves paralyzed to improve their condition, we have higher knowledge. Any person with at least one day clean and sober has expertise on this topic that is still beyond the reach of many thousands of others. If you are looking for a group of practical engineers of personal sobriety, and are willing to listen to about as many different correct answers as there are individuals, you have come to the right place.

We cannot pretend to the same collective expertise on the issue of theology (religion and/or spirituality). Nothing in our life experience, on the whole and on the average, has made us more clever than the median on this front.

You will find here the usual spectrum of believers, semi-believers, and disbelievers as elsewhere – although perhaps more of the latter – and the usual degrees of theological enlightenment, more or less. Accordingly, we do not pretend as a group to offer you spiritual, moral, or religious guidance.

If it should happen that in the course of your recovery you feel an urge to modify your theological positions, the soundest course may be to consult with the established experts in that area. Ask your friends, look on the Internet, or check in the Yellow Pages; for example, try "A" for Associations or for Astrologers, "C" for Churches, "R" for Religious Organizations, "S" for Schools (Religious) or for Spiritual Consultants or for Synagogues. In the major population centers there is a large and extremely diverse selection of providers of spiritual, moral, and religious guidance.

In LifeRing, we do not sit in moral judgment over who you are or what you do. We can show you by many living examples that you can become a clean and sober person using whatever resources of character and spirit you already possess, good, bad, or indifferent. There is a section of the *Recovery by Choice* workbook that addresses "using what you have" to get clean and sober. (See Workbook Ch. 6, Sec. 18.)

It has been my experience that when people become clean and sober persons, at some point their innate goodness grabs hold of them and they strive to become better persons by whatever yardstick they hold dear. If they stole horses when in their addiction, once sober they will think more clearly and are likely to enter a more honest line of business. However, such a transformation cannot be forced, and we will not try to force it upon you. You may find among us many models of sobriety. But we do not presume to hold ourselves up as ethical or spiritual models for you, either individually or as a group. We are humans, not saints. We know our limits.

12.12: Recovery as Liberation of the Spirit

Recovery is in one sense a mundane project, like learning to ride a bicycle or doing a mountain of laundry or writing a piece of software. The secular approach helps the recovering person get properly focused on the parameters of the task – the here and the now, the interconnectedness of thoughts and actions, the reshaping of relationships with things and with people along new, sober lines. Secularity lets people find the handle and get a grip on their recoveries in much the same way that the secular approach is fundamental to progress in the sciences and the practical arts.

Along another dimension, recovery is a liberation of the spirit from the hideous dominion of addiction. It is along this dimension that secularity truly shines. Any effort to define "the spiritual" and distill it into a catechism for group guidance ends up merely forging another cage. The most strenuous efforts to define a non-sectarian, pan-religious "spiritual" theology end up only creating the narrowest of religious cults. Only secularity, with its strict abstinence from theology, preserves an open sky for the spirit. Only secularity delivers on the promise that recovery from addiction shall be a liberation.

Chapter 13: Self-Help

13.1: About This Chapter

This chapter discusses the third "S" of the foundational Life-Ring philosophy, self-help. Self-help is as familiar in the American vernacular as the Lincoln penny. The LifeRing convenor faces no public comprehension gap with this term, no "huh?" problem, as we do with "secular." The problems lie in clarifying its meaning, establishing its legitimacy, and endowing it with flesh and bones.

13.2: Two Dimensions of Self-Help

In LifeRing, the third "S" has two dimensions. Self-help is the organizational principle that underlies the entire network of meetings both separately and collectively. It is also the basis of LifeRing's therapeutic strategy of empowerment of the sober self by building personal recovery programs (PRP).

Chapter Ten, on the Meeting of Meetings, has already outlined the basic structure of the LifeRing network. This chapter briefly expands on that topic, and then focuses in depth on the strategy of building personal recovery programs. The convenor may encounter some skepticism about therapeutic self-help and can draw on this discussion for reinforcement.

13.3: Self-Help As An Organizational Principle

Self-help as an organizational principles means that all LifeRing participants, including all convenors, directors, and officers, are peers in recovery. There is no physician, therapist, counselor, or other professional in charge of the meetings or of the organization at any level.

Physicians and other professionals not themselves in recovery may visit and observe the meetings, and are usually bid welcome as guests. Meeting convenors appreciate the courtesy of a self-introduction by a visiting professional before a meeting commences.

Convenors are usually happy to cooperate with the professional guest, but occasionally there may be items on the meeting's agenda that the participants would feel more comfortable handling in the absence of an outside observer.

Professionals who are themselves in recovery are always welcome to participate in the meetings in their capacity as recovering persons. Of course, their role in the LifeRing meeting is not that of providing treatment to the other participants.

LifeRing convenors may act as their own physicians and counselors in the same way that all recovering persons do, but, as was pointed out in the second chapter, the convenor role is not one of healer or teacher, but of facilitator, bringer-together, builder-of-connections.

The LifeRing organizational structure is one of government by peers in recovery. LifeRing as an organization values its good relations with physicians and other treatment professionals, seeks counsel and advice from professionals, refers members to professionals' books and other publications, and may invite professionals to speak at our functions, but the governance of LifeRing is in the hands of laypersons who are themselves in recovery from a substance addiction. This requirement is codified in the LifeRing Bylaws at Sec. 6.5. In this respect, LifeRing is organized along the same lines as the twelve-step organizations.

Self-help is also a question of economics. No LifeRing recovery meeting charges a fee or requires a donation. Most do pass a basket, but contribution is voluntary. Meetings are independent economic entities; see the chapter on the Meeting's Money.

What goes for meetings also applies to the LifeRing organization as a whole. We own and administer our own assets. Self-help means that the LifeRing organization nationally has to live within its means. No one can sell off the membership's voting rights to a big donor or lead the organization down the road of financial sponsorship. Although we operate on the thinnest of shoestrings, it is our own shoestring and we tie it ourselves.

Self-help also means that we avoid outside entanglements. LifeRing meetings and/or the Service Center may rent space from treatment centers, hospitals, churches, libraries, colleges, banks, title companies, and other entities, but they are autonomous from and avoid affiliation with any such institutions. LifeRing meetings are affiliated with each other via the international LifeRing network.

LifeRing may on occasion enter into coalitions or joint working relationships with other groups, but we retain our independence. LifeRing is not affiliated with any political party or movement, and is not the front group, fifth column, subcommittee, or subsidiary of any ideological, cultural, philosophical or other organization. Self-help means organizational independence.

13.3.1: Our Spiritual Ancestors, the Washingtonian Total Abstinence Society

The LifeRing approach is not a splinter or spin-off from the twelve-step movement. Our spiritual ancestors in recovery are the Washingtonians. They began as six artisans and working men who left the Chase Tavern in Baltimore in April 1840, and formed the Washingtonian Total Abstinence Society. On the first anniversary of the society's founding, it held a parade of 5,000 persons.

The *Baltimore Sun* wrote that the drunkard had become the protagonist of his recovery: he had "taken his cause in his own hands – analyzed his disease and wrought his own cure." (White 1998: 9)

The Washingtonians were secular. They came under attack from traditional temperance preachers for committing "the heresy of humanism – elevating their own will above God's by failing to include religion in their meetings." (White 1998:13)

The Washingtonians believed that "social camaraderie was sufficient to sustain sobriety and that a religious component would only discourage drinkers from joining." (White 1998:13) They were missionaries, but secular ones. (White 1998:9)

Two years after its founding, the Washingtonian Society's branch in Springfield, IL, had Abraham Lincoln as a guest speaker. (Lincoln 1842)

Their numbers grew so explosively that their fragile organizational timbers were blown away in a few years, but their energy and enthusiasm continued as a movement in other organizational forms well into this century. (White 1998:14)

One of these successor forms was the fraternal temperance orders. These also were secular. Like the Washingtonians, the fraternal societies relied on mutual support. They looked for the good within. One of these groups, the Sons of Temperance, who counted 73,000 members in 1882, were formed as

> A society ... which should, by its living spirit of love and fraternity, unlock the wards of their heart and reach the elements of humanness which lay buried there and rehabilitate and re-enthrone them. (White 1998:15)

It was a society formed, in other words, to empower – to re-empower! – the innate sober self.

A similar fraternal order, the Good Templars, had initiated more than 2.9 million persons, and in 1876 counted more than 400,000 reformed drunks in its membership. (White 1998:16)

White gives a fascinating history of the Boston Washingtonian Home. It originated in 1840 as a sleeping room under the meeting hall of the Boston Washingtonian Total Abstinence Society. It exists still as the Washingtonian Center for Addictions.

In the Home's approach to treatment of the inebriate, the emphasis was on "drawing out his inherent goodness of character." (White 1998:247) The LifeRing approach, in a nutshell.

It seems to me that it is time to revive the Washingtonian spirit: the vision of innate goodness within the alcoholic/addict, the therapeutic strategy of building on the person's strengths, the respect for the person as the protagonist of their own recovery. We can do without the Washingtonians' disorganization and chaos, but this country and this recovery movement urgently need the renewal of the Washingtonians' vision and energy.

In our small, quiet way, we in LifeRing are engaged in a Washingtonian revival. Everything we do centers on the vision of the recovering person as the protagonist of their own recovery. We define abstinence from alcohol and drugs (in sharp contrast to moderation) as a practical, doable project.

Like other mundane tasks, we can take this project into our own hands, and with hard work and perseverance we can rebuild our lives on this foundation.

We have a meeting format well adapted for the purpose.

We have a clear, practical understanding of how our process works to produce recoveries. We have much else. Let us only hope that our growth is gradual and measured.

13.4: Self-Help as a Therapeutic Strategy

Self-help in LifeRing is also the basic method by which individuals get free of their entanglement with alcohol and other drugs and begin to lead full and productive lives. It may seem odd to insist on the role of self-help in an organization whose entire effort is based on providing mutual aid. But, as will become clear, neither social reinforcement nor any other putative engines of uplift, such as divine intervention, can achieve a lasting result unless there is a motivation for betterment within the individual. It is like the old joke: How many psychologists does it take to change a light bulb? Answer: One, but the light bulb has to want to change. Substitute any other person, group, or force for "psychologist" and the answer remains the same.

To get clear about self-help recovery, it is useful to go back to basics. In Chapter Two, I sketched an elementary schematic map of the addicted brain, Drawing 1, showing the "A" and the "S." Here it is again, for reference (below, right). The "A" is the addiction, or the addict self; the "S" is the survivor, the island of sanity – the sober self.

If the "S" did not exist, if the entire map were occupied by the "A," then self-help would be impossible. There would be no "self" that could be helped or do helping. On the other hand, without the "S" there would also be no living person. If the "S" loses all traction, the person soon dies.

There is no great mystery where the "S" comes from. It is how we were born. Virtually all of us were born sober; we were born 100 per cent "S." If it helps to visualize it, look at Drawing 0 here, to the left.

The small number of unfortunates who were born drugged or intoxicated via the umbilical cord went through detox immediately following birth. Practically everyone remained 100 per cent "S" at least through the kindergarten years, when (it is said) our basic personality, our emotional range, our social skills, our fundamental knowledge of the world, and much else, first take shape. Any sober time beyond kindergarten is gravy.

Many people developed on a 100 per cent "S" basis throughout primary school, middle school, and even high school. These formative sober years make up the sober core or base of the personality. Sober is how we are born and how we are formed and take our initial shape.

The sober self is the original self, and it is always present inside and underneath the newer layers of the personality that have been formed by the addiction.

There are many reasons why people start drinking/drugging, and it is useful to know about them, but they don't fundamentally matter. All the roads, if sustained long enough, lead sooner or later to the same place. A sustained high dose of addictive substances reliably produces addiction in mice, rats, monkeys, and many other mammals. (Gardner 1998:51) It does so in humans as well. "Addiction occurs as a result of the prolonged effects of abusable drugs on the brain." (Leshner 1998:ix)

It's as if the overload blows a fuse in a control circuit deep in the brain. The place where the damage occurs lies far below consciousness. You know that you're addicted only after the fact, when the brakes no longer respond to the pedal.

The key to understanding recovery is that when the "A" gets the upper hand, the "S" doesn't vanish from the map. It is merely displaced from the top and forced into an underdog role. Much like a governing party that's deposed by a military coup, it goes into opposition. Thrown out of the seats of power, it becomes the resistance.

If the "S" becomes totally overwhelmed, then the person soon dies from overdose, disease, or suicidal recklessness (drunk driving, climbing ladders, crossing the street, etc.). How long it takes depends on the drug and on the circumstances. That fatal outcome happens more than a hundred thousand times every year in the U.S., but it is exceptional.

The much more typical scenario, involving millions of lives, is a protracted war of position, maneuver, and attrition between the "A" and the "S." It would take volumes to describe all the skirmishes, battles, negotiations, promises, betrayals, coups, counter coups, compromises, upheavals and agonies that mark this war within even one brain over a single life span. My "two-egg" drawings (in the apt phrase of LifeRing convenor Martin C.), in their crayon-like static simplicity, can give no clue to the volatile, dynamic, chaotic, exceedingly complex nature of the conflicts inside the addicted person's head.

The main points that arise from this short review of the basics are these:

• Self-help recovery is not "bootstrapping." The base of self-help recovery is the portion of the person's original, native self (the "S") that has survived during the regime of addiction.

• Participation in a recovery group is the continuation by other means of a protracted struggle that has been going on and continues to go on inside the person.

• The ultimate aim of the recovery process is to help the person recover themselves, to return as far as possible to their original sober base and make a new, sober start on the existing foundation.

With these points in mind, you can see that "empowerment of the sober self" (the LifeRing slogan), which sounds vaguely like internal revolution, is actually *re*-empowerment. It is not revolution, it is restoration.

The sober self has been "in there" all the time; it is the original us. The addiction has hijacked the airplane that is our life. The recovery project is to take ourselves back.

13.4.1: Honor Thy Original Sober Self

Sometimes newcomers in recovery are taught to look back on their pre-drinking years with contempt. They have heard the lecture that drinking/using arrests their emotional development. Suppose they started drinking at seventeen. Now they are 30, 40, 50, or whatever, and they are on their first day sober. The lecturer admonishes them that despite their chronological age, they have the emotional maturity of a teenager. They are made to feel that this is a very bad thing, of which they ought to feel thoroughly ashamed.

I see it differently. Whatever else might be said about that pre-drinking teenager, in one important respect this adolescent was more mature than the adult who followed him: the adolescent was sober.

A sober adolescent is certainly higher in the Great Chain of Being than a drunk grownup. For the drunk grownup to "regress" to their sober adolescence would actually be progress.

Sometimes well-meaning drug abuse counselors stereotype all adolescents as impulsive, egotistic, short-sighted, etc. This is unfair. To be sure, such teenagers exist. But adolescents come in all types. There are many who are thoughtful, idealistic, far-seeing, and who have many other admirable qualities – often diminished or lost as they advance in years.

Even if the person started drinking/using at age eleven, returning emotionally from a drunk age of 60 to a sober age of ten would be an improvement. Lots of ten-year-old kids are very smart and can make good decisions. Certainly they can make better decisions than a drunk grownup.

13.4.2: You Have More Sober Time Than You Think

When people calculate their clean and sober time, they normally count continuous clean and sober days since their last drink/use. This is an important and useful measure and there is nothing wrong with it.

But in a larger perspective, we should count also the clean and sober time between relapses, if any. And we should also count the original clean and sober time we had from birth. Thus, for a complete profile, a person might keep up to three separate odometers.

In viewing the big picture of your life, you could add up all your sober time on one side, and all your dirty time on the other. For example, you are 35. You started drinking at sixteen. You drank and drugged for eight years. You got clean and sober for two years. Then you relapsed for five years. You now have four years clean and sober. Lifetime balance sheet: 22 years clean and sober, thirteen years not. You have been clean and sober 63 per cent of your life. How does that feel?

Quite possibly, the recognition that you have spent the solid majority of your life clean and sober can give you a boost of confidence that you can maintain your sobriety for the rest of your life. To be sure, it's important not to become complacent. But it's also helpful to know that sobriety is a challenge you can probably handle because you have been doing it most of your life.

Even if you have just a few days clean and sober now since your last drink/use, consider that you managed to stay clean and sober, and handle lots of issues and problems, as a child. If you could handle sober life as a child, how hard could it be to do it again as a grownup? Again, the point is not to take the challenge of sobriety lightly – that's dangerous! – but rather to recognize, appreciate, and utilize your inner strengths.

13.4.3: Building on Strength

When we LifeRing convenors look for the "good" in a "bad person" we are not indulging in a wishful fantasy. The sober core or base is always there.

The fact that the person is still alive is proof positive that there is a sober self active within them. If addiction is a disease, then the sober self is the immune system. The fact that the person is not dead proves that their immune system, however burdened and battered it may be, is still kicking and doing its job. When the immune system collapses, death follows shortly.

This knowledge shapes my attitude as a convenor. It's not only a matter of acknowledging my peers. Thelma and Louise in their car going over the cliff recognized one another as peers, for all the good it did them. It's a matter of owning hope. I am not, we are not, one hundred per cent zero. There is goodness and strength in us and it is our own.

Yesterday evening in a LifeRing meeting a young man, nudged hard into treatment by a family intervention, acknowledged that he was an alcoholic and that he had to stop drinking. He then said, "I am confident that I can do this. I am a good man. I have met other challenges and overcome them. I can win this one."

Should we have pounced on him? Should we have told him he was in denial, that his confidence was his disease speaking, that he was powerless and he could never manage to change his life by his own effort? No.

His belief in his native goodness, his confidence, his energy, are precious assets for his recovery. If we destroy those, we convert an alcoholic filled with hope into a hopeless alcoholic; we convert an alcoholic filled with determination into an alcoholic filled with despair; we change an alcoholic ready to go to work into an alcoholic waiting on heaven to pick him up.

If we force this young man into the "powerless" mold we break his bones and set his feet in cement with the water rising.

That is not the LifeRing approach. In a LifeRing meeting, if there is one percent strength inside of you and 99 per cent toxic waste, we recognize, applaud, support, and build on that one per cent.

13.5: Some Clinical Examples

Treatment professionals with open minds who listen to their patients and are willing to do whatever works, doctrine be damned, may come to adopt a similar, LifeRing-style approach. Lonny Shavelson's book, *Hooked*, about present-day drug treatment in San Francisco, describes three such positive pragmatists, unchartered LifeRing-style treatment providers.

13.5.1: Dr. Stewart

Meth addict and schizophrenic Darlene, in her first interview with Dr. Pablo Stewart, resident psychiatrist at the Haight Ashbury Free Clinic, is telling Dr. Stewart that if an addict doesn't want to get off drugs, "you can just talk at them until your eyes turn blue, and they'll just tell you to fuck off."

This is not news to Dr. Stewart, and he has an answer. Holding up his thumb and forefinger pinched together, he says, "Just possibly, that person who you're speaking about may have the teeniest of desires" to deal with her drug problem.

Darlene joins in the game, holding up her fingers and pinching them together harder. "Well, what if that person only has the teeniest, teeeniest, tiniest wanting to be off drugs?"

"Then," says Dr. Stewart, standing up and offering her his hand, "I would think that such a person would do very well in this clinic." (Shavelson 2001:281)

What gets Darlene to come back for treatment is the doctor's solemn acknowledgment that something within her, something of her own, no matter how concealed and tiny, is right and good. He bonds with that quality in her, no matter how fragile it may appear, and builds a therapeutic alliance on it.

In the nonprofessional context of our LifeRing meetings, we take that same approach in building alliances of mutual support – "S" to "S" connections – with one another.

13.5.2: Evelyn

Glenda was basically kidnapped off the streets and into treatment. A Lakota Indian off the reservation, she was Number One on the City's list of homeless alcoholics most likely to die on the street. She winds up in Friendship House in the care of counselor Evelyn.

> Evelyn tells me, 'Glenda, you're a strong, wise lady.' She says all kinds of things about me that make me feel really good. (Shavelson 2001:204)

The counselor Evelyn is a strong, wise lady herself, and she knows that focusing on Glenda's many deficiencies and shortcomings would be a pointless and abusive therapeutic exercise. Glenda has been beaten up enough.

Healing cannot come by reopening her wounds; it must begin with recognizing and reinforcing her positive, sober side.

In the self-help setting of our LifeRing meetings we take that same healing approach toward one another.

13.5.3: Marillac

Marillac is a Drug Court counselor. Author Shavelson watched her run a meeting, and was surprised. He thought Marillac would talk tough to the Drug Court patients, because they were mandated to be there.

Marillac shakes her head. 'It's just the opposite.' She smiles. 'I have to be more relaxed with them here. The fact that they're mandated to be in rehab doesn't make their treatment easier, it makes it harder. They have to show up, but then I have to win them over to wanting to change their lives. If I act tough, all I get is an addict who's pissed at another authority figure. So I've got to grab at what good they have inside of them, and they have to see me grabbing it, bringing it out – accepting them.' (Shavelson 2001:232)

Seeing what good we have inside us, recognizing that good in each other, grabbing it and bringing it out in one another, accepting each other as valid persons – those are primary moves in the LifeRing process. They follow from the basic insight that we have a sober base to build on; we are sober in our core.

13.6: Denial of the Sober Self

A long-time member of AA in Southern California found his way to LifeRing online, read our literature, and became enthusiastic about the LifeRing motto, "Empower your Sober Self." He took the idea that we have a sober self within us to his home meeting. He did not bring up LifeRing, which would have violated a group tradition against extraneous matters. He merely asserted that alcoholics in recovery have a sober self within them.

Much to his surprise, he met with complete rejection. They did not want to hear it. They laughed at the idea, they hooted him down, they silenced him.

LifeRing convenor Steve W.:

Have 8 ½ months sober and have been a convenor for a couple months. I LOVE LifeRing – wow, such a refreshing change from my past attempts with AA. I couldn't relate to all the God talk, powerlessness, moral failings, etc. I was depressed and hopeless after every meeting. For me, the hands-on, empowered, positive approach of LifeRing is far superior.

It's easy to see that denial of the sober self comes from the text and spirit of the twelve steps. These all describe the alcoholic in purely negative terms: unmanageable, insane, morally deficient, toxic to others, clueless, etc. There is no hint in this program that there may be positive qualities within the addicted person.

What's difficult to see is how this denial squares with the existence of the twelve-step organizations. The basic and only requirement for membership is that the person have within them a "desire to be clean and sober."

The desire to be clean and sober does not exist within the "A," the addict self. The basic and only desire of the addict self is to drink and use, regardless of consequences.

The desire to be clean and sober is the shining hallmark of the sober self. It is the sober self within the person that is the root and the source of the desire to be clean and sober.

Without the sober self, no one could form the desire that is the basic requirement for membership in a twelve-step organization, or for that matter, in any voluntary mutual aid recovery group, including LifeRing.

Moreover, the presence of the sober self within the alcoholic/addict is the secret of that person's survival. Without this inner survivor, the addict self would face no limit on its drinking/using, and before very long the individual would be dead.

Denial of the sober self is simply not logical. It can also take a psychological toll on the individual. Denial that one has any positive qualities can promote depression, feelings of helplessness, despondency, and other negative mood states that pave the way toward relapse.

13.7: Protagonists of Our Own Recovery

The indefatigable Marty Mann, the first woman to credit her recovery to Alcoholics Anonymous, crisscrossed the country telling audiences that the alcoholic was not a bad person who had to be punished, but a sick person who could be helped. (White 1998:186)

That was great progress. But it still casts the alcoholic/addict in the passive role: one who can *be helped*.

Self-help means something more. We are not only people who can be helped, we are people who can help ourselves. We are not only patients, we are and must become our own therapists.

"Relapse prevention is most successful when the client confidently acts as his or her own therapist following treatment." (Dimeff & Marlatt 1996:177) We not only plead, we decide and dispose.

As Dr. Herman wrote in her classic study of trauma victims, the patient "must be the author and the arbiter of her own recovery." (Herman 1992:133)

We are not only victims or villains of our addiction, we are heroes of our recovery. We who are in recovery have the right to hold up our heads, take off our masks if we choose, and wear the white hats. Self-help recovery means to see the recovering person in the role of protagonist.

When you meet a sober alcoholic
You meet a hero.
His mortal enemy slumbers within him.
He can never outrun his disability.
He makes his way through a world of alcohol abuse,
In an environment that does not understand him.
Society, puffed up with shameful ignorance,
Looks on him with contempt,
As if he were a second-class citizen
Because he dares to swim against the stream of alcohol.
But you must know:
No better people are made than this.
— Friedrich von Bodelschwingh,
   German social worker and reformer 1831-1910. From the German.

13.8: The Clinical Verdict: Alcoholics Recover Because They Heal Themselves

George Vaillant MD of Harvard University is the author of the most comprehensive longitudinal study of alcoholics ever conducted. He and his colleagues spent decades researching and treating alcoholics and addicts at a Boston clinic.

After a careful statistical analysis, he was forced to the melancholy conclusion that the results of their treatment were no better than the natural recovery rate for this disorder. (Vaillant 1995:352).

This does not mean that treatment is useless. It does mean, Vaillant argues, that clinicians need to learn about and make use of the patient's own inherent natural healing forces – what I am calling the "S" – inside the recovering person.

Vaillant cites by way of analogy a 1940 textbook on healing tuberculosis, a disease for which there was then no known cure. "Treatment rests *entirely* on recognition of the factors contributing to the resistance of the patient." (Cited in Vaillant 1995:353, original emphasis).

Along the same lines, an exhaustive 1975 study of alcoholism treatment programs concluded that the dominant role in determining success or failure was the role of the patient, and not the kind of treatment used on him. (*Id.*).

Another careful research study of different treatment approaches concluded that the key task for clinicians is to capture and make use of the "natural forces" of recovery within the patient. (*Id.*)

Vaillant's own data, he wrote, "bear powerful witness that *alcoholics recover not because we treat them but because they heal themselves*." (Vaillant 1995:384, emphasis added) What clinicians should do is to "redirect therapeutic attention toward the individual's own powers of resistance." (385).

The object of treatment, in other words, is to mobilize self-help.

I submit that the LifeRing approach, in focusing attention on the recovering person's own "S," and in shaping the format so as to make mutual reinforcement of the sober selves the core of the group process, is based on the soundest clinical wisdom.

Self-help is, at bottom, the only thing that works.

13.9: Open Architecture on an Abstinence Foundation

In classical Greek folklore there was a roadside innkeeper named Procrustes, who had a bed that was absolutely the perfect size. If the travelers were taller or shorter than Procrustes' bed, it was they who were deficient, not his bed. Therefore, if they were short, he stretched them until their limbs tore out of their sockets; and if their feet hung over the end he cut them off. He did this only for their own improvement.

Dr. George Davidson of Ontario, Canada, points out on his web site that

> Procrustes kept his overhead down considerably by investing in but one bed. Had his unfortunate guests been alcoholics and addicts they surely would have been accused by him of 'denial' or 'codependency' when they protested in vain the severance and extension of their limbs to accommodate the infamous bed. (Davidson 1999)

LifeRing is unique among recovery groups in rejecting the "perfect bed" approach. We really, truly, do not have a patented, guaranteed fail-safe program that we want you to fit into. We do not believe in a magic bullet approach to curing addiction. Our pride is in diversity. We provide encouragement and support for each individual to build a personal recovery program (PRP) that works for them. Make a bed that fits you.

We provide the platform: Sobriety, Secularity, Self-Help. What you build on that platform, what path you trace for yourself, is up to you. We practice open architecture.

Even the hefty *Recovery By Choice* workbook does not contain a suggested program for everyone to follow. It is nothing more than a scaffolding – a temporary rig that you can use in the process of building a personal recovery structure of your own. Then you can discard it.

To be sure, "building your own program" is not a panacea either, and it isn't intended for everyone.

Some people want to include drinking or using in their "recovery" program. They've misunderstood the bedrock foundation of LifeRing, abstinence. All of the diverse Personal Recovery Programs that LifeRing participants construct are based on the foundation of complete abstinence.

Some people say, "I don't want to do what I want to do, I want you to tell me what to do!" Of course, as soon as someone tells them what to do, they rebel. Such people find the LifeRing approach terminally frustrating. It contains no authority figure to which they can shift blame.

Others say, "I don't want to figure out what will work for me, that's too much thinking." They don't want to do recovery, they want to have it done to them, like a patient anesthetized on an operating table.

Some people are so down on themselves that they cannot get their minds around the self-help concept, on which building a personal recovery program is founded. Poor me, I'm too sick (dumb, crazy, etc.) to figure out what's good for me. I've tried "my way" and I've always failed. Such people are in denial about the "S" inside themselves. Possibly they been taught to pose as helpless and powerless, and to reject their inner strengths.

Fortunately, there are other groups where they can be served. LifeRing does not aspire to be all things to all people. We are for that special population that tends to be anti-authoritarian, inclined toward rebelliousness, fiercely self-reliant, and insists on

figuring out everything for themselves – in short, the typical alco-
holic/addict and the average American.

13.10: The Approach Needs to Fit the Person

Recovering people are notorious for anti-authoritarianism. The
founders of AA were already well aware of it. Everyone who works
with recovering populations knows how many hard, rebellious
heads can be found here.

The obvious reason for this quality is that we have just emerged
from the inner dictatorship of our addiction. We are sore and
tired of our inner drug-lord jerking us around.

Authority is a reminder of the bad place from which we just escaped. A strong impulse for remaining sober is to stay free of that
choke chain, which would have killed us.

The recovering person's anti-authoritarianism is a healthy streak;
it comes from deep within the survival centers of our brain. Even
if we could break it, we would crush a principal motive that sustains many people's sobriety.

It is counterproductive, therefore, to try to cram a recovery
program down people's throats. Roll with the resistance. (Miller
1996:87, 96) Let people create their own recovery programs.

People really and truly have a place inside of them that wants to
get clean and sober and stay that way. Have confidence in their
"S." If you allow them and expect it from them, they will figure
out what they need to do for their own recoveries.

The psychologist Daniel Goleman speaks of "the Pygmalion effect," the dramatic change that overcame hard-core low performers in the U.S. Navy when their supervisors dropped the usual
abusive tactics and started expecting the best of them, treating
them more like winners.

"Expecting the best of people can be a self-fulfilling prophecy." (Goleman 2000:150)

We recovering people are also very diverse. The notion of a uniform "addictive personality" holds no water.

> Fifty years of both psychological ... and longitudinal studies ... have failed to reveal a consistent 'alcoholic personality.' Attempts to derive a set of alcoholic psychometric personality subtypes have yielded profiles similar to those found when subtyping a general population. ... That is, alcoholics appear to be as variable in personality as are nonalcoholics. (Hester & Miller 1996:90; see also Vaillant 1995:380).

Even the mainline twelve-step advocate Katherine Ketcham admits that the idea of a pre-existing alcoholic personality "has been debunked" by numerous studies. (Ketcham 2000:65)

Addiction ranges high and low, across the spectrum of gender, ethnicity, nationality, language, religion, sexual orientation, and everything else. It seizes many different types of individuals.

It stands to reason that if our objective is to reach the whole person, and not just some generic quality they all have in common, then we have to vary the approach to fit the individual.

In a comprehensive study of what works and what doesn't work in chemical dependency treatment programs, the National Institute on Drug Abuse (NIDA) found that the number one feature of successful programs was that they fit the treatment to the individual.

> No single treatment is appropriate for all individuals. Matching treatment settings, interventions, and services to each individual's particular problems and needs is critical to his or her ultimate success in returning to productive functioning in the family, workplace, and society. (NIDA 1999)

The same finding emerged from an academic analysis of hundreds of treatment outcome studies: the best design for a recovery program is based on "informed eclecticism," offering the patient a choice of different evidence-supported methods, looking for a good fit for the individual.

> There does not seem to be any one treatment approach adequate to the task of treating all individuals with alcohol problems. We believe that the best hope lies in assembling a menu of effective alternatives, and then seeking a system for finding the right combination of elements for each individual. (Hester & Miller 1996:33)

The editors of *Substance Abuse: A Comprehensive Textbook*, state the obvious:

> Each patient or client develops problems in unique ways and forms a unique relation to the substance of choice. Common sense dictates that treatment must respond to the needs of each individual. (Lowinson 1998:xi)

Combine the diversity fact with the anti-authoritarian fact, and you have an arrow pointing to the LifeRing approach. No compulsory program. Let each person create their own personal program. Result: a diversity of personal programs matching the diversity of people.

13.11: Lessons from Learning Theory

As it happens, modern developments in learning theory based on experience with non-addicted adult populations converge toward the same result. People who make their careers educating and training adults in organizational settings found that running everyone through the same program, assembly-line style, didn't cut very deep.

Summarizing research on the effectiveness of training programs used in Fortune 500 corporations, Goleman writes: "The standard training program, where everyone goes through a cookie-cutter experience, turns out to have the worst return on investment." (Goleman 2000:266)

One-size-fits-all may be adequate for transmitting dry academic knowledge, but it doesn't work when the aim is to change deep-seated feelings, attitudes and behaviors. That requires an individualized fit and individual initiative in creating the learning plan.

> The assembly-line approach ... may work when the content is purely cognitive. But when it comes to emotional competencies, this one-size-fits-all approach represents the old Taylorist efficiency thinking at its worst. Particularly in this domain of education, tailoring – not 'Tayloring' – maximizes learning.... We change most effectively when we have a plan for learning that fits our lives, interests, resources, and goals. (Goleman 2000:266)

When people create their own plans, they reach deeper into themselves. They become more emotionally committed to the plan and invest more resources into carrying it out.

Making one's own action plan is now a mainstream strategy in evidence-based corporate and other organizational training programs. "At American Express [among other firms] everyone designs their own action plan." (Goleman 2000:266)

Years of study and experience with people in complex organizations led MIT professor Peter Senge to the same conclusion.

Author of *The Fifth Discipline: The Art and Strategy of the Learning Organization*, Senge studied how adults learn in social settings, and how organizations either facilitate that learning, or become rigid and brittle.

The strongest organizations, he found, encourage people to develop their own learning paths and thrive on the resulting diversity.

> Don't impose a favored mental model on people. Mental models should lead to self-concluding decisions to work their best. Self-concluding decisions result in deeper convictions and more effective implementation. People are more effective when they develop their own models – even if mental models from more experienced people can avoid mistakes. It's important to note that the goal is not agree-

ment or congruency. Many mental models can exist at once. Some may disagree. All of them need to be considered and tested against situations that come up. (Senge 1994: 174)

Action programs that people author by their own efforts are more likely to be carried out to completion, and their diversity is a source of resilience for the whole organization.

13.12: Choice Is the Mother of Motivation

An important product of the LifeRing self-help approach is motivation. Everyone knows how central motivation is to recovery. If a person doesn't want to get clean and sober, they won't. The central problem for treatment professionals is how to raise and maintain motivation.

Study after study shows that the mother of motivation is *choice*. When people choose a particular program from among a list of alternatives, they work at it harder and are more likely to complete it successfully, than when it is assigned to them as the only thing.

A strong and consistent finding in research on motivation is that people are most likely to undertake and persist in an action when they perceive that they have personally chosen to do so. One study, for example, found that a particular alcohol treatment approach was more effective when a client chose it from among alternatives than when it was assigned to the client as his or her only option. ... When clients are told that they have no choice, they tend to resist change. When their freedom of choice is acknowledged, they are freed to choose change. (Miller 1996:93-94).

The blood banks discovered twenty years ago two magic words to reduce donor fainting and nausea, and dramatically improve donor returns: "Which arm?"

Giving the donor a choice, even such a simple one, converted the experience from something like being victimized by a vampire into performing a civic act of generosity. (Chase and Dasu 2001:83)

Choice redefines the patient as a protagonist, as one who disposes and decides, and this transformation releases powerful positive energy.

In LifeRing, each participant can say: My recovery program is me, and I am it. No one else has a program precisely like this one. It works for me because I built it myself; I know it intimately; I own it and I operate it; I made it; it is mine. With those feelings comes investment and commitment – motivation.

There is a growing movement in the chemical dependency treatment profession today toward modernization and diversification of treatment approaches.

New published approaches such as William Miller's Motivational Interviewing (Miller 1996:89), Doug Althauser's *You Can Free Yourself From Alcohol & Drugs* (Althauser 1998), Dr. Joseph Volpicelli's "Pennsylvania Model" (Volpicelli/Szalavitz 2000), and William White's "New Recovery Movement" (White 2002) are among the more visible signs of a wider stirring and heaving within the industry, moving slowly from a tunnel vision to an open-field, choice-based approach.

The LifeRing approach resonates strongly with much that these newer professional voices are saying.

As a light network of self-help groups – and not an entrenched institutional heavyweight – we can respond to recovering people's evolving needs much more quickly than the treatment profession and the treatment facilities.

The motivating vision of the recovery environment as a "milieu of opportunity, choice, and hope" (White 1998:342) will be some time coming in the institutions. In our LifeRing groups it is a reality here and now.

13.13: Dealing with Cognitive Distortions

In early recovery, it is not uncommon for people to be blind to the obvious, to add two and two and get three or five, to be forgetful, to procrastinate, to have a limited horizon, to be unreasonably irritable, ecstatic, absent-minded, or any number of other bubbles in the lens. But, as every teacher knows, the same kinds of cognitive distortions arise in every population at every age group from a variety of causes, and yet learning and transformation manage to occur.

Scientists constantly battle distortions of the most extreme and subtle kind in their instruments of observation (witness the Hubble space telescope, launched with the wrong shape mirror), and yet science progresses.

The key thing to understand is that plucking one's eyes out is not the best solution to cognitive distortions. One discovers and learns to compensate for the distortions in the lens by viewing and comparing many different subjects in various lights and perspectives.

The solution to cognitive distortions is not to give up on cognition, but to become more active and wide-ranging as an observer.

This self-help principle holds true even when the cognitive distortions stem from severe mental illness. In the film, *A Beautiful Mind*, based on the life of the brilliant mathematician John Nash, the Nash character suffers persistent hallucinations: people who seem real and who control his life, but exist only in his mind.

His psychiatrist tries to persuade him to submit to heavy chemical shock treatments that risk turning him into a vegetable. Says the doctor: "You can't use your mind to get out of this because the problem lies in your mind to begin with."

But Nash persists, and eventually he prevails. He finds an island in his mind that is not damaged and he works from there. He stops isolating, begins to accept the support of those who love him, and finds companionship among professional peers. He keeps working, exploring, problem solving, learning, teaching. He gradually learns how to render his hallucinations small and harmless, and to resume a normal and productive life.

This moving film is a tribute to the power of self-help even in the face of the most severe cognitive distortions.

Dr. Judith Herman's classic study of trauma explores a different class of cognitive distortions: the feelings of profound depression, heightened vigilance, sudden flashback memories and other emotional injuries that haunt victims of traumatic events such as trench warfare, rape, domestic violence, child abuse, and political terror.

She warns the therapist who has such patients that the patients will present themselves as utterly helpless, but that this belief is a delusion arising from the trauma. Recovery requires shedding the lie that the patient is powerless to help herself.

> The first principle of recovery is the empowerment of the survivor. *She must be the author and arbiter of her own recovery.* Others may offer advice, support, assistance, affection, and care, but not cure. Many benevolent and well-intentioned attempts to assist the survivor founder because this fundamental principle of self-empowerment is not observed. (Herman 1992:133)

To put it in other words, self-help is not merely a possibility, it is the only genuine possibility for escape from the many mind-warping distortions that afflict the person beginning recovery.

13.14: You Make the Path by Walking

Doing recovery, at all crucial points, is not like solving an algebra problem or learning the dates of the Civil War.

Beyond the generic prime directive, "Don't Drink Or Use No Matter What," there are many possible correct answers to the "recovery problem." This means that the individual will not necessarily win by peeking and copying someone else's solution.

There's really no Answer Book. You're doing it right when you're stringing clean and sober days together and living your life. If you're relapsing or having a string of near-relapse experiences, it's a sign that you need to debug your program and change something.

You can find the correct answer only after you understand what the correct question is. The question is not, "How Did People in the Past Get Sober," nor "How Do People in General Get Sober Today?" nor "How Do *You* Get Sober?" It is, "How Do *I* Get Sober?" No one else can have the blueprint for that particular project. It's never been done before.

A poem by the Spanish writer Antonio Machado (1875-1939) says this well:

Caminante, no hay camino	Traveler, there is no trail.
se hace camino al andar.	You make the trail as you walk.
Al andar se hace el camino,	By walking you make the trail,
y al volver la vista atrás	and when you look behind you
se ve la senda que nunca	you see the path that you never
se ha de volver a pisar.	need to walk on again.

You can learn from others, you can draw strength from others, you can accept help from others. But in the last analysis, it is your road, only you can walk it.

Chapter 14: Building a Personal Recovery Program

14.1: Two Methods

Building one's personal recovery program is the major activity that is going on in most LifeRing meetings. As people report on their week in recovery and their coming week, they are, in effect, giving status reports on their personal program-building project. Here are the issues I confronted last week, here is what I did and am doing to solve them in a clean and sober manner; here is what I will be facing next week, here is what I intend to do in order to prevail as a clean and sober person.

We may not always call it that, but what people are doing is writing their own recovery plan, week by week, in their heads. They are answering the essay question, "How Do *I* Get Sober?" without using pencil or paper.

This method of building a personal recovery plan relies on serendipity. In the meeting, the person voices the concerns that happened to come up for them during the previous week or that will come up next week. The other participants similarly voice the concerns that happened to come up for them. Whether these issues are relevant to other participants is mostly a matter of chance. This is a more or less random-access way of building a personal recovery program.

There's nothing wrong with the random access method. It works perfectly for many people and they ask for nothing further. However, as with any other approach, it doesn't satisfy everyone. Some people want a more structured, directed, organized, even linear pathway. That's where the *Recovery by Choice* workbook comes in.

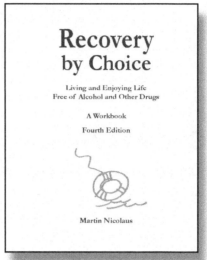

Recovery by Choice

Living and Enjoying Life
Free of Alcohol and Other Drugs

A Workbook

Fourth Edition

Martin Nicolaus

The *Recovery By Choice* workbook is a tool that allows people to do the same program-building work that they would do in a meeting, except in a structured manner.

Working in a book has advantages and disadvantages. Among the disadvantages is that the book costs money; it's only a book and can't hug you, give you feedback, or tell you it understands; and writing in a book is usually more effort than just talking.

But book work also has advantages. The money spent on the book is money not spent on alcohol or drugs. Because it's a book, it can always be there with you when you want it. You can say anything you want in the book, even things you're not ready to say at a meeting. And the very effort of writing often brings the reward of more effective mastery of the material.

Many people, including myself, are muscle learners and don't really take in an idea until we've run it out physically through our arms and fingers and written it down.

Working with a book also has other features that can be useful. When we speak at a meeting, or hear someone else speak, the words aren't recorded anywhere and we may soon forget them. When we write them in a book, they're preserved for future reference.

When we only work on our program orally, from meeting to meeting, we become dependent in our work on who happened to be at the meeting and what we happened to talk about.

Using the book, we can decide the whole sequence and content of our recovery planning in a comprehensive way. Working with the book gives us the advantages of permanence, organization, and control – in a word, structure.

14.2: Origin of the Workbook

Three of us LifeRing convenors had just finished a presentation on LifeRing at a residential treatment center in Oakland, California. In the question period, one young man said he liked what he heard, a lot. But do you guys have a workbook?

He was looking for something more than general principles like the Three "S" philosophy. He wanted nuts and bolts. That was a legitimate request.

Writing the workbook was a bit like sorting a huge mountain of laundry. Each piece represented something that someone had brought up in the decade of LifeRing meetings I had attended at the time I started writing. When I was done sorting, arranging, sorting again and rearranging, I ended up with nine piles – nine clusters of issues that people had fairly consistently brought up when reporting on their week in recovery.

Of course, "nine piles of laundry" would not have been a sexy title for the project. In the first edition of the workbook, the preferred term was "nine work areas." That was still a bit too dry, so after some discussions about marketing, by the fourth edition it evolved into "nine domains."

By whatever name, the raw material in the workbook comes straight out of many hundreds of LifeRing meetings, face-to-face and online. Working the workbook is a little like participating in a sequence of LifeRing meetings. But these would be highly unusual meetings, where everyone is on topic all the time and speaks in short, pointed sentences.

14.3: Exercises for the Choice Muscles

But obviously, there is more work to be done than listening.

The active ingredient in the workbook's architecture is *choices*. The reason people bring these issues up again and again is because they present the person with dilemmas. Shall I do this or that? How do I handle this situation? What do I do when I feel this way? How do I relate to this person? People sense that sticking with their big decision to stay clean and sober involves handling a long string of small decisions about everyday issues. Nuts and bolts.

The word 'addiction' has the same root as 'dictatorship.' The person suffering from addiction finds that their inner "A" is dictating its priorities to them, and they are experiencing atrophy in the decision-making muscles of their sober self. They're making too many decisions based on impulse, and not on sober impulse, either.

Some treatment strategies, aware of this problem, replace the dictatorship of the inner addict with the dictatorship of the external program. The program imposes a thick set of written and unwritten rules to cover every microscopic eventuality. That works fine so long as the client remains in the program setting. But as soon they leave, they crash.

What's the problem? The treatment hasn't done anything to build up the person's sober self. Their sober decision-making muscles have never been exercised. They're totally unarmed for dealing with the real world.

Exercising those sober decision-making muscles is the core strategy of *Recovery by Choice*. The book is called *Recovery by Choice*, but it could equally have been called Recovery *of* Choice.

14.4: A Tool for Making Sober Choices

The DNA of the workbook is in the opening chapter, before entering the nine domains. It has a big letter "T" at the start.

Suppose you're driving on a road and you come to a T. If you turn left you'll pass a spot where your dealer usually stands, and where you've scored a hundred times. If you turn right, you're clear. You have a choice to make.

Turning left will put you in a situation where you'll probably be triggered to use. The sight of your dealer and the force of habit create a danger zone for your sobriety. So, turning left here is likely to empower your inner addict, your "A." Turning right will tend to empower your sober self, your "S."

That one's a no-brainer.

The other day in a LifeRing informational meeting at an inpatient program, one participant was mulling the decision whether to buy a new car. I drew a T-shape on the whiteboard, with an "A" on the left side and an "S" on the right. How would buying a new car affect his "A" and his "S"? The whole group participated in a lively discussion about it, and I wrote down the ideas on one side or the other of the T as they came up.

Until that moment, this meeting participant had never considered whether buying a new car would have an impact on his recovery, one way or another. The T-chart made him think about the decision. It activated his mental muscles of sober decision-making.

The workbook didn't tell him whether buying a new car was a good idea or not. The workbook gave him a tool for making that decision in a sober way. The same tool can be used any time we have a decision to make, no matter how small. If we get into the habit of always evaluating every decision in this manner, our minds will be focused on sobriety and our power to make sober decisions will in time become awesomely strong and sharp.

That's the core concept of the workbook. In fact, if you use this approach in everything you do, you probably won't need to work any of the domains. The domains are little more than applications of this core dynamic to particular clusters of issues that come up in most people's lives. The domains don't tell you what to do. They make you think.

14.5:   The Nine Domains

• First Domain: My Body. This is a checklist for giving oneself a comprehensive health checkup. It covers a broad range of issues, such as visible and invisible body damage, doctor visits, teeth and gums, nutrition, exercise, sleep, medications, depression, anxiety, and much else. You can flag the issues that apply to you, if any do, and make a plan to get more information and/or treatment.

• Second Domain: My Exposure. Here you can take a survey of the alcohol and other drugs in your environment and do a risk assessment. Work out your options in the face of your exposure. Make a plan to get more safe space and safe time, recognize your personal triggers, and turn the trigger mechanism to your sober advantage by using daily affirmations.

• Third Domain: My Activities. When you stop drinking/drugging, you'll suddenly have a hole in your usual daily schedule. In this domain you work on filling that hole with sober activities. What activities should you avoid? Which ones do you need to learn to do sober? You may feel the need to reprogram your whole day.

• Fourth Domain: My People. You may want to change your relationships with people as you progress in your recovery. In this domain you sort the people in your life into three groups: those who support your sobriety, those who don't know, and those who oppose your sobriety. Here you decide who is who, and make a plan for dealing with each of these types of people so as to empower your sobriety.

• Fifth Domain: My Feelings. An important goal in recovery is to feel good clean and sober. This domain begins with a section on recapturing and increasing the pleasures in life. It then turns to other kinds of feelings. You can identify and label your own feelings, spot vicious circles of feelings that may trap you in drinking/using, and use a menu of options for surviving strong trigger feelings without drinking/using. You can make a plan for working on these and other emotional issues you may have identified.

• Sixth Domain: My Life Style. Recovery may involve changes in your work situation, your housing, living situation, social life, sex life, finances, and so on. This chapter contains a series of checklists for spotting problems in these areas so that you can make a plan to address your life style issues, if any.

• Seventh Domain: My History. Before you became addicted you were clean and sober, and that gives you a base to start from. Charting how you got into the pickle can be a clue to ways and means of staying out of it. This chapter briefly discusses why addiction happens, and lets you try to sum up how much drinking/drugging has cost you. It lets you draw a general balance sheet of your life, both pluses and minuses, as a basis for tying a knot around the past and moving forward.

• Eighth Domain: My Culture. Our world is filled with messages that concern drinking/using, and part of recovery is learning to live sober in a culture that, to a great extent, is not. This domain has worksheets for thinking about heroes and villains and for analyzing your culture and your subcultures. If you have a plan for improving the chances of people's recovery in your culture, here is the place to sketch it out.

• Ninth Domain: My Treatment and Support Group Experience. Treatment programs and/or support groups are part of the recovery experience for many people, including obviously people who attend meetings. This chapter lets you decide what works for you and what doesn't in the treatment and support group context, and make a plan for getting more of what you need and less of the rest.

14.6: Quality Control: Relapse Prevention

If you have put together a tight personal recovery program in the course of your work in the nine domains, the threat of relapse may never be an issue for you. But sometimes we leave things out or make unfortunate choices, creating openings for possible setbacks.

Directly following the nine domains is the relapse prevention chapter, headed with a big letter "R." This is in the nature of quality control. It reviews the work you have done in the domains. It includes a series of checklists for recognizing an approaching relapse before you pick up the first drink or drug, and for spotting and squashing the mental termites that can erode even the most solid sobriety plan if left unattended. And, if you do decide to relapse, there's an exercise for planning your relapse in elaborate detail ... so maybe you'll change your mind.

14.7: Writing Your Personal Recovery Plan

The final chapters of the *Recovery by Choice* workbook contain worksheets to help you write your personal recovery plan on several time scales. Chapter 12 is for writing your PRP for one day. Chapter 13 is for your weekly plan. Chapter 14 contains a set of tools to combine all your various issues and concerns from the previous chapters into a personal recovery program for the rest of your life.

It's a good idea always to use pencil when writing in the book. The beauty of a personal program, as opposed to a factory-issue program, is that you can revise and adapt it as your life situation evolves.

When you are done, you may want to share your plan with others.

14.8: Start Point and Sequence

Most people start the domains with number one. But that isn't really necessary. There is a logic behind the sequence, but it's a logic of convenience, not of therapeutic necessity. The domains are not steps on a staircase or stations on an assembly line. They are more similar to the different exercise machines found in a gym or health club. You know, one machine works the legs, another the arms, another the abs, and so forth. It's up to you whether, when, in what order, and how hard you work them.

You could very well open the book at random, or leaf through until you find a paragraph that spikes your interest, and start there. You could work the domains in the order 3-1-8-5-9-2-4-7-6 or whatever else suits your needs and inclinations. There may be some domains where you don't need to do any work at all. You may want to work intensely in others, and maybe repeat them. It's your recovery, it's your choice.

14.9: The Workbook in Perspective

You can see from this summary that the workbook covers a lot of ground. You might have to go to a lot of meetings to encounter all of these points in weekly check-ins.

For the LifeRing convenor, the *Recovery by Choice* workbook has multiple uses. It's a gold mine of topics for times when a meeting needs a topic. It's an answer to the newcomer looking for more direction and structure. It's a way of allowing the meeting participants to take the meeting home with them.

The workbook lends validation and prestige to the LifeRing recovery approach by demonstrating that our general concept – our operating system, if you will – is powerful enough to support a big and detailed application with lots of bells and whistles.

The workbook can also help the convenor develop stronger rapport with treatment professionals, some of whom are beginning to use *Recovery by Choice* themselves. Patients can show the workbook to probation officers, judges, and other authorities as evidence of the seriousness of their recovery effort.

In some treatment facilities, the workbook now provides clients with an alternative recovery pathway. These clients are very likely to seek out LifeRing meetings when they graduate.

Although *Recovery by Choice* is a useful asset for the LifeRing convenor, and has received a wide positive reception, it may be necessary in some instances to cool people's enthusiasm for it.

People who are accustomed to the twelve-step environment sometimes jump to the conclusion that the workbook is the LifeRing "Big Book" or "Bible." This is mistaken. We are a secular group and "bibles" are not our style. *Recovery by Choice* is large but it is just a workbook that a person wrote.

Moreover, there is very little in the way of prescription or commandment in the workbook. The book works mainly by asking questions that make you think. It's more or less a Socratic approach.

There can be and one day hopefully will be other LifeRing workbooks in addition to this one. No one in LifeRing has to use the workbook and it isn't even "suggested."

The workbook is one available tool among others. It wouldn't be *Recovery by Choice* if it were anything else. The book has a limited purpose; and when that purpose is accomplished – when you have built your recovery plan, have it firmly in hand, and are able to revise it and update it as your reality changes – then you are done with the book and can discard it or put it on the shelf for the memories.

14.10: Workbook Groups

The *Recovery by Choice* workbook is designed as personal biblio-therapy. It was not designed for use by groups. Nevertheless, there have been a number of initiatives to build groups, both face-to-face and online, around the book.

I led one of these efforts. We sat around a table and each of us did each of the exercises and worksheets. After each item we shared and discussed our choices. Although there were only six of us, we found that in an hour's time we covered only a fraction of one domain. By a rough estimate it would have taken the group more than three years to finish the book. That is not a realistic time frame for book work.

Ideally, each group member would work an entire domain at home before the meeting, so that the meeting hour could be devoted to sharing and discussing the individual choices. But realistically, few people will consistently do the extensive prep work required for such a format.

The most workable group formats to date have relied on selecting, condensing, and summarizing each domain so that it can realistically be processed in an hour or two of meeting time. A synopsis prepared by Jim R. for this format is available on request from the LifeRing Service Center, *service@lifering.org*. Workbook meetings using this format operate more or less as a repeating cycle.

Other workbook group strategies also exist. Post a request on the *liferingconvenor* email list to get details.

There is an online workbook group. It is open to anyone discussing any issue in any domain at any time. That is a useful resource for people who are mainly doing the workbook alone but want occasional feedback and contact with others. You hook up with this group via the *lifering.org* website.

I have also seen instances where two people team up to do the workbook together. This is especially useful where one person has literacy challenges.

The difficulties in adapting the workbook for group use will probably resolve, by and large, once the user base increases significantly. We could then have meetings permanently devoted to a specific domain.

The person in recovery could attend a meeting focused, for example, on the first domain, and the following week a different meeting doing a different domain, and so on, until their personal recovery program is completed to their satisfaction. Convenors of such meetings would become specialists in the given domain.

14.11: Less is More

The patented, sure-fire, never-fail big-P Programs are by their nature disempowering. If the person in recovery mentally surrenders to them, adopts them, and manages somehow to stay sober through them, all the credit goes to The Program.

LifeRing Convenor Njon W.:

Jim R's notes on the workbook chapters help pinpoint the main issues in the book without requiring the group to do the actual exercises. When I convene a WB meeting I usually do just one of the simpler exercises (maybe 10 mins) to illustrate the process and discuss the other exercises and our feelings about the subject matter for the remainder of the meeting.

As a convenor, I found that a quick review of the notes 15 minutes prior to the meeting was a great way to organize my thoughts for planning the meeting. Oftentimes, things come up that derail the course I had planned but I felt it was important to remain flexible and sometimes stretch the content of a chapter over a few meetings.

The recovering person brought nothing to the table; their effort was worth zero. The Program got them sober; The Program is Great. If things happen that The Program didn't foresee, they are in deep trouble. They remain dependent on The Program, and become personally threatened and incensed if The Program is criticized. If they relapse, it's their own fault, not The Program's.

It is different in LifeRing. Because the recovering person has invested their own judgment and effort in building their personal recovery program, its success is a credit to the individual and boosts their sober self-esteem and confidence.

The recovering person's own effort was the crucial element. Having constructed their program themselves, they have the skill to modify or extend it to meet unexpected situations. They are independent, resilient, and self-sustaining. If LifeRing is criticized, they don't get defensive. If someone blasts LifeRing for not having The Program, they cheerfully agree, baffling the attacker.

They may love LifeRing and feel grateful to it, they may continue to attend meetings for many years, they may give their time and money to make it available to others, but they aren't dependent on it or powerless without it.

When you are a LifeRing convenor, your responsibilities are different than as a group leader in capital-P Programs. Other than the prime directive, abstinence, there is no capital-P Program for you to drill into the members, by one means or another. Your role, rather, is to protect and occasionally to sweep the philosophical foundations of LifeRing so that the members have a safe, clean, and well-lighted space for their own program-building activity.

You are the guardian of the meeting's process, and part of that job is to protect the group against any effort to impose The Program – any capital-P Program – on it. You are, in a word, the keeper of the flame of motivation.

As convenor, your only reward will be that on your watch the other participants in your meeting made good progress in constructing their personal recovery programs, and so did you. If, at the end of your term, they are not even aware that anyone was in charge, and believe that everything happened completely by itself and by their own doing, you did your job well.

Chapter 15: Getting Started

15.1: About This Chapter

Chapters Two through Ten of this book described a LifeRing meeting or network of meetings that are already formed and operational. This chapter assumes that the convenor stands in a territory where no LifeRing yet exists. The chapter is a guide to the prerequisites and the methods for putting a new LifeRing face-to-face meeting on the map.

Much of this material also applies to the founder of a new online meeting. Please refer to Chapter Eight and contact the LifeRing Chat Coordinator at *LifeRingChatCoordinator@yahoo.com* for further details on starting an online meeting.

15.2: What It Takes To Be a Founding Convenor

The first requirement to be a LifeRing convenor is personal sobriety. This may seem too obvious to mention, but it bears emphasizing nevertheless. The convenor must be clean and sober before founding a LifeRing meeting and during their entire watch as convenor.

There is to date no hard and fast rule how much sober time a person should have before becoming a LifeRing convenor. Making such a rule would be in the province of the LifeRing Congress.

We have been working with an informal rule-of-custom that a face meeting convenor should have a minimum of six months.

Inside the walls of a LifeRing meeting, it doesn't matter how much sober time a person has. A newcomer with one day is as valued and esteemed as an old-timer with many years. But in the case of a convenor, sober time matters.

In the usual case, the person starting a meeting has to appear before referral sources, other recovering people, and the public to recruit members. If so, the convenor has to have sufficient sober time to be credible.

We are a sobriety group and the proof of our concept lies in our personal sobriety. The convenor's basic message is, "Come to LifeRing, it works to keep you sober!" The convenor needs to be able to walk that talk, otherwise the message carries no weight.

Not only referral sources, but newcomers to the room expect the convenor to have a solid piece of sober time. A convenor with six months has the bare minimum that public opinion in this recovery subculture judges acceptable. One year is much more presentable. Two years is respectable everywhere. Anything over that is gravy.

Convenors with six months of sober time have started many a good meeting. With energy, empathy, tenacity, and good luck, they can achieve miracles. And there's no reason to wait for the six month mark before scouting meeting locations, making contacts, and other prep work.

Convenors who are not sober or who relapse while in the convenor role not only lack credibility, they can do serious, long-term damage to LifeRing's reputation.

More than seven years after the incident, I still heard from referral sources about a certain convenor of a dissident faction of our predecessor organization who conducted his meetings with brandy on his breath. His meeting was thrown out of the host facility as a result.

Even though we were twice removed organizationally from this incident, and it happened years ago, it was still thrown up to us.

As a startup organization, we are like Jackie Robinson: we need to be twice as good in order to get equal treatment.

Another reason why the founding convenor needs to have a stable and robust sobriety is that starting a new meeting in a cold territory can be a lot of stress.

Paradoxically, the effort to build a new togetherness can make the convenor more lonesome than ever. In the early days in a new territory, the convenor may and probably will spend more than one session in the meeting room alone.

We even have a joke about it. What do you call it when you sit in a room by yourself for an hour? Answer: Convenor training. (It's a joke!)

Another point to consider is that a face meeting convenor can't be "in the closet" about their recovery. You don't have to be "out" before all the world but when you post meeting notices, contact media and referral sources, negotiate for a meeting room, etc., you are revealing yourself as a recovering person to everyone you contact in your local community.

Is your recovery ready for that? Not only that, but you are promoting a recovery brand that most people have never heard of. Even the contacts who are OK with the concept of people in recovery may look at you with skepticism and sometimes hostility. Is your recovery strong enough to handle it?

You may also want to take a look in the mirror. You will be representing not only yourself but an organization. People judge people by first impressions. Have you had a haircut recently? Are your nails clean? You don't have to look like a model, but you have to look like you have your act together.

There are other significant stresses for the founding convenor. Getting a meeting room can take legwork and time. Getting the word out can be a big project. Making all the other preparations can be a serious drain on the convenor's time, wallet, and emotional resources.

Convenors may also get so absorbed in facilitating other people's recovery that they neglect their own personal sobriety program and relapse. I've seen it happen.

The bottom line is that you must be sober in order to start a meeting. Never start a meeting in order to get sober. We've tried it, it doesn't work.

This is an old story. William White, the historian, writes about Luther Benson, a 19th century alcoholic who preached temperance on the lecture circuit with impassioned eloquence in the hope that this work would help him remain sober. He was soon drinking before, after and between lectures, and concluded that trying to cure others in order to cure himself was "the very worst thing I could have done." (White 1998:7-8)

All the happy babble about "If you want to get it you have to give it away" assumes that you and the people who want it have already found one another. Until you get to that point – which can be a long, uphill struggle – the motto is, "If you want to give it away you got to have it first. Lots of it."

15.3: Bootstrapping

The person early in sobriety in a cold place who wants to start a new LifeRing may feel caught in a Catch-22. In order to start a meeting you need to be sober, but in order to stay sober you need the support of a meeting. How are you supposed to bootstrap yourself?

One ready solution: go online. Using the LifeRing email lists and forums and chat meetings for support, an otherwise isolated person just beginning their recovery can build up enough sobriety time to become a credible, robust face meeting convenor.

It's been done. Go online every day, twice a day. Engage with people. Read the literature. Soon you may feel not only connected, but overwhelmed with the amount of support that's out there for the asking.

The other solution: find a partner. Use all your online connections to advertise: "Middletown, KS, recovering person wants to start LifeRing, seeks kindred spirit." Use all your local connections by word-of-mouth. Is there someone you already know in twelve-step meetings who feels as you do?

Do you have a sympathetic counselor, minister, physician, lawyer, nurse, bartender, barber, manicurist, massage therapist, bus driver, or somebody else who sees a lot of people, and who will put out the word for you on the local grapevine that an abstinent alternative to twelve-step is forming and to get in touch with you?

When you have a partner, you already have the nucleus of a meeting. You can meet in living rooms or over coffee for a few months and recruit others by word-of-mouth until you feel solid and credible enough to go public.

Lots of social movements start in this quiet way, in living rooms. Don't be in a rush to raise the flag and make a big public display. When you are ready to make the big move, you can share the chores and the expense, and you'll never be alone in the room.

Having a partner is the best way by far for a convenor in early sobriety to bootstrap a new LifeRing meeting in a new territory.

15.4: Finding and Reaching Our People

In order to make a meeting, the convenor needs other people. The convenor's role definition, after all, is "to bring people together." To bring them together one first has to find them and reach them.

15.4.1: Who Are Our "Customers"?

It may be a useful mental exercise for the startup convenor to pretend that a LifeRing meeting is a commercial enterprise, like a grocery store or a barber shop or an auto repair shop, and to ask, where and how will we get our customers?

Thinking about the meeting as a business proposition can be helpful in coming to grips with the nuts-and-bolts issues that have to be solved in order to turn a dream into a reality. The convenor who does not confront these questions may end up spending more time in solo meditation than is necessary or beneficial.

Some startup convenors think about getting a room before they think about the "customers," but it may be wiser to think about the "customers" first, and let that analysis illuminate the search for a location.

Who is our target audience? In the heroic era of Temperance, larger-than-life reformers like Carrie Nation marched into saloons brandishing umbrellas, smashing bottles, beating inebriated sinners about the head and shoulders, driving them into the street and herding them onto the horse-drawn wagon to the revival tent to be saved.

That's not our style. Were it so, then LifeRing convenors should be hanging out in bars trying to argue the besotted sober. We know better.

Our target audience is people who already have a desire to quit drinking/drugging, or who have already quit and want support to stay quit. (I'm using the word "desire" in the loosest sense here.) We are not a reform group trying to save people from their addiction despite themselves. We are a support group to connect people who want to help themselves.

Such people are scattered all over the social and geographical landscape. Wherever people drink/drug, a certain proportion of them get sick and tired of drinking/drugging, and the urge to quit arises within them. This process goes on all the time, entirely independent of us, like a force of nature.

As long as people drink/use, there will be a percentage who get sick and tired of it and want to quit. Our potential customers, our people, are scattered here and there, everywhere. The great mother of all problems is finding and connecting with them.

15.4.2: Broadcasting and Narrowcasting

The primary way that big businesses reach a widely scattered customer base is unremitting exposure on network television. One day, if we become a large and established organization, Life-Ring will enjoy persistent favorable national network television coverage. Until then we are relegated to the cheap streets.

A few of the people who want recovery are active on the Internet search engines, hunting out all their available options. We are there for them at *www.lifering.org* and related sites and they can readily find us. Through their online LifeRing connection they may be able to find and connect face-to-face with other people who are online in their community.

The folks at the LifeRing Service Center can sometimes help make those connections for them. But a lot of people in recovery have spent their computer money on drink and drugs, or are not computer-literate, or reside for other reasons on the wrong side of the great Digital Divide. How will we reach those?

Some recovering people haunt bookstores, and they have spending money. We can covertly slip our meeting notices between the pages of recovery books in bookstores and libraries ("salting"). But a great many people in recovery are not active readers; and many bookstore owners and librarians are wise to the ways of missionaries, secular or otherwise, who mess with their merchandise.

A few LifeRing meetings started as maverick twelve-step meetings and gradually peeled off and changed their affiliation. That's fine when it happens spontaneously, due to internal pressures in the twelve-step world. But there is no effective lever from which such a result can be engineered from the outside, nor is it a wise strategy to spend energy on the attempt.

Many communities have noncommercial community channels, public access TV, free speech forums and similar openings that the local LifeRing convenor may be able to utilize. We can also put free or cheap ads and calendar notices in community newspapers, hire inexpensive services that post flyers on utility poles and in laundromats all over town, and use other affordable media that broadcast to a general audience.

LifeRing convenors have done all of that in several communities. However, most of these efforts to broadcast to a general audience using small ads in the cheap media have so far had very limited impact. The fish are too widely scattered or run too deep and the cheap nets are too small and shallow to catch many. That is why they are cheap.

Getting the local press to cover the opening of the first LifeRing meeting in a community sometimes works, particularly in small towns. It's worth trying. We've had a handful of successes. But the chances of press coverage are much better after we've already established a whole network of LifeRing meetings to gain credibility.

The LifeRing convenor is in the same situation in this regard as many other small entrepreneurs. We can't afford to broadcast via the high priced media, and broadcasting via the cheap media doesn't reach enough of the customers.

> **LifeRing Convenor Craig W.:**
> Convenors everywhere should consider approaching local media – in some ways, LifeRing is what newspapers used to call a "man bites dog" story – the existence of AA is not news, but the existence of alternatives to AA is, at least in the minds of most news people.

This dilemma, however, is far from hopeless. The solution is to switch from broadcasting to narrowcasting or focused marketing. Instead of trying to cover the whole sea where the fish are widely scattered, narrowcasting focuses effort on limited pools where the target population is concentrated.

Focused marketing in various forms is today a widely practiced business strategy used by commercial and nonprofit concerns alike.

Are there pools where our "fish" are concentrated? Yes, there are. On any given day in the United States, about nine hundred thousand people are in licensed chemical dependency treatment programs of various kinds and in various settings. (Robert Wood Johnson Foundation, 2001:106)

Based on the fact that the people are there, it can be assumed that they have some desire to get clean and sober, however fragile and temporary it may be. Practically all of these people need support groups and all of their treatment providers will refer them to support groups.

Perhaps the same number of people or more attend twelve-step meetings. They already have a support group and generally aren't in the market for another.

Apart from those two pools of concentration, people who have a desire to quit drinking/drugging are scattered thinly all over the social and geographical landscape. Those are basic demographic facts. It does no good to fight or ignore these facts.

The landscape is littered with the bones of meetings that dried up and died because they found no way to reach the pools where the people are to be found.

The LifeRing convenor who wants to turn the dream of a new meeting into a reality will need to make peace with demographic facts and build on them.

15.4.3: Twelve-step Meetings: Off Limits

LifeRing convenors or members do not attempt to infiltrate twelve-step organizations and conduct recruitment within them. If that occurs – and instances are rare – the members are acting as individuals on their own.

It happens that people who normally attend twelve-step meetings as well as LifeRing meetings share their LifeRing experience, meeting locations, and literature with their twelve-step friends. But we do not enter twelve-step meetings for the purpose of recruitment or propaganda.

The twelve-step organizations have rules against "outside" encroachment and we need to respect that. We also do not permit people to promote or recruit for other organizations inside LifeRing meetings.

LifeRing has nothing to gain, and much to lose, from provocative, antagonistic, confrontational, or invasive tactics toward twelve-step meetings.

We have everything to gain from mutual tolerance and respect. They travel their road, we travel ours. Although the roads are different, we are on the same journey.

Does this mean that we, as LifeRing convenors, are not interested in reaching the members of twelve-step groups? On the contrary.

When we are invited to share our views with audiences composed largely of twelve-step people, we happily accept. But twelve-step meetings are generally not free speech forums, nor should they be. LifeRing convenors are realists; we do not go where we are not invited.

A "hands-off" attitude toward twelve-step meetings is also important because it improves the working climate for our friends within the twelve-step community.

In the treatment industry, many of the professionals who have been most active in supporting LifeRing as a support group option are long-time participants in twelve-step groups. They want an abstinent secular option, and are willing to invest time and effort to make it happen, because it is the right thing to do.

There are twelve-step activists who want the treatment industry and the twelve-step organizations to step back from one another, take down the big Steps and Traditions posters from the treatment room walls, and play a more neutral, independent role. They don't seem to be vocal on a national scale, but I hear them in treatment facilities on a local level.

Nationally, LifeRing is recognized, included on referral lists, and treated fairly by such notables as the late historian of AA, Ernest Kurtz, recovery historian and treatment consultant William L. White (*Slaying the Dragon*) and Stacia Murphy, president of NCADD (the National Council on Alcohol and Drug Dependency).

These and other figures in the twelve-step world take to heart the pluralist streak within AA co-founder Bill W., who recognized that there are many roads to recovery (Wilson 1944) and that AA has no monopoly on getting drunks sober.

As Wilson said in an address to the New York Medical Society:

> Your president and other pioneers in and outside your society have been achieving notable results for a long time, many of their patients having made good recoveries without any AA at all. It should be noted that some of the recovery methods employed outside AA are quite in contradiction to

---

LifeRing Convenor Mary S.:

We got our venue free of charge at a hospital, courtesy of the IOP director who ran a 12 step-based program. Another of our meetings takes place at a recovery community where most of the residents are heavily into the steps. I have found that most treatment professionals are delighted to discover that a viable alternative to AA is available.

AA principles and practice. Nevertheless, we of AA ought to applaud the fact that certain of these efforts are meeting with increasing success. (Wilson 1958)

Many LifeRing convenors have encountered individuals within the twelve-step world who would be happy to see an abstinent alternative emerge – "whatever works" – and are willing to help to make it happen, or at least not stand in the way.

A recent nationwide survey estimated that about 33 million Americans suffer from an Alcohol Use Disorder as defined by the DSM-5, the Diagnostic and Statistical Manual created by the American Psychiatric Association. (*http://archpsyc.jamanetwork.com/article.aspx?articleid=2300494.*) Only a tiny sliver of these (approximately one million by its own count) ever participate in Alcoholics Anonymous. There is no shortage of drunks in this country and we have no reason to try to pilfer them from other organizations.

15.5: Sobriety Is the Key to the Door

Unlike participants in twelve-step meetings, patients/clients in treatment programs are a perfectly proper and legitimate audience for our outreach. There they are, nearly a million of them each day, clustered together at locations where you can find them, all needing support groups. We have support groups.

LifeRing Convenor Patrick N.:

In Victoria we grow because of the grassroots efforts of the members here. We place our meeting schedules and brochures in the main locations where addiction is addressed, at community health centers and at some doctors offices. We announce meetings starting up at new locations by producing a flyer and posting it around the community. We also hold a weekly meeting at the hospital detox unit. Most feedback from people, albeit anecdotal, is that their LifeRing experience is positive. Word of mouth brings people back and we get affirmative referrals from addiction workers.

The LifeRing convenor who wants to fill a meeting room with people who want recovery will want to do everything possible to reach the patients/clients in treatment programs.

In the San Francisco Bay Area, the earliest convenors already took the trouble to get their local meeting announcements into the major chemical dependency treatment programs.

These efforts made a big difference in my life. When I arrived for my intake interview with the medical director of the Kaiser program on my first day clean and sober, he already had a sheet of paper with the meeting schedule to give me.

At that meeting, I met some other patients from the same treatment program. We banded together and we would speak up, politely and respectfully, at strategic moments.

For example, when a counselor asked the group, "And how many twelve-step meetings have we attended this past week?" We would say, "None." When the scolding began, we would add that we had been to two secular, non-twelve-step, abstinence support group meetings.

This game went on for quite some time, and I suppose the counselors thought we would just relapse and go away. But, instead,

---

LifeRing Convenor Mona H.:

I wanted to share that I met with the Hospital staff and managing Head Physician on Tuesday morning. The hope was gaining their extended endorsement and expanding our Lifering outreach to additional outpatient treatment centers. Wow, was it successful. Dr. U. was his charming self and will stand behind whatever we need, but he has very little additional time. The best help was a surprise. The head of the ARC (Addiction Recovery Center), is HIGHLY endorsing Lifering as a secular choice and is going to introduce us to two addiction directors on the East coast at a meeting on Monday.... I will be on a "meet and greet" basis and along with my handouts I will just need to be professional. I'm feeling VERY strongly that the approach of the hospital professionals is a good one here in the NE and I hope this experience will be a good expansion model to report back.

we stayed very much sober, and also attracted other patients to our informal caucus. While many of the patients who relied on twelve-step were dropping like flies all around us, we stayed rock steady through thick and thin and were obviously enjoying ourselves. After a while, our cheerful sobriety wore down the ranks of the staff skeptics.

The Permanente Medical Group, Inc.
CHEMICAL DEPENDENCY RECOVERY PROGRAM
969 BROADWAY
OAKLAND, CALIFORNIA 94607
(510) 251-0121

Antioch	Rancho Cordova	
Davis	Redwood City	
Fairfield	Richmond	
Fremont	Roseville	
Fresno	Sacramento	
Gilroy	San Francisco	
Hayward	San Jose	
Martinez	San Rafael	
Milpitas	Santa Clara	
Mountain View	Santa Rosa	
Napa	S. Sacramento	
Novato	S. San Francisco	
Oakland	Stockton	
Park Shadelands	Vallejo	
Petaluma	Walnut Creek	
Pleasanton		

PAUL T. MCDONALD, M.D.   PRESTON MARING, M.D.   JOHN LOFTUS, M.D.
Physician-in-Chief   Associate Physician-in-Chief Associate Physician-in-Chief

RICHARD BROWN, M.D.   ANANSE TAHARKA, M.D.   SHEILA MACKEL, M.D.   J. DAVID ARTERBURN
Assistant Physician-in-Chief   Assistant Physician-in-Chief Assistant Physician-in-Chief Medical Group Administrator

April 25, 2000

To Whom It May Concern:

I am writing this letter in support of LifeRing Secular Recovery. Kaiser Oakland's Chemical Dependency Recovery Program has been at 969 Broadway, Oakland since May of 1995. Ours is a regional program, drawing participants from Alameda and Contra Costa Counties and occasionally from Solano, and San Joaquin Counties. The Oakland CDRP offers four levels of care for chemically dependent people. Our population is a mix of voluntary and mandated patients. Some of our patients are struggling with addictive disease only, while others are dually diagnosed.

All the CDRP patients are required to go to outside support meetings. We offer traditional meetings such as NA and AA. We also offer LifeRing for patients who are not comfortable with the format of 12-step programs. LifeRing meetings have been offered on Tuesday and Wednesday since our program began. Last April LifeRing began a Saturday morning group. LifeRing meetings have always been well attended but the Saturday group has been so popular that at times we have had to open a second meeting room to accommodate all the people who wish to attend.

I am happy to state that LifeRing has always been able to coexist harmoniously with other support meetings. Patients report being satisfied with the format and some say they attend LifeRing and 12-step support meetings. I am happy to recommend LifeRing to any drug treatment program.

Sincerely Yours,

Jeffrey Blair MS MFCC
Day Treatment Co-coordinator

KAISER PERMANENTE

Today, LifeRing enjoys something like a level playing field at this treatment facility, and at a growing number of others. As a support group we are treated more or less on a par with twelve-step groups, and the patients enjoy all the benefits of choice.

At such facilities, program literature and forms such as sign-up sheets have been modified to speak of attendance at "outside meetings" instead of "twelve-step meetings." All patients are given the choice of LifeRing or twelve-step attendance, or a combination thereof, from the outset.

Using variations on this same basic sobriety-centered approach, LifeRing convenors in the San Francisco Bay Area built a network of more than 25 LifeRing meetings, at least two meetings every day of the week.

Similar networks have grown up in other cities. The recovering person who wants or needs to do "90 in 90" (90 meetings in 90 days) can do that entirely in LifeRing if that is their preference.

The basic point of this story is that if you have sobriety, then you need not be afraid to rattle the cages of treatment programs. Sobriety is the key to get in the door. You could make a big difference in someone's life when you make the effort.

LifeRing Convenor Jeff C.:

I just finished week eight of our Sunday meeting. After four weeks of sitting by myself, a few people started attending. Tonight we had eight in attendance. It was exciting to hear the newest participants saying "see you next week" to the other members. All attendees were from the treatment center where the meeting is located, but I believe that is how LifeRing started in the first place, so it is a proven model.

I am starting to meet with addiction providers and the reception has been warm. Currently sending mailings to local providers. I will also be meeting the clinical director at a Veterans treatment center to discuss helping some of the folks there get a meeting going.

Professionals in the chemical dependency field know that relapse is very common. "The most common treatment outcome
for alcoholics and addicts is relapse." (Dimeff/Marlatt 1996:176)

If you can demonstrate that you have something that keeps
some people sober – especially people whom the professionals
expected to fail – then you have something that serious treatment
professionals want to know about.

Some LifeRing convenors have wounds in their souls from certain treatment programs, and they like the idea of approaching
those programs for referrals about as much as a doing their taxes.

In truth, some programs are abominably bad and would be shut
down in any other health care field but substance abuse. Substance abuse in some eyes seems to legitimize patient abuse.

But the convenor who simply turns away from mistreatment
and never looks back may be missing an opportunity to help other
patients in that program by getting them to a LifeRing meeting.

The LifeRing convenor who has been a patient at a treatment
facility has a valuable asset for building the ranks of the meeting:
their contact with the staff, and possibly also with other patient
graduates.

Every LifeRing member who has been in a treatment program,
and who has at least six months of sobriety, can pick up the phone,
call the counselors they knew, and set up an appointment to bring
them LifeRing literature. You can ask for fifteen or twenty minutes of staff meeting time to share your LifeRing experience.

Be sure that staff always have a suitable stack of your meeting
flyers to hand out to patients. If the program has outside speakers
come in to speak to patients, insist on being included.

LifeRing Convenor John B.:
Our newest meeting in Salt Lake is at a recovery home called
"First Step House" and the convenor is someone who just gradu-
ated from the program there.

Don't take no for an answer. Sobriety is the gold standard. If you have sobriety, you can get what you need. Rehab managers who shut the door in your face even though you have solid long-term sobriety embarrass themselves. Be patient and persistent, and you will wear them down.

The LifeRing convenor who has never been a patient in a treatment program will want to learn the ropes of this milieu for the same obvious reasons that a seller of cowboy boots will want to become familiar with rodeos.

Remember, the role of the convenor is to bring people together. That requires knowing and going wherever our people can be found.

The startup LifeRing convenor or convenor partnership, then, may want to sit down early on with the Yellow Pages and make a list of their local treatment facilities.

There is also an online national treatment locator maintained by a federal agency (Google "SAMHSA") that lists licensed and accredited facilities nationwide by zip code, with telephone numbers, addresses, and often the names of the directors, along with types of service and other useful information.

LifeRing Convenor Michael J.:

I planned way ahead and the group is (for the moment) targeted at a specific segment of the population – the LGBT community. We are tied to a local community center here that serves our community at large. It may seem foreign to some (it was to me, being from California – the Bay Area, specifically) but my community is still very much in need of resources here.

We have two advantages starting up – the backing of a known, established and trusted entity and a group of people needing support. We welcome anyone into our circle of recovery – last meeting the ages ran from 23 to 65, gay, lesbian, bi and straight, transsexual, black and white. Heroin, alcohol and "pot" were all represented. Short timers and long timers and of course, yours truly, the middle timer.

Some localities also have associations of accredited substance abuse counselors, and these have mailing lists that can be borrowed or rented. From these lists, the convenor(s) can select and prioritize the most likely looking facilities, and then plan out a campaign of approach.

The same rationale applies if you are looking to build a meeting for women only, or young women who are parents (you'll need to arrange childcare), or LGBT people, Spanish language speakers, veterans, the deaf, or other select demographics. You will want to focus on women's centers, or LGBT centers, and the like.

I sometimes talk to convenors in communities where the Life-Ring meeting is not growing and I ask them what they are doing to try to attract newcomers.

In some cases they are relying entirely on word of mouth. Word of mouth is good if your existing members are widely connected into self-renewing pools of other recovering people. Word of mouth is good also if your organization is deeply wired into the media and if every Hollywood movie with a drug or alcohol theme includes a plug for your group.

But if you are new to the scene, and if your existing members tend to stay to themselves outside of their meeting, then word of mouth may not be enough to reach new members.

In other cases, the convenors are trying to broadcast to a general audience using the cheap media, and are not finding their high expectations fulfilled. Sometimes the convenors become dejected and believe that nobody wants what we have.

LifeRing Convenor Laura M.:
I also convene meetings in a Kaiser facility. I have been impressed with how cooperative they have been in letting LifeRing have meetings and promoting those meetings to members of the Chemical Dependency program.

But when I ask them what have they done to get the word out to the pools of recovering people who are concentrated in the local treatment programs, they have assigned that a low priority.

15.6: Treatment Programs: A Convenor's Primer

Treatment programs virtually all refer their patients/clients to support groups. The basic reason is that treatment is short and recovery is long. Support groups provide the long-term follow-up or maintenance that the programs themselves usually cannot provide.

In a sense, the central function of treatment is to induce the client to take up long-term support group participation.

For historical reasons that are discussed in some detail in White's *Slaying the Dragon* (White 1998) most treatment programs in the U.S. operate on a model derived from the twelve-step groups and routinely refer their patients into twelve-step groups. This treatment model is enshrined in manuals, taught in schools, and bears the name Twelve Step Facilitation (TSF).

The symbiosis between twelve-step groups and the treatment programs is often so close that it may be impossible to tell where the twelve-step group leaves off and the treatment program begins. This long-standing connection is familiar stuff to anyone acquainted with the field in the United States.

LifeRing Convenor David R.:

Kaiser Hospital has been great about letting us have a room to meet in every Thursday night. Many of the people that come are referred from the Kaiser Chemical Dependency Program offered here in Fresno. I went through the same program three years ago.

15.7: Gaps in the Wall

The significant fact for LifeRing convenors and others is that in recent decades, cracks have developed in this relationship and there are openings for change. In my experience, six developments have stirred the pot most deeply: professionalization, internal ferment, public criticism, court decisions, patient resistance, and the growth of alternative treatment protocols.

15.7.1: Professionalization

Rank-and-file substance abuse treatment providers are underpaid, overworked, and receive little professional respect. In their own healthy self-interest many of them have formed associations to advocate for elevated and uniform educational standards, accreditation, and improved compensation.

This movement marginalizes counselors whose only credential is their own recovery, and it advances counselors who have university degrees and graduate-level accreditation. Most of the latter have been exposed to the scientific method, behavioral psychologies, and the secular outlook. These professionals, by and large, are much more receptive to abstinent alternatives. In general, the more M.D.s, Ph.D.s, and other accredited professionals a program has on its clinical staff, the more likely it is to have a LifeRing meeting.

A case in point is the Kaiser Permanente Health Maintenance Organization (HMO), the largest in the U.S. All Kaiser chemical dependency treatment centers are headed by an M.D. and require graduate degrees and/or professional licenses from their treatment staff. This level of staffing is strikingly higher than the industry average.

With a few holdouts, Kaiser chemical dependency treatment centers include LifeRing meetings among their support group offerings wherever LifeRing convenors are available to lead such meetings.

For an example, see the flyer that Kaiser management posted in the Denver area Kaiser campuses, announcing that LifeRing groups are now offered there (below).

LifeRing support groups now offered at Kaiser Permanente

Kaiser Permanente and LifeRing will offer peer-led recovery support groups to Kaiser Permanente members at no additional charge.

LifeRing is an abstinence-based, worldwide network of individuals seeking to live in recovery from addiction to alcohol or to other non-medically indicated drugs. Peer-to-Peer support is offered in ways that encourage personal growth and continued learning through personal empowerment.

Tuesdays from 6 to 7p.m.
Kaiser Permanente Regional Offices: Vohs 1 Conference Room 10350 E. Dakota Ave., Denver, CO 80247

Thursdays from 5:30 to 6:30 p.m.
Kaiser Permanente Hidden Lake Medical Offices: Rapids Room 7701 Sheridan Blvd., Arvada, CO 80003

Meetings may be scheduled in rooms provided as a community service by Kaiser Permanente; however, LifeRing is solely responsible for all services provided. The services are not a part of the Kaiser Permanente medical care program and attendance at meetings does not confer any benefits of Kaiser Permanente membership.

15.7.2: Internal Developments in the Twelve-step World

The seamless connection between twelve-step organizations and most of the treatment industry has always had critics within the twelve-step organizations.

The practice of hanging large twelve-step posters in treatment rooms, which is offensive to clients looking for a secular treatment environment, is also objectionable to twelve-step followers who take seriously the AA tradition against identification with outside entities.

The court systems in many localities routinely mandate twelve-step attendance for people convicted of drug-related offenses. Where this is the case, twelve-step meetings may be flooded with people who don't want to be there, contribute nothing, and fill the room with resentment.

Many twelve-step participants are less than thrilled by the massive influx of treatment patients into their meetings. I have written about this in more detail in Chapter 6 of *Empowering Your Sober Self.*

The rapid growth of religiously non-affiliated people in the United States, detailed above in the chapter on Secularity, has

---

LifeRing Convenor David R.:

I have been sober since 2008 and have been a LifeRing convenor here in Fresno CA for a little over five years. I owe my continued sobriety to this affiliation. It was difficult getting the word out at first, but as time went by information about LR spread.

I made contact with several rehab counselors in town and worked closely with Kaiser Permanente Hospital and their chemical dependency department. As time passed some attendees stepped forward and wanted to convene their own meetings. We now have LR meetings every night of the week except Saturday and Sunday. I also try to "table" at any community events that are appropriate.

also left its mark on the twelve-step world. By some reports, most of AA's recent growth is in the form of atheist/agnostic meetings.

Some believe that the twelve-step movement, born in the Great Depression, has experienced a hardening of the arteries and an exhaustion of its primal spirit. Although the loose organizational structure of the Anonymous groups seems well adapted to riding out change, the core program remains unaltered from when Bill W. penned it more than 80 years ago. For many modern eyes, that text has become an unreadable 1930s religious tract.

Another aspect of the problem is commercialization. Originally a volunteer-driven group with a missionary spirit, the twelve-step approach has become today a profitable business model. Rehab owners hire treatment staff whose main qualification is their own recent twelve-step recovery. These workers may see the job as "carrying the message" (the twelfth step) and are happy to be paid at all. Their low credentials and minimal wages translate into high rates of return for investors, with low success rates for the clients. More and more clients and those who pay their bills are feeling ripped off by service products sold under the twelve-step label.

15.7.3: Public Criticism

In recent years, the addiction treatment profession has come under mounting public criticism. A 2012 report by Casa Columbia, a prestigious research institute, blasted the treatment industry for its lack of professionalism and for adherence to a one-size-fits-all approach, which it called "typically a recipe for failure."

LifeRing Convenor Cindy K.:

I'm convening a 3rd weekly group in Greenwich, CT. I live nearby in Stamford, CT. Our meetings draw mostly from the addiction recovery program (from which I "graduated") at Greenwich Hospital. It's been gratifying to see LifeRing get more referrals from the staff there, plus more and more finding us from web searches.

The clear target here is the twelve-step treatment model, which relies on low-paid nonprofessional staff to operate a one-size-fits-all approach.

Bestselling author Anne Fletcher's 2013 book, *Inside Rehab* and Harvard psychiatrist Lance Dodes' 2014 expose, *The Sober Truth*, ventilate additional criticisms of the prevailing twelve-step treatment model.

A new documentary film, *The Business of Recovery* (2015), says that treatment outcomes have worsened while treatment industry profits have soared.

Criticisms of this sort have been heard before. What is new is the high level and prestige of the critics. Censure of the prevailing treatment model no longer comes only from the margins; it is becoming mainstream.

Treatment centers have been listening and, in their fashion, making adjustments.

It is now relatively rare for a treatment center to state on its website that it is locked into the twelve-step treatment approach. A decade ago, that was considered almost obligatory.

Centers today typically claim that they are multi-disciplinary, offer alternative approaches, treat clients as individuals, etc. But, as both Fletcher and Dodes point out, once inside the door the client is typically shunted onto the same one-size-fits-all railroad track as before.

Many of these centers just don't know any other treatment modality, and can't be bothered learning. Deceptive advertising is quicker and cheaper.

Other centers, by contrast, search their souls and conclude that their primary business is not to carry the twelve-step message but rather to help their clients get clean and sober by any means necessary – whatever works.

Sometimes the change at these centers runs no deeper than a token LifeRing meeting once a week. At others, real and creative changes take place, such as a two-track system, where clients have the choice of the twelve-step or the LifeRing approach.

15.7.4: Court Decisions

A string of recent court decisions is beginning to reshape treatment and referral practice wherever government funding plays a decisive role. It was and in many areas remains standard practice for courts, prison authorities, and parole agencies to require all prisoners with drug-related crimes to attend treatment programs based on the twelve-step model.

A series of federal appeals court decisions on the East Coast, in the Midwest, and on the West Coast has made it clear that the twelve-step model is religious in nature, and forcing a prisoner to participate in a program that violates their religious beliefs is a violation of the U.S. Constitution. In the most recent such case, *Hazle v Crofoot (2014)*, the prisoner obtained a $2 million settlement.

> **LifeRing Convenor Mona H.:**
> I received this email from the head of the addiction treatment program at a local hospital:
>
> "All the newest scientific literature in recovery says "one size does not fit all – and should not" implying people should have choices that will keep them coming, as it is difficult to effect change when the patient does not attend. Historically, we have viewed resistance to 12-step programs as 'denial.' We are moving away from that dogmatic approach to substance abuse counseling. This is my long-winded way of attempting to say I no longer view LifeRing as 'competition' [to twelve-step], especially given the extraordinary acceptance it has had among our IOP patients who would not have otherwise attended AA or NA.... Congratulations on a very popular treatment alternative that has meant the difference between attending or not attending self-help groups for a large number of our patients."

These cases wield leverage not only in the prison context, but in any setting where government money plays a decisive role in addiction treatment. See Section "15.17: Dealing with Obstruction" on page 319 below.

15.7.5: Patient Resistance

Undoubtedly the greatest and strongest force for change has come from the patient population. Clients today are less interested in religion and more receptive to non-religious approaches than ever before.

An analysis of research into Americans' church participation and religious faith says:

> In every region of the country, in every Christian denomination, membership is either stagnant or declining. Meanwhile, the number of religiously unaffiliated people – atheists, agnostics, those who are indifferent to religion, or those who follow no conventional faith – is growing. In some surprising places, these "nones" (as in "none of the above") now rank among the largest slices of the demographic pie....

> The so-called millennials (Americans born between 1982 and 2000) are far more diverse, educated and tolerant than their predecessors. They're also the least religious genera-

---

LifeRing Convenor Scott H.:

I'm happy to report that this month marks one year since we started our f2f in Pacifica. Having spent the first few weeks alone in the room, I can say we now have a solid group of regulars. We've had some highs and lows, but I look forward to the middle of each week for our meeting.

The staff at the Pacifica Resource Center have been a huge support. Last night I had to apologize for the noise we made. The staff member I spoke to said the applause and laughter coming from that room is always a joy to hear.

Most importantly this meeting has helped me through some tough times in my sober journey. I wanted to thank those in this group who have helped with their advice and encouragement.

> tion in American history – they're even getting less religious as they get older, which is unprecedented – and the majority of them identify Christianity as synonymous with harsh political conservatism.
>
> As older, more religious generations fade away and younger generations replace them, the societal midpoint shifts. And this trend is going to accelerate in coming years, because the millennial generation is big. They're even bigger than the baby boomers.

(Lee 2014). See also the discussion of this issue in the chapter on secularity.

The religious content of the twelve-step approach, as the twelve-step advocate Ketcham noted, has driven "many thousands" away (Ketcham 2000:202-203). With the advent of the millennial generation, those thousands are likely to multiply.

Client resistance to twelve-step is a nationwide phenomenon. Rehab workers, on the average, aren't prepared to deal with it. Some ascribe twelve-step resistance to the patient's denial. They attempt confrontational approaches to force the client into submission, with predictable results. Others simply go through the motions and blame the client when the treatment fails.

Whatever the reasons, the bloom is off the rose. The counselor whose mission it is to steer patients into twelve-step groups is facing more and more patients today who are OK with abstinence but not OK with the twelve-step approach.

As a speaker and exhibitor at addiction treatment conferences, I've polled dozens of rehab staff members from all parts of the country about this issue. Without exception, they face the prob-

---

LifeRing Convenor Dave F.:

I'm a new Convenor for a Louisville, CO LifeRing group. I've been involved with LifeRing for a couple years; most actively in a group that meets at a chemical dependency treatment facility. Each meeting has the in-patients come down and participate. Wonderful experience!!

lem of what to do with clients who want to do recovery but don't respond to the twelve-step approach.

I've written about the rehab staff worker's dilemma in some detail in the Introduction to *Empowering Your Sober Self*.

The basic problem is that the treatment program is unable to offer its clients an additional, secular pathway. It's the program managers, not the clients, who are in denial here.

Case in point: At the 2005 annual LifeRing meeting, held that year in Guelph, Ontario, Canada, the head of the major addiction rehab in the city threatened to fire any of his staff members who attended any of our sessions. A columnist for the local press got wind of it and savaged him in print as a Neandertal.

15.7.6: Growth of Alternative Treatment Approaches

One of the most encouraging developments in recent years is the growth of Cognitive Behavioral Therapy (CBT), Motivational Interviewing (MI) and other alternative (non-twelve-step) treatment modalities such as Dialectical Behavior Therapy (DBT), Choice Theory, and Solution Focused Therapy (SFT).

LifeRing Convenor Mona H.:

I wanted to share that I met with the Hospital staff and managing Head Physician on Tuesday morning. The hope was gaining their extended endorsement and expanding our Lifering outreach to additional outpatient treatment centers. Wow, was it successful. Dr. U. was his charming self and will stand behind whatever we need, but he has very little additional time. The best help was a surprise. The head of the ARC (Addiction Recovery Center), is HIGHLY endorsing Lifering as a secular choice and is going to introduce us to two addiction directors on the East coast at a meeting on Monday.... I will be on a "meet and greet" basis and along with my handouts I will just need to be professional. I'm feeling VERY strongly that the approach of the hospital professionals is a good one here in the NE and I hope this experience will be a good expansion model to report back.

The LifeRing approach is, of course, part of the broad CBT mainstream in psychology, but is not affiliated with any particular school or doctrine within it.

MI has achieved impressive recognition in the addiction counseling literature. The MI approach is highly congruent with the LifeRing way of thinking. Some of the formative concepts that underlie the LifeRing approach come directly from the writings of leading MI authors.

Psychologists will also readily recognize in LifeRing elements of the client-centered approach pioneered by the great Carl Rogers. The obvious difference is that we apply Rogers' seminal ideas in a peer leadership context.

The self-efficacy research of Albert Bandura and colleagues tends to be strongly supportive of the LifeRing approach. Strength-based methods in the social work fields also speak a language that resonates with LifeRing.

The growth of each and all of these approaches generally and within the addiction treatment field in particular is helpful to the development of LifeRing. All of these approaches are secular and hold out hope that individuals have the power change their lives for the better by their own concerted efforts.

LifeRing Convenor Mahala K.:

We now have four meetings here in Salt Lake City (where, yes, there is a large and diverse recovery community!). We're getting an increasing number of referrals from therapists, and also from the outpatient program I was part of in 2011. When they (the outpatient program) started referring folks to LifeRing, I knew we had turned a major corner. Interestingly, we have a number of artists, writers, teachers, and musicians in our groups.

I've found 1:1 outreach to be the most effective way of talking to the professional community. And even then, it's been difficult to get buy-in – until a client finds LifeRing to be a "fit." Then the referrals start coming.

So, patience is a good thing to have in your quiver at all times.

15.8: Clients as Educators

Clients are among the leading educators in the addiction treatment industry. Many times when a treatment professional contacts LifeRing for the first time, they have heard about LifeRing from a patient.

Patients tirelessly search the Internet for alternatives. They read everything they can get their hands on. They are highly motivated to find an approach that is going to work for them. It is their own lives that are at stake.

When they meet with their physician or counselor, they are energized and prepared. Many times, it is the patient who broadens the professional's horizon and drives progressive change.

15.9: A Two-Way Street

The upshot of these changes is that the LifeRing convenor today has opportunities that have not existed for many decades. The old stereotype of the U.S. treatment industry as an impenetrable and monolithic fortress of twelve-step dogma has developed significant cracks and, in a number of places, is crumbling or has crumbled before our eyes. Behind those walls there is a small and

---

LifeRing Convenor Jeff C.:

I just finished week eight of our Sunday meeting. After four weeks of sitting by myself, a few people started attending. Tonight we had eight in attendance. It was exciting to hear the newest participants saying "see you next week" to the other members. All attendees were from the treatment center where the meeting is located, but I believe that is how LifeRing started in the first place, so it is a proven model.

I am starting to meet with addiction providers and the reception has been warm. Currently sending mailings to local providers. I will also be meeting the clinical director at a Veterans treatment center to discuss helping some of the folks there get a meeting going.

growing number of professionals who are not only open to Life-Ring, but who actively seek us out.

There is a substantial and growing number of patients who welcome LifeRing with enthusiasm because the twelve-step approach has simply not worked for them.

It follows that the relationship between LifeRing and the treatment industry today is a two-way street.

• One: LifeRing has much to offer the treatment industry. Our meetings provide a vitally needed service for the growing ranks of the program's patients/clients who want another abstinence flavor besides twelve-step. In so doing, we perform an essential service for the treatment programs themselves. We make it possible for them not to fail those clients. We give patient rebellion a safe, abstinent place to go, and we ease internal tensions and frictions in the clinical setting. We improve the programs' outcomes balance sheet, if they keep one. Offering the

---

LifeRing Convenor David R.:

When I started here in Fresno five years ago, there were many times only a handful of people came to the meetings. Sometimes only one or two. At first I took it personally and kept thinking it was something I was doing wrong. Then I took the position that it didn't matter if the number of attendees was small. What mattered was establishing a place where people could come to talk about their addictive behavior without being judged or made to feel bad about their behavior. A place where they could count on someone being there to listen to them when their addictive behavior started causing problems in their lives. Over time people heard about the meetings from other people, or from going on the internet, and attendance slowly increased. Even when only one or two people came, I tried to see it as chance to have a real and meaningful conversation between our sober selves. Many times they wouldn't return the next week, but would show up six months later. Now we have four weekly LR meetings here in Fresno. I am sure other convenors will have some ideas for spreading the word in your community. It may take time to build your attendance, but I encourage you not to give up.

patient a choice of support groups is the hallmark of a modern professional-quality program. Having a LifeRing meeting available as an option makes a treatment program look good.

• Two: The treatment industry has much to offer LifeRing meetings. Treatment professionals are gatekeepers who funnel patients/clients into other resources in large numbers over time. Channeling people into support groups is at the core of their function. The LifeRing meeting that has a place on the local treatment professionals' referral list will experience a steady stream of newcomers.

LifeRing Convenor John D.:

Two months ago, I started a new meeting at Diablo Valley Ranch, in Clayton CA., which is a sixty man plus live-in treatment facility.

The facility conducts a very full schedule, so fitting a new meeting in required some creative thinking. It was decided that it would be best to fit the meeting in on Monday evenings at 6:30. This is, coincidentally, at the same time as a bible study in a different location on the ranch. Also, to add to the challenge, there is/was a mandatory AA meeting thirty minutes after the LifeRing meeting.

Well, the first meeting was fairly successful with fifteen men, but as time went on, it began to fall off a bit. Finding this a little puzzling, I asked the men what they thought was the reason for the drop off in the numbers. This is when I found out about the mandatory requirement for attending the AA meeting, while LifeRing was a voluntary extra credit meeting. What? You say that isn't fair? Well, that is exactly what I thought, so I put on my diplomatic hat and made a phone call to the Doctor that initially approached me about starting the meeting. I diplomatically voiced my concern to him. He was very receptive to my suggestion that LifeRing should be on even par with AA's mandatory status. He said that he would bring the topic up at the staff meeting later in the week, but he couldn't promise anything.

Well, guess what? When I showed up for the next meeting, there were thirty-one men in attendance, out of the forty-seven currently at the ranch. LifeRing is now an optional mandatory meeting on Monday night at DVR. I don't know if this will the typical meeting, but what a good feeling. I love being a part of moving LifeRing forward.

The cracks in the twelve-step-treatment-industry nexus spread in an uneven, irregular manner. They are not visible everywhere or to the same degree.

Even in the San Francisco Bay Area there are doors that remain closed to us. Nevertheless, LifeRing convenors everywhere who still stand alone in the cold outside the walls where recovering people are concentrated, rather than inside among our people, may have mainly themselves to blame.

The doors may not have opened because the convenors have not knocked on them, or not often and persistently enough.

15.10: Abstinence, Abstinence, Abstinence

In areas with a large and growing number of LifeRing meetings, LifeRing convenors have given dozens of presentations in treatment programs. We have addressed patients, staff, mixed groups of patients and staff, and high-level program directors. At a number of the larger treatment facilities, LifeRing presentations are scheduled every eight weeks, or at a similar interval synchronized with the facility's treatment cycle.

Sometimes the LifeRing speakers have the whole hour to ourselves; sometimes we share the platform with speakers from other support groups. Sometimes staff gives us only a few minutes. We have learned to scale our presentations to fit the time available.

> **LifeRing Convenor Garry M.:**
> One of the problems is that LifeRing is relatively new and professional therapists and counsellors will be reluctant to recommend us until we have a proven track record. This is not a personal slight against us. They need to keep their clients well being as their primary priority. We found that we have to win them over one by one and by that I mean individual therapists and health boards. I have found that the health boards [in Toronto] are the hardest to win over, but it can be done with patience, preparation and a good presentation.

If I have an audience that knows nothing about LifeRing, and I have only one brief chance to get the LifeRing message across, I will hammer on three points only: abstinence, abstinence, and abstinence.

The most pervasive and damaging myth about recovery alternatives is that only twelve-step is abstinent, and that all the alternatives promote moderation or controlled drinking. We need absolutely to sweep aside this misconception in order to be heard.

Effective LifeRing presentations begin with stating the speaker's clean and sober time. If the presenter has at least two years of clean and sober time, all achieved in LifeRing, that alone can stand as the central message. The rest of the presentation is a footnote.

Effective explanations of the LifeRing philosophy begin with the first "S," Sobriety, defined as abstinence. Write it on the board if there is one, "Sobriety = Abstinence." If I have time, I make a joke. I say that we considered abbreviating our philosophy as one "A" and two "S," but "Three S" sounded catchier.

Effective outlines of the difference between our approach and the twelve-step approach begin by noting the identity of our views on the issue of abstinence, expressly rejecting moderation and controlled drinking.

Effective discussions of any recovery-related topic benefit from using the word "abstinence" as many times as will reasonably fit into a sentence.

If the only thing that the audience remembers from a short initial LifeRing presentation is "LifeRing = abstinence," the presentation has been a success. Of course, there are many other topics to cover as well; but in a brief first meeting, the abstinence message is the most vital part of the LifeRing philosophy to get across.

15.11: The Strategic Goal is Choice

The LifeRing convenor's strategic goal in the treatment industry is always choice. We do not want to supplant the twelve-step approach but to be a supplement to it.

It's helpful to our cause that LifeRing has operated for years in a variety of treatment facilities without any friction with twelve-step groups or twelve-step group leaders. Although we clearly have a different approach and we obviously reject some propositions that are fundamental to the twelve-step world view, we have coexisted peacefully with twelve-step meetings for a long time, sometimes literally next door.

We know very well that the LifeRing approach is not intended for everyone and it is not our ambition to become the only program. We are glad that the twelve-step groups are there so that people who don't resonate with the LifeRing approach can have an alternative. We respect the twelve-step group leaders and members because we are all working on the same project, leading our lives clean and sober.

It's also useful to point out that the LifeRing option is not an either-or choice. In a 2005 LifeRing membership poll, about one third of the respondents said that they attend both twelve-step and LifeRing meetings, and we have no problem with that.

LifeRing is not a cult and we do not demand exclusive possession of our members' soul.

Therefore, what LifeRing offers to a treatment program and to its clinical staff is "another arrow in the quiver." The aim of having LifeRing meetings included on the professionals' referral list is to allow patients a wider choice of abstinence support groups.

We are a plus; we represent an enrichment of their program; we allow them to help patients who would not otherwise be helped. We offer an additional channel on their set; one more road to recovery; more tools in their box; more healing resources for the patient to select from. The key word is choice.

15.12: Accent on the Positive

In approaching treatment professionals, the LifeRing convenor not only needs a credible term of personal sobriety, but also a positive explanation of how LifeRing works to keep people clean and sober.

Presentations to treatment professionals are not occasions to criticize other approaches. They are occasions to put our own best foot forward and to lay out our basic philosophy and practice.

The convenor will want to be familiar with our "Three S" and with the main points of our usual How Was Your Week meeting format. We have a great deal to talk about, and the practiced convenor can easily fill an hour speaking positively about recovery the LifeRing way and answering questions.

Each convenor will have to work out a presentation that works well for them and for the audience.

Generally, if the audience is composed of people whose horizon is defined by the twelve-step world, it will be helpful to include those elements of LifeRing that are identical to or similar to twelve-step practice. For example, abstinence and group support: basic principles in both approaches.

At the same time the convenor can highlight positive features of our own approach that, as it happens, contrast with the twelve-step approach. For example,

• The LifeRing poly-abstinence approach is a point that most treatment professionals accept as solid and obvious, and that they have long embraced in their own practice. They have to backpedal hard in order to justify segregating the community of recovering people into different organizations based on "drug of choice."

• Our inclusion of crosstalk in the meeting format provides feedback, which most counselors know to be a highly effective motivational tool.

• Our support for members' voluntary efforts to quit nicotine, if and when they are ready, resonates affirmatively with most professionally trained counselors.

• Our underlying "You can do it" attitude – otherwise known as building self-efficacy – is an outlook that counselors in all the helping professions (at least outside substance abuse) know as essential for healing and progress.

And so on. It is not necessary to draw the contrasts explicitly; the listeners are painting the picture in their own minds.

When the convenor has hewed strictly to the positive, and has succeeded in portraying LifeRing as a viable and coherent recovery approach, the listeners will sometimes surprise the convenor by voicing their own spontaneous doubts about the twelve-step method.

This phenomenon occurs frequently in presentations to patients. The convenor has not said one cross word about any other approach, but in the question period some of the patients spontaneously cut loose with strong criticisms of the twelve-step meetings they have experienced. The LifeRing convenor then needs to take the high road and gently restrain the attacks with a reminder that there are many roads to recovery.

This paradoxical phenomenon also occurs with treatment staff. When the convenor's presentation has been entirely positive, staff will often vent their frustration that "patients just don't get the Higher Power thing, maybe we should try something else," and similar fertile thoughts.

Twelve-step fatigue is deep and widespread beneath the surface. Occasionally, after the presentation, in confidence, a twelve-step counselor will bare their professional soul: they see nothing but relapse after relapse, the Promises don't come true, it's just not working, why are we even here?

The reason for high staff turnover in addiction counseling is not only the low pay, the long hours, and the lack of respect, but the high rate of client relapse. Counselors, like everyone else, want to feel that they are doing some good in the world. If LifeRing can help the treatment professional get a positive feeling more often in life, they may be ready to give it a try.

15.13: Team Presentations

When I first started doing treatment center presentations in 1995, I did them alone. Gradually I got smarter, and for the past few years practically all the treatment presentations in this area have been done by speaker teams.

Doing a presentation with one other person gives us two angles of approach into the minds of the audience, and it helps the person get training as a speaker.

There is only one way to learn doing presentations, and that is by doing them. Some of our most successful presentations have been with three, four, five, even six speakers dividing the speaking time. This way we get multiple angles of approach. We are very likely to get a broader resonance than any single speaker. When they speak as part of a team that includes people with two or more years of LifeRing sobriety, newcomers with just a few weeks of sobriety can deliver very effective presentations.

There's no need to rehearse anything ahead of time; people can just talk on the topic of "What I like about LifeRing."

When there are three or more presenters, it's a good idea to put the two most experienced LifeRing speakers first and last. Sandwich the first-timers and the less-experienced speakers in the middle. Audiences best remember the first thing they hear and the last thing.

15.14: Using LifeRing Press Literature

LifeRing convenors approaching treatment professionals will want to come armed with literature. This will consist not only of a local meeting flyer – good for posting and handing out – but also of other literature designed for the program's patients/clients, particularly the three main handouts that outline the "Three S" philosophy.

In addition, convenors will want to bring at least a few copies of the *Recovery by Choice* workbook and of *Empowering Your Sober Self.* Although economics forbids distributing these free to all professional staff, donating one copy to the center's library is usually feasible.

It is a good practice to circulate a display copy of the workbook among the audience while the LifeRing presentation is in progress so that they can heft it and leaf through it. The book tends to underline the convenor's positive message that LifeRing is a well thought-out, structured approach that can help their clients achieve long-term abstinence.

15.15: Approaching Others

If the ranks of the addiction counselors in a given area are closed to alternatives, the convenor has the option of approaching other physicians and medical staff, particularly in hospitals. General practitioners in private practice are also often approachable. Almost every kind of counselor (marriage and family, occupational

> **LifeRing Convenor Mary S.:**
>
> When our group was starting, I asked the director of the Intensive Outpatient Program if I could come in to speak with her participants. Once she saw the workbook, and was confident that I wasn't a flake, she started bringing her folks to our meeting once every 6 weeks. Many therapists are thrilled to discover that they can offer their clients choice.

therapy, physical therapy and many others) has clients with substance use issues, as do nurses, mental health workers, DUI lawyers, and staff at Goodwill, Drug Court and probation departments, among others.

They all see their share of people with substance issues and may be more open to hearing about LifeRing. A face-to-face appointment with one or a few such practitioners may lead to an invitation to present at a staff clinic or other professional meeting.

Most large employers have Human Resources departments that run Employee Assistance Programs (EAP). The convenor with a connection to their EAP may be able to win an opportunity to brief the EAP managers about the LifeRing approach and about local LifeRing meetings. EAP managers care about getting their employees back to work and aren't (or shouldn't be) picky about what works.

15.16: Other Ways to Reach Out

There are local, state, and national organizations of treatment professionals, and they hold annual conferences. Whenever possible, LifeRing convenors can and should play a role in these

---

LifeRing Convenor Joe M.:

The CAADAC conference LifeRing exhibit table was, I would say, a success. We had lots of folks stop by and thank us for being there, and four folks at treatment centers in the San Diego area told us they wanted to start meetings and support them (one was willing to get a counselor trained to run a meeting, another was willing to pay rent for the first six months of a meeting in order to rent meeting space), and 24 individuals signed up to be on a mailing list/outreach list. We also sold a bunch of books and gave out a bunch of fliers....

We also had a chance to talk to a bunch of STUDENTS who passed by. I made a special effort with each of them. It would be great, I think, if we could get a foot in the door at one or two places that train students....

events. On some occasions, LifeRing convenors have been speakers. LifeRing has mounted and staffed exhibit booths. At some events, LifeRing meetings have been put on schedule early in the program day.

These events pull together large numbers of counselors and offer an excellent opportunity for LifeRing convenors to learn their views, become familiar with their problems and needs, and expose them to the LifeRing name and materials.

Gaining name recognition is a key to acceptance. Participation in these events is also a great learning opportunity and usually a lot of fun for LifeRing convenors.

One effective way to get the word out about LifeRing is by writing letters to potential referral sources, such as treatment programs, psychiatrists, psychologists, and other health care professionals. The LifeRing Service Center has conducted and/or assisted with a number of targeted mass mailings of this kind and can be a valuable source of information and advice.

Some of the most effective outreach work, particularly in early days, involves person-to-person communication. It makes a difference for a key individual in a referral position to see a real person in recovery face to face. Letters are most effective when followed up by a personal visit.

LifeRing convenors staffing the LifeRing exhibit table at the 2006 annual conference of an addiction counselors' association.

The LifeRing booth at the 2010 San Francisco LGBT Pride Parade.

A helpful tool for the convenor's one-on-one outreach is a Life-Ring business card. The LifeRing Service Center provides templates for such cards; contact *service@lifering.org*. There are several online print services that produce business cards quickly and inexpensively.

Some communities have online registries of human services agencies. There is even a nationwide network of such listings called 2-1-1, *www.211us.org*. LifeRing convenors can make certain that their meetings are included in the list for their locality.

Nationally, Recovery Month events are staged every September. These include lectures, slide shows, picnics, barbecues, recovery walks, bike rides, musical performances and more. The federal government and local behavioral health agencies sponsor these events. LifeRing is perfectly entitled to participate, and the events are well suited to getting the word out. The SAMHSA website (Google it) usually carries detailed schedules, including links to local events.

Many local governments have advisory boards on alcohol and other drugs. These are often a division of the Behavioral Health

> **LifeRing Convenor Byron K.:**
>
> One thing that we can do is to plan to participate in local celebrations of "Recovery Happens." It is a fun event that is celebrated nationally throughout the month of September every year. It is a government sponsored event. In the past this event has been dominated by "brand X."
>
> We participated in the Sonoma County, CA event last year and had a blast. There was food, softball, kids stuff, and fun. We showed the LifeRing banner, distributed literature, shook hands, made friends, and had a lot of fun.
>
> You can check for your local event at http://www.recoverymonth. gov/. It is sponsored by the Substance Abuse and Mental Health Services Administration (SAMHSA) of the federal government. They can not legally exclude us. Many states already have events scheduled. If your state does not already have an event scheduled, start one. There is not a good reason for other brands to have an exclusive relationship with this event.

Department at the city or county level. In the past, representatives of the alcohol industry and of the twelve-step organizations have dominated these bodies. However, there is no reason why LifeRing members cannot also participate. You could begin by attending one of your local agency's public meetings. These bodies are an excellent way to get to know people in the local recovery world, and (not incidentally) getting referrals to LifeRing meetings.

Some communities have free publications specializing in health and wellness issues. These will tend to reach a narrower, more focused audience where the LifeRing approach is likely to find appreciative readers.

Some communities stage events on streets or in parks where nonprofits put up booths, sometimes combined with colorful parades, and large numbers of people visit. LifeRing convenors can raise the organization's profile, make new friends, and have an enjoyable experience by participating in these events.

> **LifeRing Convenor Mahala K.:**
>
> We also launched a year-long advertisement and listing Salt Lake's "healthy living/green/alternative health" monthly magazine. Our listing in the community resources section is online as well as in the print edition.
>
> I happened to be in the yarn shop today and learned that the woman helping me there is (small world) the art director for the magazine. She apologized profusely for the placement of this month's ad ... it ran on a page that included two cocktail recipes. (I had contacted the advertising manager to suggest that might not be ideal placement ...) Who knows, it might be just the right page for our ad – but I think we'll try to avoid such irony (intentional or unintentional) in future months!
>
> It's an expensive commitment for the year, but it seemed like consistent advertising for a year's time would be better than a one-time deal. It's being funded from one of our members, not from funds collected at meetings. We're also hoping that being an advertiser might lead to getting a story placed about LifeRing during the course of 2015. The reader demographic is perfect ...

Is there a college in your community? Many universities have courses in addiction, or courses where addiction is one of the units in a broader behavioral health syllabus. Some LifeRing convenors have obtained invitations to present in these classes. You reach people who, a few years from now, may be treatment staff.

TV and radio frequently carry programs about addiction and recovery. Some of these allow call-ins. A caller who mentions LifeRing positively in this kind of setting may reach a lot of people. Most print media are also online now, and when they run stories relevant to what we do, the online comments section is a platform where a brief and appreciative reference to LifeRing can help people find us.

When LifeRing is already established in a community, the chances are better that a newspaper will take notice of LifeRing and publish a favorable article, causing a spike in meeting attendance.

Some LifeRing groups have mounted their own local websites. These should be listed and linked on *lifering.org*. Note, however, that a local website does not magically solve the problem of publicizing the meeting, because there is still the task of driving traffic to the website. The impact of local websites tends to follow, rather than lead, the growth of the meeting. Nevertheless, it may be an

LifeRing Convenor Martin C.:

I got an article done in a local paper by looking to see which of the staff writers wrote about health issues, and then emailing her to say that a change was happening in which healthcare professionals were recommending groups like Lifering as an alternative to AA. I believe that I tacked on the We Come Recommended and the Welcome to Lifering flyers and links to the websites and said I would be happy to talk to her about it.

That's not a press release, but it worked to get us a story, by basically making life easy for the writer (giving her a subject and sources).

effort worth doing in order to gain credibility. In this day and age, if you don't exist on the web, you don't exist at all.

Some LifeRing convenors have put listings in their local YellowPages.com.

The online *meetup.com* platform may be useful for announcing LifeRing meetings. Note that *meetup.com* charges for listings.

Some LifeRing groups create a page on Google+ and post their meeting announcements and contact information there. The same can be done and is done on Facebook, Craigslist, LinkedIn, and other net platforms. Convenors need to update these postings frequently to keep them fresh.

The Google Calendar app can be used to synchronize meeting announcements between different websites and to send out reminder messages.

Google Voice provides a free phone number that can used as a contact number for the local group. Calls to that number can be redirected to other numbers and messages accessed from anywhere. This can be very helpful in setting up networks of convenors in a community.

Some LifeRing convenors have created and posted short videos on YouTube. Again, this may be helpful but is not a magic solution, because you still have to drive traffic to those videos.

One LifeRing group, in Vancouver B.C. Canada, has produced its own 35-minute movie DVD as orientation for new convenors. A shorter version of the movie for outreach purposes is in the works.

> **LifeRing Convenor Byron K.:**
> The recent article in the Santa Rosa *Press Democrat* has caused a noticeable spike in interest in LifeRing. Attendance in Sonoma County LifeRing meetings is up at least 50% this week. Many of the new attendees have specifically expressed excitement and relief at finding LifeRing.

Outreach can take surprising leaps. A prison in Tucson, Arizona, asked for a LifeRing presentation and started a LifeRing meeting because the prison has a contract with Hawaii to house the overflow from Hawaiian prisons, and some of these prisoners had participated in the LifeRing meeting at a detention facility in Honolulu.

Kaiser in Denver, Colorado, decided to publicize LifeRing meetings after a new administrator arrived there who had been familiar with LifeRing at Kaiser in Northern California. You just can't predict where the seeds you sow today will sprout tomorrow.

LifeRing Convenor Troy S.:

I've been sitting on the Stanislaus County Advisory Board for Substance Abuse Programs for over a year now. I'm also its liaison to the Mental Health Board. I have been able to get LifeRing acknowledged begrudgingly by the County, but not at a sufficient speed.

What does this have to do with convening? Nothing and everything. Getting participants is key. The government is uniquely situated to give our meetings free publicity. However, they are monopolized by twelve-steppers and their supporters. I have felt a bit lonely in LifeRing trying to use local government to get people to our meetings. I haven't heard of anyone else doing it.

Anyway, in California, recovery outpatient programs have to come to our Board, hat in hand, to get recommended for approval as a PC 1000 deferred judgment program. There's big bucks in it.

A program that wouldn't acknowledge LifeRing attendance came for such approval this afternoon. I quickly looked through the application to note the program required a minimum of two AA/NA meetings a week. I asked them to include LifeRing, because as an arm of the state, they are forbidden from coercing their clients into religious programs.

The Director of the Mental Health Department told me they were just using language their department approved and that they would change it to allow other types of recovery program. I abstained from the vote to make it clear that I would wait to see if the department made good on its promise.

The *liferingconvenor* email list (accessible via the *lifering.org* website) contains additional suggestions, reports, samples, templates, and other resources for getting the word out. Every convenor and every person contemplating becoming a convenor should be a member of that list.

15.17: Dealing with Obstruction

In some localities, members of twelve-step organizations have effectively taken over key positions in the courts, social service agencies, medical institutions, and other authorities that have referral powers. They obstruct any effort to introduce choice of support groups. Heedless of the twelve-step traditions that mandate separation between AA and other organizations, they wield governmental and quasi-governmental authority to enforce a twelve-step monopoly in their jurisdiction.

The LifeRing convenor faced with this type of obstruction will normally begin with sweet reason: emails and letters to the responsible parties and their higher-ups emphasizing the positive qualities of LifeRing and the value of patient choice. If these efforts meet with stonewalling, it may be necessary to go to Plan B: calling on legal counsel.

Here, by way of example, is a letter written at the request of LifeRing convenor Byron K. by Monica Miller, staff attorney for the American Humanist Association, to a referral agency in Orange County, California.

The referral agency had just revised its rules in such a way that its clients could no longer attend LifeRing or other secular meetings but had to attend religious meetings. (Names and local details have been redacted.)

> The American Humanist Association (AHA) is a national nonprofit organization with over 400,000 supporters and members across the country, including many in California. The mission of AHA's legal center is to protect one of the

most fundamental principles of our democracy: the constitutional mandate requiring separation of church and state.

The First Amendment's Establishment Clause "commands a separation of church and state." *Cutter v. Wilkinson*, 544 U.S. 709, 719 (2005). It requires the "government [to] remain secular, rather than affiliate itself with religious beliefs or institutions." *Cnty. of Allegheny v. ACLU*, 492 U.S. 573, 610 (1989). Not only must the government not advance, promote, affiliate with, or favor any particular religion, it "'may not favor religious belief over disbelief.'" *Id.* at 593 (citation omitted). The Establishment Clause "'means at least' that [n]either a state nor the Federal Government" can "aid one religion, aid all religions, or prefer one religion over another." *Hartmann v. Cal. Dep't of Corr. & Rehab.*, 707 F.3d 1114, 1125 (9th Cir. 2013) (citation omitted).

For "the government to coerce someone to participate in religious activities strikes at the core of the Establishment Clause of the First Amendment." *Inouye v. Kemna*, 504 F.3d 705, 712 (9th Cir. 2007). See also *Torcaso v. Watkins*, 367 U.S. 488 (1961) (ruling that the government could not require persons who qualified for office to declare their belief in the existence of God). In *Torcaso*, the Supreme Court made clear that "[n]either a state nor the federal government can constitutionally force a person 'to profess a belief or disbelief in any religion.'" Id. at 495.

The courts have been unanimous in concluding that the Establishment Clause is violated when the state requires attendance of religious-based substance abuse programs.[1] The state may only offer religious-based substance abuse programs if a "secular alternative ... is provided." *Miner v. Goord*, 354 Fed. Appx. 489, 491-92 (2d Cir. 2009) (citing *Cox v. Miller*, 296 F.3d 89 (2d Cir. 2002); *Griffin v. Coughlin*, 88 N.Y.2d 674 (1996)).

Not only must secular alternatives be available, but the "secular alternatives must, of course, be meaningful, rather than available in name only." *Bausch*, 139 F. Supp. 2d at 1033, n.4. In addition, the government has an affirmative duty to make such alternatives known. See *Warner*, 115 F.3d at 1075 (finding it coercive to sentence probationer to AA "without suggesting that the probationer might have any option to select another therapy program, free of religious content"); *Rauser*, 1999 U.S. Dist. LEXIS 22583, at *19 (W.D. Pa. 1999); *Griffin*, 88 N.Y.2d 674; *Arnold*, 956 S.W.2d at 484 (Tenn. 1997). See also *Bausch v. Sumiec*, 139 F. Supp. 2d 1029, 1034 (E.D. Wis. 2001) (Establishment Clause violated where state presented 12-step program as a condition of parole, even though plaintiff may not have objected, because the religious program "was presented to plaintiff as the only available and feasible alternative to revocation, he faced the 'force of law' and the 'threat of penalty.'").

An individual cannot "be considered to have a choice when the available options are unknown to him." *Id.* at 1035. Indeed, it is the "government's obligation always to comply with the Constitution, rather than to do so only upon request." *Id.* The court in *Bausch* explained: "Defendants' assertion that they stood ready to provide a secular alternative, if asked, would reduce the evil of government inducements to participate in religiously-based programs only for 'those brave or resourceful enough to assert their rights but [not for] the untold number who feel they have little choice but to comply.'" *Id.* (emphasis added).

In view of the above, the removal of the online secular sobriety program will have the unconstitutional effect of coercing individuals to attend religious programing in contravention of the First Amendment. I am hopeful that you will take the appropriate steps to ensure that such a clear constitutional violation will not occur. I ask that you confirm this in writing.

[Signed]

References:

[1] See *Inouye*, 504 F.3d at 710 (9th Cir. 2007); *Warner v. Orange County Dep't of Probation*, 115 F.3d 1068, 1074-75 (2nd Cir. 1997) (it was unconstitutional to impose participation in AA/NA as a probation condition); affirmed, 173 F.3d 120, 121 (2d Cir. 1999); *Kerr v. Farrey*, 95 F.3d 472, 479-80 (7th Cir. 1996); *Alexander v. Schenk*, 118 F. Supp. 2d 298, 301-02 (N.D.N.Y. 2000); *Warburton v. Underwood*, 2 F. Supp. 2d 306, 318 (W.D.N.Y. 1998); *Ross v. Keelings*, 2 F. Supp. 2d 810, 817-18 (E.D. Va. 1998); *Messere v. Den-*

nehy, 2007 U.S. Dist. LEXIS 65529, 17-18 (D. Mass. Aug. 8, 2007); *Arnold v. Tenn. Board of Paroles*, 956 S.W.2d 478, 484 (Tenn. 1997) (where program is religious and is the only one available, forced participation violates Establishment Clause); *Griffin*, 88 N.Y.2d at 691-92 (same); See also *Armstrong v. Beauclair*, 2007 U.S. Dist. LEXIS 24008 (slip op.) (D. Idaho 2007) (striking down AA/NA requirement as parole condition where no secular alternatives were offered); *Turner v. Hickman*, 342 F. Supp. 2d 887, 895-97 (E.D. Cal. 2004) (failing to offer the inmate a secular alternative for parole eligibility violative of Establishment Clause); *Nusbaum v. Terrangi*, 210 F. Supp. 2d 784, 789-91 (E.D. Va. 2002); *Bausch v. Sumiec*, 139 F. Supp. 2d 1029 (E.D. Wis. 2001); *Rauser v. Horn*, 1999 U.S. Dist. LEXIS 22583, at *19-*20 (W.D. Pa. Nov. 2, 1999) (coerced participation in NA/AA violated Establishment Clause), *rev'd on other grounds*, 241 F.3d 330 (3d Cir. 2001); *Pirtle v. Cal. Bd. of Prison Terms*, 611 F.3d 1015, 1024 (9th Cir. 2010) (noting that requiring prisoner to attend AA as a condition of parole would "likely" violate the First Amendment). Cf. *In re Garcia*, 106 Wn. App. 625, 634-635 (Wash. Ct. App. 2001) (agreeing that "mandating attendance at [A.A.] classes" violates the Establishment Clause but finding no violation where "alternative classes without religious-based content were provided").

The receipt of this kind of letter, especially when combined with a reminder of the $2 million award in *Hazle v Crofoot*, is likely to make the targeted agency reconsider the cost-benefit ratio of continued obstruction.

15.18: If We Build It, They Will Come

The LifeRing convenor who advocates choice of support groups may encounter skepticism from some counselors that patients will actually attend something other than twelve-step. Some counselors just don't listen to patients; if they listen they don't hear; if they hear they don't believe.

LifeRing convenors themselves may be unsure on this vital point. How many will come to a LifeRing meeting if it is offered as a choice side by side in the same time slot with twelve-step meetings?

In the San Francisco Bay Area we now have more than a decade of practical experience with situations where the LifeRing meeting runs side-by-side with twelve-step meetings in the same time slot. This is the situation at the Kaiser Chemical Dependency Recovery Program and at the Merritt-Peralta Institute, both in Oakland, and at a growing number of other centers. Clients have the

---

LifeRing Convenor Byron K.:

I was scheduled to meet this morning with Mike K., Sonoma County Director of Behavioral Health Services. Our meeting was scheduled for 11 AM.

I arrived about 10 minutes early, introduced myself to the receptionist, and took a seat in the lobby area.

After a few moments, a woman walked into the lobby and said to me, "Hello." It was Phyllis G., the Deputy County Counsel that I had been communicating with for almost two years. Mike had obviously invited her.

The three of us met in a small conference room and after some brief small talk, I once again made the request that I have repeated over the last two years. That request was for the County to remove specific mention of mandatory twelve-step support attendance from all county policy and replace the language with neutral language mandating attendance in "abstinence-based, self-help support" instead.

In separate referral literature, I recommended the County refer county clients to all available sobriety support groups on a clear and equal basis, including LifeRing, SMART, and twelve-step.

The County agreed to all requests immediately. All county documents and policies will be changed to reflect clear and equal choice of support for all.

This is the culmination of almost two years of letter writing, face to face meetings with legal and health officials, and determination.

We can effect change if we try.

choice which meeting to attend. LifeRing meetings consistently attract good attendance in this situation.

Patients in treatment programs want choice. If we build it, they will come. The record of LifeRing convenors' work leaves little doubt on this score. At the time the first edition of this manual appeared, LifeRing had multiple meetings only in the San Francisco Bay Area. Since that time, meeting clusters have sprung up in territories that were previously thought unreachable: Sacra-

---

Treatment Services

February 24, 2003

To Whom It May Concern:

I am writing this letter in support of LifeRing Secular Recovery. MPI was established in 1979 and is the oldest chemical dependency treatment facility in the San Francisco Bay Area. MPI's multi-disciplinary treatment team provides patients with a full range of treatment modalities, including medically supervised detoxification, 24-hour nursing care, education, group therapy, individual counseling and family therapy. In addition, we offer five different levels of care, or programs, to meet client needs:

- ❖ **Detoxification**
- ❖ **Inpatient Treatment**
- ❖ **Residential Treatment**
- ❖ **Day Treatment**
- ❖ **Morning Outpatient**
- ❖ **Evening Outpatient**
- ❖ **Counseling and Education**

As part of our Continuing Care program for clients who have completed our program, we require that all attend one outside meeting. LifeRing has been extremely popular with our clients, and we offer it every Wednesday evening. MPI would recommend LifeRing with enthusiasm and full support to any other drug treatment program.

Sincerely,

Terry Arnold
Manager
SG

South Pavilion, 6th Floor, 3012 Summit • Oakland, California 94609 • (510) 869-8850 • Fax (510)869-8820 & 869-6880
(A Division of Summit Medical Center)

96-3092-3

mento, Fresno, and Santa Rosa, California; the greater Denver area; even Salt Lake City, Utah; and the beat goes on.

A key benchmark is having meetings seven days a week. At that point, treatment counselors who demand that their clients go to a meeting every day lose a key argument for steering clients away from LifeRing. Growth snowballs as more meetings are added.

However, starting a new meeting without a solid convenor, just to inflate the number of meetings, can backfire and injure the reputation of the whole network in the local area. Convenors should also be cautious about taking on too many meetings. Convenor burnout is a real danger. Quality ahead of quantity!

15.19: Leveraging Outreach

Once you the LifeRing convenor have established a stable connection with some of the pools where our target audience concentrates, you may find that your other "nets" gradually become more effective.

Most people who have attended treatment programs go out into the wide community and tell at least some of their family, friends, and co-workers what they heard and learned. If they have heard of LifeRing in treatment, they will spread the word wherever they go.

If they have personally benefited from their LifeRing involvement, they will become walking LifeRing advertisements. There is no better promotion for your meeting than someone who credits LifeRing with a role in helping them get themselves clean and sober.

The next time someone reads the word LifeRing in your calendar notice in the local community throwaway, or sees your bookmark salted into the pages of a recovery book in a bookstore or library, there may be that little spark of recognition that raises the item above the blur.

When you have become a presence in treatment programs, your word-of-mouth circuits will start working for you. Conversations that mention LifeRing run into fewer terminators – people who say "Eh what? Lifething? Never heard of it!" – and more repeaters, people who continue the circuit because they have name recognition, as in, "Yeah, LifeRing. My sister's ex went to that, she said it did the bum some good."

Focused outreach to the places where our fish are pooled gives all of our other outreach nets positive leverage.

15.20: The Meeting Room

Once you the convenor have decided where your people can be found, the next step is to find a location where you can meet with them.

In theory a LifeRing meeting can be located anywhere, even in a cathedral. Churches have budgets. Renting meeting space implies no organizational affiliation.

There are LifeRing meetings now that meet in churches, coffee houses, burger joints, public libraries, municipal and county community centers and recreational facilities, meeting rooms of banks and title companies, hotels, college classrooms, therapist offices, general hospitals, student clinics, parks, beaches, and in people's living rooms.

All of these and other locations can and do serve the basic purpose. The founding convenor may have very little choice in the matter of rooms and needs to be creative, flexible, and opportunistic. Take whatever you can find.

If you have the option, however, consider the advantages of locating your first meeting in or near a chemical dependency treatment facility.

- Foot traffic. Your people are right there, within walking distance, or very near. An excellent location for a LifeRing meeting is in one of the group rooms of a large treatment facility. Arrange your meeting schedule so that your meetings start as soon as the treatment program's own group sessions close, or fit into time gaps in the program such as the lunch hour. The next best location is in close geographical proximity.

• Referral contacts. Your referral sources are on location and you can contact them frequently. They can see that your meetings are active. If necessary they can drop in to reassure themselves that you are not roasting babies. When you are in their view, you are in their minds, and they will not forget you when making referrals.

• Economy. Most treatment centers provide meeting spaces for recovery groups without cost. The reason for this is solid: the groups provide a valuable service to their patients. In some cases your meeting literally frees up hours of staff time and allows staff members to catch up on their paperwork or help other patients. They are usually sincerely grateful that you are there.

LifeRing Convenor Byron K.:

I guess I would say the key to finding meeting locations is to keep knocking on doors. There will be some that will say no initially, only to say yes some time later. There will be a few definite "no"s, and in those cases, just move on. Consider all options. Hospitals, rehab facilities, public recreation facilities, government facilities, and churches.

Yes, churches. Many churches are supportive of any alternative to 12-step. Churches have in some cases been victimized by other meetings. Rent may be free or very reasonable.

Look at where other types of groups are meeting. Meetup groups might provide ideas for locations we might not consider otherwise.

I don't hesitate to look at the local AA/NA meetings list and approach the same locations. There is one LifeRing meeting that occurs within an Alanon facility.

It may take knocking on 100 doors to get just a few to open. It gets easier after the first few doors open.

Therefore your LifeRing meeting in a treatment facility rarely has rent to pay. This greatly simplifies the convenor's job; see the chapter on the Meeting's Money.

It may be well to remember that a meeting requires the coordinated motion of physical bodies in space, and this requires investing energy to overcome inertia. A location with short transportation lines maximizes the average number of bodies you will have in your meeting and the number of sober minds that will be able to connect with one another.

Many facilities require groups to fill out paperwork to reserve a room, and this paperwork may need to be repeated every year. Part of the convenor's job is to calendar that renewal. We've had several experiences where other groups (typically, AA) have claimed that a room at a certain hour belonged to them, but on checking with the facility manager it turned out they forgot to renew their paperwork, and the room was rightfully ours.

15.21: The LifeRing Charter

The LifeRing charter is a useful piece of paper that convenors can use to demonstrate the bona fides of their meeting to meeting space providers and referral sources.

LifeRing Convenor Byron K.:

Last night the inaugural meeting of LifeRing in the City of Napa, CA took place. The location was the Napa United Methodist Church, which received over two million dollars of damage during the recent Napa earthquake. The convenor set up the assigned room for the LifeRing meeting and shortly thereafter an AA group showed up claiming that the room was theirs. The convenor politely disagreed and invited the group to attend the LifeRing meeting. They declined and offered some impolite words.

This morning the secretary of the Napa UMC called to apologize. She assured me that LifeRing did nothing wrong and was impressed with how we responded.

LifeRing is launched in Napa.

Some space providers can only rent meeting space to nonprofits and require proof that your meeting is part of a nonprofit entity.

Some space providers will rent to nonprofits at a discount.

Some are just cautious about who they rent to and want to see paperwork.

Some referral sources don't require paperwork, but papers would help to establish your pedigree.

When you're a local unaffiliated group, you're sometimes regarded as nobody. National affiliation establishes your identity and gets you recognition.

The meeting charter serves all of the above purposes. You can use it alone or in combination with supplementary documentation, such as LifeRing's 501(c)(3) tax exemption letter or LifeRing's corporate charter (both available for download on *www.lifering.org*) to establish your bona fides wherever required.

LifeRing Meeting Charter

LifeRing, Inc. hereby grants the _____ (location or Internet address) meeting this charter to display the LifeRing logo and to use the name, "LifeRing Secular Recovery" and any short forms thereof, to promote abstinence, secularity and self-help. This charter is valid so long as the Meeting remains actively dedicated to these goals.

For the duration of this charter, LifeRing Secular Recovery Service Center promises to list the Meeting on the LifeRing meeting list, to notify the Meeting of any publications or events that may affect it, to include the Meeting in the democratic internal decision-making process of LifeRing Inc. pursuant to the LifeRing Bylaws, and to serve the Meeting's needs to the best of its ability.

In turn, the Meeting promises to keep the LSR Service Center informed of the current name, address, phone number, and, if applicable, email address, of at least one contact person for the Meeting, to notify the Center promptly of any change in its meeting time, place, Internet address if applicable, or description, and to support LifeRing Inc. financially to the extent the Meeting sees fit.

LifeRing, Inc., owner of the LifeRing logo and of the service mark "LifeRing Secular Recovery," is chartered as a nonprofit corporation to serve recovering alcoholics and addicts, and the general public, by organizing meetings dedicated to sobriety, secularity and self-help, and by providing educational information toward that end. By "sobriety" LifeRing means complete abstinence from alcohol and illicit or non-medically indicated drugs.

For LifeRing Inc.:   For the Meeting:

_____ (Director or Officer)   _____ (Convenor)

LifeRing Service Center   _____ (Mail Address)
1440 Broadway Suite 312
Oakland CA 94612-2023   _____
www.lifering.org
service@lifering.org   Phone: _____ Email: _____
510-763-0779

If these documents are still not enough, contact the Service Center (*service@lifering.org*) with your needs. "Serve the Meetings" is the Service Center's mission.

The meeting charter is also helpful within LifeRing to establish your bona fides as a meeting. If questions arise at an annual LifeRing Congress about your meeting, such as whether your meeting is entitled to be listed on the web, or to receive referral services, or otherwise to be included in the LifeRing internal process, the charter document can help to decide the issue.

The LifeRing Service Center keeps a photocopy of meeting charters and the volunteers there very much appreciate the record keeping clarity and simplicity that comes from having a charter document.

You get a charter by downloading a blank charter form from *www.lifering.org*, filling in the meeting information and the contact information, and sending it to the LifeRing Service Center. (You could also phone the Service Center and ask to have a blank sent to you.) Your original with the countersignature of a LifeRing director or officer will be mailed back to you.

Although having a charter paper is useful and recommended, it would be a mistake to make a fetish out of the document. The charter paper only memorializes the underlying agreement between the meeting and the larger LifeRing network.

You enter into that agreement by the act of using the LifeRing name and/or logo. In legal terms, each meeting that uses the LifeRing name and/or logo enters into an implied license to use the name and logo only in a manner consistent with the basic purposes of the organization.

This license is legally enforceable whether it is recorded on a piece of paper with signature or not.

Thus, if you make "a few little modifications" to your local meeting format so that it now begins with a sacrifice to Baal, continues with compulsory Scientology exercises, and ends with a pitcher of beer at the local tavern, you could be sued in court to make you stop using the LifeRing name and logo, regardless of whether or not you have a charter document. Hopefully such a situation will never arise.

The charter document can also serve an informational function. If members are ever in doubt about the organization's basic philosophy – its reason for existence – the charter document is the most authoritative and succinct statement available. A meeting that has no other LifeRing literature but the charter can still find its way. If you are permitted to do so by your meeting space provider, you might frame a copy of your charter and hang it for display in your room.

15.22: Leases, Insurance, Rent

Venues differ greatly in the formality of their room assignments. Some operate on a handshake, others require a written application procedure and signatures on a lengthy room lease or space use agreement, subject to annual renewal.

Some rooms are free, some want a regular weekly or monthly rent, a percentage of the basket, an unspecified monetary donation, or a periodic donation of common supplies such as toilet paper, napkins, etc.

Many room providers are willing to negotiate a reduced rent for a new meeting; it pays to beg. The *liferingconvenor* email list is a valuable resource for issues in this area.

Some room providers want proof of LifeRing's liability insurance. You can obtain the required certificate from the Service Center, *service@lifering.org*.

15.23: Growing the Meeting

Once the LifeRing organization becomes fairly well known in a community, meetings may grow quickly. Recent LifeRing convenors in areas where a network of LifeRing meetings is already established have no experience of sitting in a room by themselves.

Where the local treatment facility gives LifeRing meetings a level playing field with referrals and facilities, the room is full from day one. By the second month these convenors are worrying about whether to get a larger room and/or a second room because of the overflow.

While writing the first edition of this book I started a lunchtime meeting at an outpatient facility in downtown Oakland. We had eight people the first week, 18 the second, and then averaged between 16 and 24 people steadily. This experience is not unusual for new LifeRing meetings at major treatment facilities.

Still, a thriving meeting consists of more than a room full of bodies. There has to be chemistry between them. In a treatment setting, turnover in meeting attendance can be as rapid as turnover in the facility's own program. The challenge for the convenor there is threefold:

• Guide the participants to the other LifeRing meetings in the area so that they can settle in a meeting nearer to where they live after they leave treatment

• Plant the seeds so that people will take LifeRing with them to areas where no LifeRings exist yet, and perhaps start new meetings there

• Develop a core group of regulars.

The first objective requires distributing current meeting schedules and talking up the existence of the other meetings. People who attend other LifeRing meetings should be encouraged to report on their experiences there.

Convenors will benefit from visiting one another's meeting, being recognized there, and inviting members to come check their meetings out. As much as possible, we want to encourage participants to see and use LifeRing as a network of meetings, not only as a single point.

Regularly distributing LifeRing literature in the meeting is also a key to encouraging participants to start LifeRing meetings in areas where there are none. This goal may be many months off for them, and it is not a realistic objective for everyone, but it is not too early to talk it up, get the literature into their hands, and plant the seeds.

Most important for the convenor of any new meeting is retaining and building a core group of people who participate on a regular basis. Without the core group, the convenor has to work hard to re-establish the ground rules at almost every meeting.

A core group carries the meeting and makes the convenor's work light. The chemistry between the core group members sets the tone for the meeting and models the process for newcomers.

Newcomers are often attracted to a meeting because of its core group, provided that the group is open and welcoming to newcomers. Some hints and ideas for welcoming newcomers are in the chapter on Newcomers.

Developing a core group requires a little bit of luck and a lot of common sense. You need luck to draw a set of people who get along and have good chemistry. Common sense tells you to give people talking time, listen carefully and empathetically to what they have to say, avoid giving unsolicited advice, give them responsibility, and be there for them between meetings if that seems appropriate.

In other words, building a core group largely means applying the basic convenor skills discussed in the initial chapters.

15.24: Turning it Over

Now you are a convenor, you have a room, you have people in it, and you are exhausted and exhilarated. You have brought them together in recovery. The peer-to-peer bonds are forming. Sober-to-sober communication is flowing. Synergy is surging. People are feeling their sober power growing inside of them. They are weaving their personal recovery programs in the quickness of the here and now. They are taking charge of their recoveries and making plans to prevail against the challenges of the coming week. The pulse of your own sobriety is going strong. Everything that you dreamed of is becoming a reality. Is your work finished now?

No. You have one more task ahead of you: turning it over.

15.24.1: Convenor Candidates

Somewhere in the ring of faces in the room there is at least one, perhaps quite a few more than one, who will be ready in a few months to become convenors themselves. From the first meeting, and every meeting thereafter, you need to be scanning the room to identify them. How can you tell the likely convenors of the future?

• They are clean and sober. If they relapse they quickly get up again. They don't repeat the same mistake more than twice. They make whatever life changes they need to make to achieve a stable recovery. They are actively building and implementing their personal recovery program. Sobriety is their personal priority.

• They are regulars. They arrive on time just about every time, and stay for the whole meeting. If they go on vacation, they announce it ahead of time. If they unexpectedly miss a meeting for some reason, they try to phone somebody to let people know.

- They participate. You can count on them to give a vivid highlights-and-heartaches newsreel of their past week in recovery, and to lay out their personal challenges ahead. They get and give crosstalk. They ask helpful questions, and make people laugh in a good-natured way. They show empathy. They refrain from talking too much. They model how to make the best use of the LifeRing meeting format.

- They have something extra. They explain things well, or they have a bigger reserve of empathy, or they are more energetic or more patient, they volunteer to help, they take responsibility, they defuse sticky situations, they listen really well, they make friends well, they help people between meetings, they show leadership ability, they have a great sense of humor, they have creative ideas – some combination of passion, insight, and salesmanship.

The LifeRing meeting format, with its participatory nature and its open architecture, is an apt one for potential convenors to develop themselves and to display their qualities.

The current convenor sometimes only needs to observe and let matters take their course. Over a period of a few months or a year or so, depending on the situation, a natural new convenor, or several of them, will usually emerge, and all the current convenor has to do is get out of the way at the appropriate moment.

Meetings need not be limited to a single convenor. A number of meetings use a rotating convenor system where two, three, or even four convenors take turns.

15.24.2: On-the-Job Training

The current convenor may want to create opportunities for others to develop in the convenor role. As early as possible, the convenor could, for example:

- Decide that the meeting today is too big and needs to split into a second room. Whoever emerges as the "split" convenor will be developing the skills to become the main convenor.

- Hand the clipboard to a likely successor and excuse themselves to go to the restroom … and take a long time before returning.

- Announce that they will be late to the next meeting, and ask for a volunteer to start the meeting off.

- Announce that they will be absent for the next meeting, or the next two, and ask someone to take over temporarily.

The ingenious convenor can craft other similar opportunities for regulars to obtain in-the-water convenor swimming practice.

It also helps if the convenor spends extra time with the people who are developing toward the convenor role and does whatever may be helpful to them to come along. Perhaps the convenor can lend them a useful book, or go have coffee, or arrange to meet for lunch between meetings, or some other positive effort.

It doesn't hurt at all for the convenor to say publicly and privately that the LifeRing system is to pass the convenorship along and to ask others to think about stepping into the role one of these days.

In the San Francisco Bay Area, where we have periodic convenor workshops, the current convenor of each meeting will want to bring along at least one, if not more, other meeting participants.

These workshops are useful not only in developing meeting leadership skills but also in developing the theoretical understanding of why we do what we do. Every LifeRing convenor needs to be able to explain the basic LifeRing philosophy and to relate it to everyday practice.

15.24.3: When to Pass It On

There can be no hard and fast rule about how long a convenor should remain in the role before turning it over. It depends entirely on the circumstances. In one meeting I started, I was able to turn it over within a couple of months. In another, it took more than three years.

The convenor needs to find a middle ground between "too early" and "too late."

Walking away from a meeting before another convenor is at all ready to take over amounts to abandonment. The meeting could disband, or continue but merge into the twelve-step background, or go off on a wild tangent and self-destruct. Walking away prematurely is irresponsible.

On the other hand, if the convenor holds on too long, members will become frustrated and people who are ready to become convenors may become hostile or go away. Such a convenor no longer brings people together but drives them away.

In my observation, convenors are more likely to underestimate than to overestimate the readiness of others to step into their role. In one instance the convenor held on for many months longer than the usual six to eighteen months or so, arguing that the meeting had high turnover and nobody was regular and stable enough to take over.

LifeRing Convenor Martin C.:

That's how its supposed to work. A person convenes a meeting for a while, then passes it on. If they can, they start a new meeting. Then that makes two meetings. If the person who took over the first meeting passes that one on, they can start a new meeting too. Then there are three meetings. And so on. I'm always on the lookout for people who can take over. We had our first meeting in the West End tonight (good meeting with five people there) and I was already asking about people who would be willing to step up (we have had some offers of space for new meetings).

When this convenor finally did relinquish the reins, it turned out that there were at least four people in the meeting ready, willing, and able to be its convenors, but too polite to suggest that it was time for a change. The convenor role has its gratifications and convenors may be reluctant to let them go.

If the founding convenor of a community-based meeting (as distinct from a meeting in special settings, see that chapter) cannot find a successor after two years or so, my intuition says that something may be wrong; let's have a look.

• If this meeting has lots of newcomers but no core of regulars, that is a red flag. Perhaps the convenor could do more to retain people. Generally, people come back if they feel that their participation is welcome and valuable. One of the most meaningful ways of communicating this message is to invite people to become convenors themselves when they feel ready.

• In other cases, the convenor is doing all the right things within the meeting, but something is wrong in the meeting's time, location, or supply lines (referrals, outreach, word of mouth). The local convenor workshops, if they exist in that region, or the online channel (the convenors email list) are good venues for analyzing problems of this kind in detail and getting feedback from other experienced convenors.

If the meeting is doing well and a core group has developed, the actual handover to a new convenor can occur in any number of ways. If there are several people who are clearly candidates for the convenor role, and if they cannot come to an informal agreement about sharing or taking turns, the meeting could hold a quick vote.

Most of the time formal votes are unnecessary. The outgoing convenor hands the new convenor the clipboard and the other tools of the role, and sits back. The new convenor starts or continues the meeting.

It may be appropriate to begin with a few words of thanks and a round of applause for the outgoing and incoming convenors. A card of thanks to the outgoing convenor signed by all those present may be appreciated. The less ceremony, the better.

It's usually a good practice for the former convenor to continue to attend the meeting as a regular member for a period of time. This can be good for the convenor in the same way that a cool-down walk after a strenuous run is good for the body.

It may be good for the meeting because the experienced convenor can be there as a backup if the new convenor runs into an unexpected snag.

Once the transition is complete and the meeting is in cruise mode with the new pilot, the convenor's job as convenor in that meeting is finally done.

Congratulations!

Now it's time to start the next one.

Chapter 16: About This Book

This book has a bit of history. Its history is intertwined with the conception and birth of LifeRing.

16.1: Pre-history

In 1988, an unsigned guidebook for group leaders of what was then called Secular Sobriety Groups (SSG) circulated in photocopies in the San Francisco Bay Area. Its author was Janis G., a follower of SSG founder James Christopher. Janis was a prodigious organizer who founded the first meeting of SSG in the San Francisco Bay Area on March 17, 1988.

In 1990, the organization that was then called Council for Democratic and Secular Humanism (CODESH), a breakaway from the American Humanist Association (AHA), acquired SSG, converted it into a subcommittee of CODESH, and renamed it SOS (Secular Organizations for Sobriety). CODESH published a 12-page pamphlet largely based on Janis' work under the title SOS *Group Leader's Guidebook*.

When I got sober in October 1992, SOS was headquartered in Los Angeles, but its largest cluster of meetings was in the San Francisco Bay Area. It was due to the energy and tenacity of local SOS convenors like Karl S. and Mike B. that a schedule of these meetings was in the hands of my intake counselor at the Kaiser Chemical Dependency Recovery Program (CDRP) in Oakland on the day I checked myself into treatment.

In 1996, Florida SOS group leader Tom Shelley and I, who was then an SOS group leader in Oakland, learned that CODESH was going to revise the Group Leader's Guidebook, and that none of the SOS group leaders was going to be consulted in the revision. We and other group leaders felt that we had a few things to contribute.

With the unanimous support of an informal national gathering of SOS group leaders in the spring of 1997, we wrote our own group leader's guidebook and established our own Press to publish it. This was the birth of LifeRing Inc. and of LifeRing Press and its maiden title, *Sobriety Handbook: The SOS Way*. It was an odd little book, part textbook, part grab-bag anthology, part crusading broadside, but there was a great deal more in its 100 pages than in the 1990 pamphlet. I was the book's editor and the author of some of its chapters, as well as the publisher, typesetter, and the order fulfillment, mail room, and bookkeeping departments. With an attractive cover, Maurits Escher's "Hands," the book was well enough received and served its purpose. It has long been out of print.

16.2: A Period of Ferment and Frustration

The 1996-2001 period was a time of ferment and frustration in SOS. The Internet was growing and many of us were going online. Tom Shelley founded our first email list in 1995 and I launched our first website a year later. Many of us were frustrated by the interminable delays on the part of the SOS center in getting online. Also, when people ordered SOS books, there were long delivery delays because all the printing and distributing was done by CODESH in New York. The list of SOS meetings put out by the SOS Clearinghouse turned out on closer examination to be a work of fiction; fewer than ten per cent of the listed groups actually existed. Communications to the Clearinghouse typically went unanswered. There were constant appeals for money, but never a financial report.

A hard chill descended on a convenor meeting in September 1999, when we learned officially that the leadership of SOS was appointed by CODESH and not elected by the SOS membership. As a wholly-owned subcommittee of CODESH, SOS and its members had nothing to say about it.

The simmering discontent might have dragged on for some years longer without resolution, but a federal court decision forced the issue. At the time I attended my first meeting in October 1992, I found a schism brewing within the Northern California SOS network. A cluster of meetings centered in Marin County had incorporated separately as SOS West.

The SOS West leadership took the view that an alcoholic, after an interval of abstinence, could learn to drink again normally, and further, that people only needed to abstain from drugs to which they believed themselves addicted, but were free to use all others.

One of the leaders of this faction, who convened a meeting at the Kaiser hospital in San Rafael (the main town of Marin County), was caught and admitted drinking before the meeting, with the result that the hospital evicted the meeting from its premises.

This schism landed in federal court, with national SOS and SOS West battling over the right to use the SOS name. In this contest, SOS West unexpectedly (and in my opinion unjustly) prevailed, and the judge issued an injunction forbidding the Northern California groups affiliated with national SOS – the largest cluster of SOS groups in the country – from using the SOS name.

Shortly thereafter, a council of local SOS group leaders met at the home of Geoff G. in Albany, California, and voted to adopt the name LifeRing.

The founding convention of LifeRing Secular Recovery as a national organization occurred in February 2001, organized by Tom Shelley, at a Universalist-Unitarian retreat center in rustic Brooksville, Florida.

SOS West, although it had prevailed in court, lost the battle on the ground and, with the death of its chief spokesperson, disintegrated and disappeared.

16.3: New Energy, New Publications

The founding of LifeRing cleared the air and brought a surge of new energy. When a detailed history of LifeRing is written, it will show important breakthroughs in this period in starting new meetings, establishing a lively and diverse online presence, winning acceptance by referral sources, launching new publications, and developing the organization's democratic inner life. Both the *Recovery by Choice* workbook and the current book went into "alpha" and "beta" editions in the early oughts. These were posted online and circulated as photocopies to informal focus groups of LifeRing members to get feedback. *How Was Your Week* Version 1.00 was launched in July 2003 as the successor to the 1997 *Sobriety Handbook*.

Besides the external organizational changes, the six years between the publication of the 1997 edition and the first edition of the present work brought a great deal of additional experience and some important internal evolutionary changes.

An important evolution had taken place in the typical meeting format. The 1997 edition described the main body of the meeting's time as spent in "discussion completely at random" or else organized around the "topic system." In fact, those SOS meetings were often a forum for people venting their unhappiness with their twelve-step experience. There was not much recovery work going on there. The "topic system" in those days, ironically, was copied from twelve-step meetings. It meant that at the end of each meeting someone had to volunteer to prepare a topic for next week and to lead the discussion. Crosstalk was not usually allowed in a topic meeting. Frequently the person charged with preparing the topic failed to show up, and getting volunteers to take on this task became like pulling teeth.

Today in LifeRing some meetings do occasionally focus on topics, but in an open, flexible, informal manner. Discussion completely at random is also unusual, and discussion that criticizes other recovery approaches is always Off Topic within the walls of LifeRing meetings. Most LifeRing meetings today use the How Was Your Week format described in earlier chapters of this book. These evolutions in meeting format came about purely through collective trial and error. Nobody decreed or decided them.

The 2003 edition also contained entirely new matter for which there was little or no precedent in the 1997 book, including the chapters on the role of the convenor, openings and closings, nuts and bolts, handling money, convening in special settings, convening online, dealing with the treatment profession, the annual meeting and Congress, and much more.

The core and most enduring legacy of the 1997 edition was the "Three S" philosophy, which the book formulated for the first time. It remains the core of the 2003 edition and of the current update. The "Three S" concept has proved durable and productive. The three parts of the philosophy are central to what we do, and they throw our distinctive features into clear relief. They integrate well with each other, and the bundle is scalable: you can deliver it in thirty seconds, or unpack it and spend three days.

16.4: Sobriety Becomes the Priority

The 2003 edition not only developed the "Three S" in much greater detail than the 1997 version, it marked an important shift in priority. The 1997 edition placed secularity in the first position, ahead of sobriety and self-help. This prioritization reflected the influence of CODESH, the parent organization of our predecessor. CODESH's mission was secularism, and it had no interest in sobriety; in fact, as I saw with my own eyes, wine flowed copiously at the dinners of its governing board, with SOS issues on the agenda. After LifeRing found its feet as an independent national organization in 2001, prioritizing secularity appeared backward. The 2003 edition put sobriety in the first place in the philosophical triad, where it belongs and where it must always remain.

16.5: The Need for an Update

While the philosophical core of the 2003 edition only matured and grew stronger in the years that followed, many of the circumstances described in the book changed, and it became clear already in 2010 that the book sorely needed an update. In that year, as one of my last acts before retiring from LifeRing leadership, I posted a How Was Your Week Wiki – an online text of the book that could be edited by anyone, similar to Wikipedia. However, participation was slight, and after a couple of years the Wiki effort was abandoned.

The book lingered in that slowly aging state, and might have continued to do so, had it not been for the Swedes. In late 2014, the Swedish LifeRing group obtained a small grant to translate the three LifeRing Press books. As I reviewed the text of the 2003 edition, I recoiled in dismay at the prospect that this stale bread was going to be translated and served up to a Swedish readership. Thus energized, I undertook this 2015 edition.

16.6: What's Different

Much of the text in the current edition remains exactly as written in 2003, except that anachronisms, such as reliance on books now out of print and references to websites no longer in use, have been corrected. Where relevant, references have been added to current texts, such as the *Recovery by Choice* workbook and *Empowering Your Sober Self.* There are other changes:

• The chapters on money, on online meetings, on meetings in special settings, on the annual meeting, and others, have been updated to bring them in line with new experiences, new research, current practice, and current issues of interest.

• Graphics have been refreshed.

• Some material has been rewritten for greater readability. Some sections have been moved into other chapters.

• The extended personal meditations and anecdotes in the chapter on secularity, as well as some other autobiographical digressions elsewhere in the book, have been deleted.

• The material on newcomers has been expanded and put into its own separate chapter.

• The material on building a personal recovery program also has been expanded and broken out as a separate chapter.

• The introductory chapter has been greatly expanded into a brief summary of the book, so that prospective convenors who do not have time or inclination to read the whole thing can get the gist of it in a few pages.

• The chapter on starting new meetings contains much more material than before.

• The whole book has been reset in a larger, more readable typeface, with a bit more white space and larger pages. It is also bound like a regular paperback, not produced in a copy shop with a plastic comb binding like the 2003 edition.

• The most important update is the inclusion of numerous short contributions by other LifeRing convenors, gleaned from the *liferingconvenor* email list. I had the pleasure of reviewing the more than 7,500 messages posted to this list from its opening in January 2008 until mid-June 2015.

The list archive is not only a gold mine of insights and experiences. It is also a startling and revealing testimonial to the power of one or a few convenors to put LifeRing on the map.

Typically, it begins with a timid sign-on by a newcomer, liking the LifeRing approach for their personal recovery, and wondering if there might be a way to share it with others in their community.

Three years later, that community has half a dozen, a dozen, or two dozen LifeRing meetings, is recognized by the local addiction treatment heavyweights, and perhaps plays host to the LifeRing annual meeting. The energy, imagination, and tenacity of these convenors – I almost want to call them super-convenors – is inspirational, even legendary. You can see here vividly the truth of what Margaret Mead said about small groups of persistent people changing the world. You will see the voices of these convenors in gray rectangles scattered throughout the pages of this edition.

Almost all of this took place after my retirement in mid-2010. Those who worried that LifeRing would crumble "after Marty" can forget it. Marty will indeed crumble one of these days, but LifeRing will prevail.

16.7: The Experience Base of This Book

The personal experience on which I drew in writing the 2003 edition of this book stems mainly from participating in about a thousand face-to-face meetings of LifeRing and its predecessor since my sobriety date of Oct. 2, 1992. I attended my first meeting that week and attended about two or three face meetings a week on the average in the years leading up to the first edition. If you add participation in LifeRing email lists and LifeRing online meetings, my experience at that time amounted to well over four thousand sessions.

I took turns leading some of the established face meetings in the Oakland and Berkeley area after about a year of sobriety.

In 1995, when I had three years' sobriety, I founded a new meeting, on Tuesday nights, at the Kaiser Chemical Dependency Recovery Program in Oakland CA.

In January 1999, I went across the Bay and started the first Life-Ring meeting in San Francisco, and a year after that I co-founded the first LifeRing meeting in Marin County.

In 1999 also, I was the founding convenor of the first LifeRing meeting in special settings, namely the locked dual diagnosis crisis ward at a local hospital. The following year I co-founded the first LifeRing meeting at a 28-day inpatient drug treatment program.

In the fall of 2002, I founded the second lunchtime LifeRing meeting ever – Mark C. in San Francisco founded the first – and the first in downtown Oakland.

During the writing of the first edition, I regularly convened one face meeting; started, convened and turned over a second; and regularly attended a third. At the time of the 2003 edition, I led two hours of online chat meetings per week, and moderated the online Forum.

I was one of the first dozen or so members of the nationwide email list that Tom Shelley in Florida started in 1995. Reading and writing to this list was my "Daily Do" for several years, and I sifted through the first approximately thirty thousand posts on this prolific list to compile and edit the book *Keepers: Voices of Secular Recovery* (LifeRing Press, 1999, now out of print).

I co-founded a separate email list especially for convenors, so that convenors could give one another support and share experiences specifically related to convenor work. (That list, *lsrcon*, unfortunately crashed and burned due to human error in 2008. The *liferingconvenor* list is its successor.) In June of 1996 I launched the *www.unhooked.com* website (today: *www.lifering.org*), the entryway into our organization for many people all over the world.

I launched the first LifeRing online chat room linked to the website, and then set up, trained, and hosted weekly chats in the more sophisticated multi-room facility that succeeded it. I created and occasionally moderated the LifeRing Recovery Forum, an online bulletin board also linked to *www.lifering.org*. I started up the LifeRing pages on Facebook and on Ning.

My experience with face-to-face intergroup meetings began in 1996, when I attended a gathering of convenors of our predecessor organization in Mexico City. The following spring I participated in a national membership retreat in Florida.

In September 1999 I was coordinator of the Secular Recovery Conference in Berkeley, CA, which brought together convenors and members from a number of states and featured a lively internal discussion. I have led several convenor workshops and convenor round tables in Oakland.

I was an active member of the Bylaws Committee that drafted the LifeRing constitution.

At the historic Brooksville Congress in February 2001, where LifeRing was officially formed as a national organization, I became one of the first elected directors of LifeRing Inc. and its CEO, services I performed until my retirement in 2010.

16.8: My Convenor Mentors

I had the privilege of learning the elements of the convenor's role early in my recovery from two San Francisco Bay Area convenors, Karl S. and Mike B., who modeled the qualities that an all-around convenor needs to have. They were of course solidly clean and sober. They were reliable at opening and setting up the room and skillful at facilitating the participation – more or less the minimum tool kit that every convenor needs to have. They had much more.

- They saw themselves as part of a larger network of convenors and meetings, and actively participated and involved other members in conferences, intergroup meetings, social events, Internet groups, and in organizational governance, such as it was in those days.

- They understood that philosophical clarity, particularly about the core concept of sobriety, is the foundation of each group's survival, and they fought hard to defend the sobriety priority against subtle erosion and outright assaults.

- They were practical people versed in organizational nuts and bolts such as budgets, copy machines, phone lines, and many other vital details.

- They understood that recovery support groups, such as ours, need to have inputs and outputs that connect them with the treatment professions, with various institutions, with other recovery organizations, with media, and with the general public.

- They were avid readers who studied the recovery literature and could talk intelligently on many of the controversies in this field, and tried to keep up on the latest findings of scientific researchers.

- They understood and practiced the convenor's Rule One: pass it on.

These two, who were more or less my direct mentors as convenors, were themselves already the second generation of our movement. They were carrying on from figures like Janis G., the prodigious convenor who started the first meeting of this type in Northern California in 1988 and drafted the first organizational manual, and from the writer James Christopher before her, who started this branch of the alternative abstinence movement in Los Angeles in 1986. I had the experience of meeting Janis briefly and I got to know Christopher well over the course of several years.

I've had the privilege of meeting and learning from other veteran convenors of this movement, such as Tom S., Paula B., Laura L., and the late Nick A. of Florida, Ed B., Larry B., and Luisa B. of Los Angeles, and others.

I've worked with and learned from many of the other San Francisco Bay Area convenors of my own third generation, including Geoff G. (who has ten days more sobriety than I do and doesn't let me forget it!), Bill C., Mike F., Rich R., Fred and Elly S., Sue T., Craig M., John D. and Lisa E., Rick and Karen F., Sherry F., and others, all still sober but many gone on to other pursuits.

It's been a privilege to sit in with and learn from many of the 2003 generation of LifeRing convenors here in the San Francisco Bay Area, including the late Bill Somers, Gillian E., Dennis T., Amy L., Teresa B., Gary E., Raphael E., Mark C., Alicia B., Sharon B., Aram A., Chet G., Marjorie J., Tracey D-T., Larry S., Lori A., Meg H., John O., John H., Dave W., Robbin L., Bettye D., Syl S., Marylou B., the late LouAnthony G., Owen P., Charlotte G., Lin L., Susan S., Laura H., Gary B., Dennis M., and others. It's a delight to realize that we've grown so large that I no longer know them all in person.

I've worked closely with and learned a great deal from many of the online convenors, including Tom Shelley (the listmeister of LSRmail), Glo M. and Paula B., (former online coordinators); chat convenors John R., Rick B., Ben G., Angela N., Steve S., Mona H., Jack P., and others, and from many active participants in the chats, lists, and the forum.

One of the guarantees of LifeRing's future is the caliber and breadth of talent that has come together around this recovery vision.

After my retirement from the leadership of LifeRing in 2010, I scaled back my meeting attendance. Currently, while working on the update of this volume (2015), I lead one weekly LifeRing meeting at an inpatient treatment center and another in a dual diagnosis crisis ward at a local hospital.

16.9: Treatment

My entry into the groups that are now LifeRing came via referral from my case manager at the Kaiser chemical dependency treatment program where I was a patient. Because of this history and my interest in it, I have been keenly aware of the symbiosis between support groups and the treatment industry.

I was part of an informal group of patients who agitated for years within our treatment program to obtain recognition for our secular support group as a legitimate option alongside the traditional twelve-step groups. At the same time I have been an unabashed cheerleader for that treatment program. For several years I appeared there every eight weeks in the role of successful alumnus to speak to incoming patients about LifeRing.

Since those years, I have given presentations to staff and/or patients in a variety of settings, including the national and California associations of addiction counselors (NAADAC, CAADAC). I have led all-day LifeRing training sessions for clinicians in the U.S. and in Canada.

Based on this experience, I edited and produced a booklet, *Presenting LifeRing Secular Recovery* (LifeRing Press, 2000) now out of print, that served at the time to introduce the LifeRing option to potential referral sources in the treatment professions across the country. I also produced a glossy booklet based on the Life magazine format containing material for rehab professionals; this also is now in the dust bin.

With my degrees in comparative literature, sociology, and law, I have taken a keen interest in the literature of addiction. In this pursuit I owe much to my LifeRing friends who have steered me toward interesting new titles. Through such friends I found William L. White's *Slaying the Dragon*, Lowinson's *Substance Abuse* textbook, Reid Hester & William R. Miller's *Handbook of Alcoholism Treatment Approaches*, Doug Althauser's *You Can Free Yourself From Alcohol and Drugs*, Lonny Shavelson's *Hooked*, and others. One of the recreations of my career as a LifeRing convenor has been to write reviews of these and other books. Through the relationships created by these reviews, some of these authors became speakers at our LifeRing congresses, so that other convenors and members could hear them and see them in person – again the convenor's Rule One in action.

In these and other ways, I have tried to live up to the description of the convenor role that my informal mentors modeled. Even though they have meanwhile gone on to other pursuits, they passed on the good stuff about convening before they went. With this book, I hope to pass the good stuff on to you.

16.10: Acknowledgements

Many people reviewed the drafts of the 2003 text, made suggestions, contributed specific sections and/or ideas, and enriched the development of the book from draft to successive draft. Special acknowledgements are due to the following:

Patrick Brown of Austin TX contributed the section on organizing in prison to the Special Settings chapter, and updated that section for this 2015 edition.

Glo M. of MN and Jacquie J. of VA contributed several paragraphs to the chapter on Online Meetings in the 2003 edition.

Marjorie Jones, then a director of LifeRing and its CFO, and one of LifeRing's most seasoned and thoughtful convenors, read the entire first draft and contributed numerous ideas both on paper and in conversations to its inception and to its final form.

Scott Newsom, Ph.D., of Dallas TX contributed early comments and suggestions.

Charlotte G. of San Rafael CA helped with feedback on the sequence of chapters.

Bill Somers of Vacaville CA (while he was still with us) gave me useful insights into the secularity chapter.

Syl Scherzer of Emeryville CA reviewed the chapter on meetings in special settings and offered detailed feedback.

Mark Connors and Gillian Ellenby of San Francisco offered detailed feedback on the whole of version 0.76. Ellenby, then a director of LifeRing and its Secretary, and herself a meeting founder, experienced presenter and convenor, followed up with a close reading of later versions, and made valuable suggestions on the book's over-all organization, approach, title, and appearance.

Additional thanks are due to the following for contributions to the 2015 edition:

Craig Whalley, a member of the LifeRing Board of Directors and former Executive Director, made major contributions to the chapter on the LifeRing annual meeting. He also read and proofread numerous other sections of the book and contributed his decades of experience in the book industry to improving this product.

Mary A. in South Africa brought her professional proofreading skills to bear on the manuscript. She caught and flagged numerous issues of punctuation, capitalization, hyphenation and style which the average person might never notice, but which would have lowered the product in the esteem of the discriminating reader. I am very grateful.

Robert Stump, Executive Director of LifeRing, reviewed and edited the chapter on handling meeting money.

Patrick Brown updated the section on organizing in prisons. Tim Reith, LifeRing Secretary, contributed additional material on LifeRing in prisons.

Njon Weinroth, Board Chair, Steve S., Craig W. and Melly K., Online Coordinator, contributed extensively to the chapter on online meetings.

Special thanks are due to all of the LifeRing convenors whose messages to the *liferingconvenor* email list over the past few years enormously brighten and enrich this edition: Adam H., Betsy Y., Bob O., Byron K., Carola Z., Chet G., Cindy K., Craig W., Dale B., Dan C., Dave F., David R., Dona B., Garry M., Greg H., Jack M., Jeff C., Jeff K., John B., John D., John O., Joseph M., Laura M., Mahala K., Martin C., Mary A., Mary S., Michael J., Mona H., Njon W., Patrick N., Pernille F., Peter H., Rob M., Robert M., Scott H., Steve W., Susan K., Thomas H., Tim R., Tom S. and Troy S. These messages appear in gray boxes scattered throughout the book. I have made minor edits for relevance, confidentiality, and style.

A special thanks also to cartoonist Matt Diffee, who gave permission to reprint his *New Yorker* cartoon in the chapter on Secularity.

To all of these and to the numerous others who contributed ideas and pointed out areas for improvement, I am very grateful. Needless to add, final responsibility for the content, including all errors and omissions, remains with me.

– MN 7/15/15

References

Althauser, Doug, *You Can Free Yourself from Alcohol & Drugs, Work a Program that Keeps You in Charge*. New Harbinger, Oakland, 1998.

Atkins, Randolph G and James Hawdon, "Religiosity and Participation in Mutual-Aid Support Groups for Addiction," *J. Subst. Abuse Treat.* 2007 October; 33(3): 321-331.

Baugh, Laura, with Eubanks, Steve. *Out of the Rough*, Rutledge Hill Press, NY, 2000.

Bufe, Charles. *Alcoholics Anonymous, Cult or Cure*, See Sharp Press, Tucson AZ, 1998.

Chase, Richard B. and Dasu, Sriram, "Want to Perfect Your Company's Service?: Use Behavioral Science," *Harvard Business Review*, June 2001.

Cloud, William and Granfield, Robert. *Recovery from Addiction: A Practical Guide to Treatment, Self-Help, and Quitting on Your Own*, New York University Press, 2001.

Council for Democratic and Secular Humanism, *SOS Group Leader's Guidebook*, 1990.

Davidson, George, MD. Steps, Staggers, Lurches, And Lunges, website at http://www3.sympatico.ca/gdavidson/home.htm

Dimeff, Linda & Marlatt, Alan. "Relapse Prevention," in Hester/Miller, *Handbook of Alcoholism Treatment Approaches*, 2 ed. 1996.

Fletcher, Anne. *Sober for Good: New Solutions for Drinking Problems – Advice from Those Who Have Succeeded*. Houghton Mifflin, New York, 2001.

Gardner, Eliot. "Brain Reward Mechanisms," in Lowinson et al., eds., *Substance Abuse: A Comprehensive Textbook*, 3ed., 1997, Williams & Wilkins, p. 51.

Goleman, David. *Working With Emotional Intelligence*, NY Bantam 2000

Herman, Judith MD. *Trauma and Recovery, The aftermath of violence – from domestic abuse to political terror*. Basic Books 1992.

Hester, Reid and Miller, William, *Handbook of Alcoholism Treatment Approaches: Effective Alternatives*. 2ed. 1996 and 3ed. 2003. Allyn & Bacon, Boston.

Hurt, Richard MD et al. *Mortality Following Inpatient Addictions Treatment*, JAMA 275:1097-1103 (4/10/1996).

Kasl, Charlotte. *Many Roads, One Journey: Moving Beyond the 12 Steps*, Harper, 1992.

Ketcham, Katherine, et al., *Beyond the Influence, Understanding and Defeating Alcoholism*, Bantam Books 2000.

Knapp, Caroline. *Drinking, a Love Story*. Dell, 1997.

Kurtz, Ernest: *Not God: A History of Alcoholics Anonymous*, Hazelden 1980.

Lasser, Karen MD, "Smoking and Mental Illness, a Population-Based Prevalence Study," JAMA 2000:284:2606-2610 (11/22/2000).

Lee, Adam. "Godless millennials could end the political power of the religious right," *The Guardian*, 26 Oct. 2014.

Leshner, Alan, Ph.D., Director, National Institute on Drug Abuse, *Foreword* in Lowinson et al. *Substance Abuse: A Comprehensive Textbook*, 3ed., 1998

LifeRing Secular Recovery, *The LifeRing Bylaws*, Adopted by the LifeRing Constitutional Congress, Feb. 17, 2001, Brooksville FL. LifeRing Press, 2001.

Lincoln, Abraham. Address to the Washingtonian Temperance Society, 1842, online at http://www.assumption.edu/ahc/LincolnTemperanceAddress

Lind, Michael, *The New York Times*, Dec. 9, 2001.

Lowinson, Joyce H., et al., "Methadone Maintenance," in Lowinson et al., *Substance Abuse: A Comprehensive Textbook*, 3d ed., 1997, p. 406, 411-412.

Lowinson, Joyce, et al., editors, *Substance Abuse: A Comprehensive Textbook*, 3ed., Williams & Wilkins, Baltimore, 1997.

Milam, James R. and Ketcham, Katherine, *Under the Influence, A Guide to the Realities and Myths of Alcoholism*, Bantam 1983.

Miller, William R. "Increasing Motivation for Change," in Hester, Reid and Miller, William, *Handbook of Alcoholism Treatment Approaches: Effective Alternatives*. 2ed. 1996. Allyn & Bacon, Boston.

Morse, Gardiner and Goldsmith, Marshall: "Behave Yourself: A Conversation with Executive Coach Marshall Goldsmith", *Harvard Business Review*, Oct. 2002, pp. 22, 24.

National Institute on Drug Abuse (NIDA). *Principles of Effective Treatment*, National Institute of Mental Health, Washington D.C., 1999. Online at http://www.nida.nih.gov/PODAT/PODAT1.htm

Nicolaus, Martin, editor. *Sobriety Handbook: The SOS Way*, LifeRing Press, 1997.

Nicolaus, Martin. *Empowering Your Sober Self: The LifeRing Approach to Addiction Recovery*. 2ed., LifeRing Press 2014.

Nicolaus, Martin, editor. *Presenting LifeRing Secular Recovery, A Selection of Readings for Treatment Professionals and Others Interested in an Abstinent Alternative to Twelve-Step Support Groups*, LifeRing Press, 2ed., 2002.

Nicolaus, Martin, editor. *Keepers: Voices of Secular Recovery*. LifeRing Press, 1999.

Nicolaus, Martin. *Recovery By Choice: Living and Enjoying Life Without Alcohol or Other Drugs, a Workbook*. LifeRing Press, 2002 – 2011.

Order-Connors, Bernice, LSCW, CADC, CPS. *Smoke Screen, Professional Counselor* Dec. 1996

Pew Research Center, "America's Changing Religious Landscape: Christians Decline Sharply as Share of Population; Unaffiliated and Other Faiths Continue to Grow." May 12, 2015. *http://www.pewforum.org/2015/05/12/americas-changing-religious-landscape/*

Presser, Stanley, and Stinson, Linda. "Data Collection Mode and Social Desirability Bias in Self-Reported Religious Attendance," *American Sociological Review*, Vol. 63, No. 1, Feb. 1998

Resnick, Michael P. Treating Nicotine Addiction in Patients with Psychiatric Co-morbidity, in *Nicotine Addiction: Principles and Management*, C. Tracy Orleans MD and John Slade MD, eds. 1993

Robert Wood Johnson Foundation. *Substance Abuse: The Nation's Number One Health Problem, Key Indicators for Policy* ("Chartbook"), Princeton NJ, 2001.

Roizen, Ron, "The Great Controlled-Drinking Controversy," pp. 245-279 [Chapter 9] in Marc Galanter (ed.), *Recent Developments in Alcoholism*, Vol. 5, New York: Plenum, 1987. Available online at http://www.roizen.com/ron/cont-dri.htm

Senay, Edward C. "Diagnostic Interview and Mental Status Examination," in Lowinson et al., eds., *Substance Abuse, a Comprehensive Textbook*, 3ed..

Senge, Peter. *The Fifth Discipline: The Art and Strategy of the Learning Organization*, NY Doubleday, 1994.

Shavelson, Lonny. *Hooked: Five Addicts Challenge Our Misguided Drug Rehab System*, The New Press, NY 2001.

Tonigan, J. Scott; Rice, Samara L., Is it beneficial to have an Alcoholics Anonymous sponsor?, Psychology of Addictive Behaviors, Vol 24(3), Sep. 2010, 397-403. http://dx.doi.org/10.1037/a0019013

Vaillant, George, MD. "Interview: A Doctor Speaks," *AA Grapevine* May 2001. http://aagrapevine.org/archive/interviews/GVMDInterview.html

Vaillant, George, MD. *The Natural History of Alcoholism Revisited*, Harvard University Press 1995.

Volpicelli, John R., MD, and Szalavitz, Maia. *Recovery Options, The Complete Guide*, John Wiley & Sons, NY 2000.

Walsh, Andrew. "Church, Lies, and Polling Data," in *Religion in the News*, Fall 1998, Vol. 1, No. 2. The Leonard E. Greenberg Center for the Study of Religion in Public Life, Trinity College, Hartford CT. Online at http://www.trincoll.edu/depts/csrpl/RIN%20Vol.1No.2/Church_lies_polling.htm

White, William. *Slaying the Dragon: The History of Addiction Treatment and Recovery in America*, Chestnut Health Systems, Bloomington IL,1st ed. 1998.

White, William. "The Rhetoric of Recovery Advocacy, An Essay on the Power of Language," 2001, online at *http://www.williamwhitepapers.com/papers/*

Wilson, Bill. Address to the General Service Conference, 1965. Online at http://www.historyofaa.com/billw/gsc1965.htm

Wilson, Bill. "The Impact of Alcoholism," Hearings before a committee of Congress, July 1969, online at http://www.a-1associates.com/AA/testimony.htm

Wilson, Bill. Address to the New York Medical Society, April 28, 1958. Online at http://www.historyofaa.com/billw/med1958.htm

Wilson, Bill.*The Grapevine*, Vol. 1, No. 4, Sept. 1944.

Witbrodt, J., Kaskutas, L., Bond, J. and Delucchi, K. (2012), Does sponsorship improve outcomes above Alcoholics Anonymous attendance? A latent class growth curve analysis. Addiction, 107: 301–311. doi: 10.1111/j.1360-0443.2011.03570.x

359

Index

A

Abstinence. *See also* Sobriety
  demand for 1
  foundation of PRPs 249
  from the "easy ones" 199–200
  main topic of talk 305
  poly-abstinence 198
    rejection of 343
  popular choice 193
  sustainable 197
  versus moderation 193–195
  Washingtonians 233
Adam H. 69, 356
Addiction
  and animal models 226
  myth of addictive personality 226, 251
  no universal cure 27
  the result of use 237
Addict self
  in brief 2
  names for 15
  not just an urge 15
Alcoholics Anonymous
  Agnostic/Atheist meetings 219–222
  and medications 153
  bashing in meetings 74
  court decisions 297
  dealing with obstruction by 319
  demand for alternatives to 1
  denial of Sober Self 244
  God at the core of program 220
  and Marty Mann 245
  most people get sober without 197
  profitable business model 295
  pushing in meetings 75
  resistance to 298–300
  and sponsorship 106–107
  and treatment programs 291
Annual meeting 185–189
  summary 7

B

LifeRing Board of Directors
  candidates 187
  powers of 188–189
  qualifications 188
  serve as volunteers 188
LifeRing Bylaws
  key points in 187–189
  online meetings in 140
  only official publication 11
  peer governance 233
  text available on lifering.org 125
Bandura, Albert 301
Betsy Y. 113, 356
Bob O. 146, 356
Brown, Patrick 172, 176, 178, 354, 355
Byron K. 120, 121, 314, 317, 319, 323, 327, 328, 356

C

LifeRing Charter 328–331
LifeRing Congress

delegates
  election procedure 187
  from meetings in special settings 183
financial report 136
founding 125, 350
generally 185–189
powers of 189
and sign-in sheet 123
voting 186
Carola Z. 105, 356
Chet G. 70, 91, 108, 194, 352, 356
Choice Theory 300
Christopher, James 341, 351
Cindy K. 84, 295, 356
Cognitive Behavioral Therapy 300
Convenor
  brings people together 13, 31
  building core group 331
  candidates 334
  can step away 31
  catalyst 25
  does not have Truth 27
  does not "own" meeting 32
  Facilitates connections 25, 28
  meeting not focused on 29
  not a counselor 27
  not a guru 27
  not an authority 3
  not a psychiatrist 26
  not a super-hero 26
  on the job training 335–336
  other-directed 28
  outreach 31

and prescription medications 203
presentations 308
  team 310
reasons to become 33
Rule One: pass it on 32, 337
word defined 13
work outside meetings 31
Craig W. 109, 128, 280, 356
Crosstalk
  and advice 56, 60
  common issues in 61–64
  and "I" statements 59
  important in LifeRing 55
  in psychiatric crisis ward 158
  in special settings 56
  involving everyone 29
  is conversation 60
  is supportive 57–58
  and laughter 60
  like jumper cables 67
  not confrontation therapy 58
  provides feedback 54, 59
  summary 4
  timing 64–65
  voluntary 56

D

Dale B. 201, 356
Dan C. 66, 356
Dave F. 299, 356
David R. 163, 291, 294, 303
Dialectical Behavior Therapy 300

disease concept 16, 23, 24, 62, 94, 95, 193, 200, 225, 226, 234, 238, 241, 247

  one-sided 24

Divided self

  Convenor's vision 23

  Jekyll and Hyde 17

  secret of recovery 25

  typical of addiction 17

Dodes, Lance 296

Dona B. 62, 356

Drunkalogues ii, 4, 52

E

Ellenby, Gillian 355

Employee Assistance Program 312

Empowerment of Sober Self. *See also* Self-help; *See also* Sober Self

  general aim of LifeRing 3

  objective not to live in bubble 102

  recovery means facilitating 23

  result of social reinforcement 22

Eye contact

  shows pattern 30

G

Garry M. 305, 356

Geoff G. 343, 352

Goldsmith, Marshall 26

Goleman, Daniel 250, 251, 252, 253, 357

Greg H. 220, 356

H

LifeRing History 341–345

Hazle, Barry 175, 176, 179, 297, 322

Herman, Judith 246, 257, 357

Higher power

  assumes addict is powerless 8, 24, 105, 173, 215, 216, 220, 221

  drives people away 220, 299

  not required in LifeRing 215

"Hitting bottom" 100

Hospitals and Institutions. *See* Special Settings

How Was Your Week format

  and different formats 79

  and newcomers 68

  and topic discussion 69–70

  asking for advice 48

  builds camaraderie 78

  check-in 40

  common topics 40–41

  convenor role

    handling problems 75

      threats of harm 77–78

    how much to talk 71–72, 73

    intervention 73–75

  and empowerment 82

  equal opportunity 81

  flexible time scope 49, 51

  and "I" statements 46

  importance of detail 43

  includes week ahead 42

  in perspective 80–83

  and life stories 50

  like an extended family 51

living room atmosphere 4, 54

low entry barrier 39

newsreel of highlights and heartaches 39

origin of 345

promotes participation 81

relevance to recovery 48

silence 68, 70

summary 3

variations on 84–86

where to start 67

I

Institutions. *See* Special Settings

summary 7

J

Jack M. 227, 356

Janis G 341, 351

Jeff C. 287, 302, 356

Jeff K. 196, 356

John B. 164, 288, 356

John D. 304, 352, 356

John O. 114, 352, 356

Joseph M. 62, 312, 356

K

Kaiser Permanente 62, 66, 114, 120, 123, 150, 285, 286, 290, 291, 292, 293, 294, 318, 323, 341, 343, 349, 353

Karl S. 341, 350

Keeley League

formula a gimmick 15

support groups 14

Ketcham, Katherine 226, 251, 299, 357, 358

Kirkpatrick, Jean 14

Kishline, Audrey 194

L

Laura M. 61, 290, 356

LGBT 152, 289, 290, 313

M

Mahala K. 301, 315, 356

Martin C. 63, 197, 238, 316, 337, 356

Mary A. 107, 355, 356

Mary S. 34, 108, 216, 222, 283, 311, 356

Meeting room

attendance slips 118

basket 127

books and handouts 124–125, 133–134

and LifeRing charter 328

chair arrangement 111–112

door signs 116

finding 326

leases, rent, insurance 331

literature display 126

outgrowing, splitting 113

signup sheet 120

summary 5

supply box 116–117

table 112

Merritt-Peralta 323–324

methadone 203, 204, 209

Michael J. 56, 289, 356

Miller, William R. 55, 58, 95, 226, 250, 251, 252, 254, 255, 319, 320, 354, 357, 358

Moderation Management 194

Mona H. 75, 92, 285, 297, 300, 352, 356

Money

options for handling 131–137

summary 6

to Service Center 136

Motivational Interviewing 255, 300

N

Native American 243

support groups 14

Newcomers 103–109

and e-Pal program 109

and sponsorship 106–109

convenor approach toward 103–104

and Recovery by Choice workbook 105

summary 5

Nicotine 204–206

NIDA 226, 251, 358

Nine domains 264–266

summary 10

Njon W. 52, 218, 270, 356

O

LifeRing Online 139–147

e-Pal program 108–109, 141

issues and tools 143–144

and newcomers 104

online meetings

summary 7

online support works 139–140

proof of attendance 145

varieties of 141–142

Opening, closing meetings 87–101

applause at closing 97

before opening statement 88

closing message 97

insufficient in high turnover settings 91

Opening statement boilerplate text 89

personal talking rituals 91–92

positive attitude toward attendees 99–100

social events after meeting 100–101

summary 5

use of "alcoholic/addict" label 93–95

P

Partners and Loved Ones 83

Patrick N. 284, 356

Pernille F. 106, 356

Personal recovery program 259–271. See also Self-help; See also Recovery by Choice workbook

and sponsorship 106

based on abstinence 249

and cognitive distortions 256

convenor's role in 271

and learning theory 252–253

random-access approach 259

structured approach 260

summary 9

treatment needs to fit the person 251–252

two methods 259

writing 266

Peter H. 195, 356

R

Recovery by Choice vi

Recovery by Choice workbook 1, 5, 10, 41, 43, 44, 70, 85, 105, 106, 107, 109, 124, 166, 167, 171, 180, 228, 260, 263, 266, 268, 269, 311, 344, 347

active ingredient: choice 261

group work 269–270

nine domains 264–265

not a bible 268

not mandatory 268

origin, sources 261

relapse prevention 265

start point and sequence 267

T-chart tool 263

Reith, Tim 176, 355

Robert M. 221, 356

Rob M. 219, 356

Rogers, Carl 301

S

SAMHSA 289, 314

Scott H. 298, 356

Secularity 211–229

compared to Atheist/Agnostic AA 219–222

engine of recovery 215

everyday practice 212

includes all beliefs and none 216

keep what you believe 217

legal right to 175, 319

lets people be real 224

liberation of spirit 229

like a family reunion 217

misunderstood 211

research-friendly 225

trending upward 213–214, 298–299

self-efficacy 301, 309

Self-Help 231–257. See also Personal recovery program

and anti-authoritarianism 250

and choice 254

and open architecture 248

as organizational principle 232

as therapeutic strategy 234–236

building on strength 241

clinical examples 241–243

clinical necessity 248

and economics 233

and Marty Mann 245

and motivation 254

and professionals 232

protagonist role 246

and the early sober self 237

and Washingtonians 233

Senay, Edward 18, 358

Senge, Peter 253, 254, 358

Shavelson, Lonny 17, 18, 48, 60, 242, 243, 244, 354, 358

Shelley, Tom 141, 342, 344, 349, 352

Sober Self

in brief 2

denial of 244

early years 239

measures of sober time 240

names for 16

origin of 236

Sobriety. *See also* Abstinence

and eating disorders 208

and process addictions 208

is the priority 201–202

key to the door 284

and medical marijuana 207

and medications 153, 201–202

in psychiatric ward 153

two-part test 202

and methadone 203

means abstinence 201–203

and nicotine 204–206

Social reinforcement

importance of 15

jumper cables 19

reaches tipping point 21

Solution Focused Therapy 300

Special Settings 149–183

and Recovery by Choice workbook 171

crosstalk in 158

defined 151

delegates from 183

high turnover settings 161

How Was Your Week format in 165

need for extended intro 162

and professional staff 153

as backups 167

as convenors 169

positive results in 159

prisoner correspondence 176

Prison in Texas 172–176

psychiatric crisis ward 154

special rewards 181

topics for use in 157

varieties of 151

Sponsorship 106–109

and Recovery by Choice workbook 108

no demand for in LifeRing 108

Starting LifeRing 273–339

bootstrapping 276

broadcasting, narrowcasting 279

founding convenor qualifications 273–275

in treatment centers 281

summary 10

target audience 278

twelve step meetings 282

Steve W. 244, 356

Stump, Robert 355

Susan K. 116, 356

T

Thomas H. 57, 356

Three-S philosophy

in brief 1

origin of 345

Secularity. *See* Secularity

summary 8

Self-Help. *See* Self-Help

summary 9

Sobriety. *See* Sobriety

summary 8

sobriety becomes first 345

Tim R. 110, 356

Tom S. 101, 352, 356

Treatment 291–296

  and LifeRing 303

  conferences 312

  strategic goal is choice 307

Troy S. 318, 356

V

Vaillant, George M.D. 18, 197, 205, 226, 247, 251, 358, 359

Volpicelli, Joseph 225, 226, 255, 359

W

Washingtonians 14, 80, 233, 234, 235

Weinroth, Njon 356

Whalley, Craig 355

White, William 14, 15, 17, 24, 27, 28, 80, 155, 204, 234, 235, 246, 255, 276, 283, 291, 354, 359

Made in USA - Kendallville, IN
704664_9781515286561
10.29.2020 1554